CCET

CENTRE FOR CO-OPERATION WITH THE ECONOMIES IN TRANSITION

OECD
ECONOMIC
SURVEYS

POLAND

1994

ORGANISATION FOR ECONOMIC CO-OPERATION AND DEVELOPMENT

ORGANISATION FOR ECONOMIC CO-OPERATION AND DEVELOPMENT

Pursuant to Article 1 of the Convention signed in Paris on 14th December 1960, and which came into force on 30th September 1961, the Organisation for Economic Co-operation and Development (OECD) shall promote policies designed:

- to achieve the highest sustainable economic growth and employment and a rising standard of living in Member countries, while maintaining financial stability, and thus to contribute to the development of the world economy;
- to contribute to sound economic expansion in Member as well as non-member countries in the process of economic development; and
- to contribute to the expansion of world trade on a multilateral, non-discriminatory basis in accordance with international obligations.

The original Member countries of the OECD are Austria, Belgium, Canada, Denmark, France, Germany, Greece, Iceland, Ireland, Italy, Luxembourg, the Netherlands, Norway, Portugal, Spain, Sweden, Switzerland, Turkey, the United Kingdom and the United States. The following countries became Members subsequently through accession at the dates indicated hereafter: Japan (28th April 1964), Finland (28th January 1969), Australia (7th June 1971), New Zealand (29th May 1973) and Mexico (18th May 1994). The Commission of the European Communities takes part in the work of the OECD (Article 13 of the OECD Convention).

The Czech Republic, Hungary, Poland and the Slovak Republic participate in the OECD programme "Partners in Transition". This Economic Survey was carried out in the framework of this programme, which is managed by the OECD's Centre for Co-operation with the Economies in Transition.

Publié également en français.

3 2280 00497 9696

Table of contents

3

Tables

Diagrams

BASIC STATISTICS OF THE REPUBLIC OF POLAND, 1993

THE LAND

Area (sq. km)	312 680
Arable land (sq. km)	143 600

THE PEOPLE

Population (thousands)	38 505	Population of major cities, June 1993 (thousands):	
Projected population growth rate (1990-2000)	0.4	Warsaw	1 643
Urban population (percentage of total)	62	Katowice area	2 069
Rural population (percentage of total)	38	Lodz	834
		Gdansk area (incl. Gdynia and Sopot)	763
		Cracow	745
Employment (thousands, excl. self employed)	8 790		
Employment (percentage of total):			
State agriculture (and forestry)	4	Labour force (percentage of total):	
Industry	37	Under 40 years of age	53
Construction	8	With technical and occupational training	54
Services	19		
Government and other	32	Private farms (thousands)	2 149

THE PARLIAMENT

Bicameral Parliamentary system	
Sejm membership (lower house)	461
Senate membership (upper house)	100
Number of political parties in Sejm	6
Share of seats in Sejm held by 3 major parties	81

PRODUCTION (preliminary)

GDP (trillion zlotys, current prices)	1 556
GDP per capita (US$, official exchange rate)	2 230
Consumption (private, percentage of GDP)	63
Gross fixed capital formation (percentage of GDP)	16

PUBLIC FINANCE

State budget deficit (percentage of GDP)	2.8
General government revenues (percentage of GDP)	47.7
Government debt (domestic, percentage of GDP)	23.0

FOREIGN TRADE AND FINANCE

Exports of good and services (national account basis, percentage of GDP)	22.2
International reserves (months of imports)	6.6
Total external debt (bn US$)	47.2
Total external debt (percentage of GDP)	64.8
Estimated external debt after agreements	
with the Paris and London Clubs (billion US$)	39
– percentage of 1993 GDP	53

THE CURRENCY

Monetary unit	zloty
Currency units per US$:	
Average, 1993	18 383
June 1994	22 450

Introduction

After a sharp fall in output during 1990 and 1991, Poland became the first country in transition to return to growth: GDP increased by 2.6 per cent in 1992 and by 3.8 per cent in 1993. Inflation was brought down quickly from near hyper-inflation in 1990 and has been held on a downward path since then; significant current account convertibility has been maintained; and the zloty has become accepted by the population as a store of value. While output in some branches declined at an alarming rate in 1990 and 1991, in others, such as services, growth began quite early and exports to the OECD area surged. The balance between expanding and declining sectors finally moved in favour of the former in 1992, and in 1993 most sectors returned to growth.

The Economic Transformation Programme, which was introduced in January 1990, sought to stabilise the economy and at the same time to initiate rapid systemic transformation. All Polish governments since that time have remained steadfast in adhering to stabilisation objectives although the emphasis given to structural reforms has varied, reflecting the difficulty in maintaining a consensus about the way forward. The major systemic reforms such as price and trade liberalisation and freedom of entry into almost all activities were implemented quickly during 1990 and 1991, and since then structural changes have developed spontaneously: the private sector has grown dynamically and financial discipline has improved steadily, even in a number of state-owned enterprises. Small privatisation is practically complete, and a number of medium-sized firms have either been sold or leased. However, the majority of enterprises which were state-owned at the start of programme remain to be privatised.

Despite these positive developments, the challenge facing economic policy is, if anything, more difficult. After an initial period in which demand was underpinned by exports, consumption became the dominant factor in 1993. If sustained this would raise issues about the adequacy of savings and whether the economy has embarked on a low-growth path. Inflation has been brought down to levels – 25-35 per cent – which in other countries have proven difficult to reduce further. The budget deficit remains a point of political contention and the burden of debt service is increasing rapidly. At the same time, there are difficult issues for policy in dealing with the costs or side-effects of the transition, and in furthering reforms. Unemployment has increased steadily to around 16 per cent and is concentrated by region, gender and age group. A widening of the distribution of income and a marked decline in employment have resulted in a high level of budget transfers in the form of unemployment payments and subsidies for early retirement. Non-performing loans by the banking system to state-owned firms are high and, as a result, financial intermediation has remained limited. Above all, four years into the transition, the way forward in transforming state-owned enterprises into profit-oriented entities remains a point of contention.

Chapter I of this second Survey of Poland analyses the recovery, focusing on structural changes in the economy and indications of evolving enterprise behaviour. Macroeconomic policy settings are reviewed followed by an assessment of short-term economic prospects.

Chapters II and III are concerned with the difficult area of structural policy. Policy measures to improve the governance and performance of state-owned firms, including their privatisation, and to create a competitive environment are discussed in Chapter II. The policy issues which have arisen in the banking sector as a result of non-performing loans to state-owned enterprises are taken up in Chapter III. Policy measures, including bank recapitalisation, are discussed, and broader issues relating to the establishment of a sound and efficient universal banking system highlighted. The rapid development of non-bank financial intermediaries since 1991 is outlined in an annex.

Success in the first phase of the transition highlights the need to solve a number of medium-term policy issues if growth is to be consolidated and strengthened. Chapter IV reviews some of these issues which include the low level of monetisation and high level of indebtedness, the need to control fiscal deficits and to ensure that these are consistent with inflation objectives, the provision of adequate savings in the economy to support an acceptable growth rate, and the necessity to ensure that growth will be consistent with unemployment and environmental objectives. Conclusions to the Survey are presented in Chapter V.

I. Macroeconomic policies, economic performance and the short-term outlook

Overview

The Polish economy has completed two years of recovery during which time growth appears to have become progressively more firmly based: it has spread to a larger number of sectors; the inter-sectoral reallocation of resources has continued; and improved supply-side behaviour has become evident. The heterogeneity of the recovery in 1992 represented a continuation of developments in 1990/1991 when the economy was characterised by strong growth in some sectors but falling output in others. Expanding sectors and private enterprises finally outweighed declining sectors and contracting state-owned enterprises so that overall growth became positive in 1992. Broadly speaking, 1993 represented a deepening of the growth process: expansion became characteristic of more branches, the losses incurred by many large state-owned firms and in significant sectors of the economy decreased, and improved financial discipline became more apparent. In both years growth was driven by the private sector. From the perspective of aggregate demand, the expansionary impulse provided by exports in 1990/1991 continued, although in late 1992 and during the first half of 1993 it was significantly weaker. Public consumption grew rapidly in both years and was further augmented by a substantial recovery of household consumption in 1993. The current account deteriorated markedly, led by a sharp rise in imports.

Economic Recovery, 1992-1993

Output and demand have expanded

After falling by 7 per cent in 1991; GDP rebounded in 1992 and 1993, growing by 2.6 per cent and 3.8 per cent respectively (Table 1). In view of its

Table 1. **Sources and uses of gross domestic product**

Constant prices [1]

	1992	1990	1991	1992	1993
	Share in GDP	Percentage growth over previous year			
Sources [2]:					
Industry	39.6	−22.0	−17.1	2.6	3.5
Construction	11.2	−14.5	6.7	3.8	4.3
Agriculture	7.3	−0.3	6.8	−12.3	3.6
Forestry	1.0	−21.9	−31.8	18.5	−
Transportation	3.6	−14.8	−19.9	0.9	−
Communication	0.8	−1.9	−21.4	14.9	−
Trade	15.0	0.7	7.9	−0.2	−
Other material sectors	1.8	−11.6	3.3	2.5	−
Community services	1.8	−10.4	24.9	−16.2	−
Housing	4.3	−5.7	−4.8	48.8	−
Education	4.2	9.4	0.4	3.3	−
Health care and social welfare	2.9	2.6	−3.8	3.4	−
Other sectors	8.8	−3.0	−20.1	−20.2	−
Imputed banking services	−2.2	n.a.	−28.0	−43.1	−

	1992	1990 [2]	1991	1992	1993 [3]
	Share in GDP	Percentage growth over previous year			
Uses [2]:					
Consumption	78.4	−11.7	7.5	3.5	4.6
Personal consumption	54.1	−15.3	6.6	1.0	5.3
Public consumption	24.2	0.5	9.5	9.5	3.0
Capital formation, *of which:*	18.6	−24.8	−20.1	−13.0	14.0
Gross fixed investment	21.3	−10.6	−4.5	2.80	2.9
Stockbuilding (trn zlotys)	−2.9	−68.9	2.2	−15.3	−4.8
Intangible investment	−	−	9.3	−28.4	17.7
Domestic demand	97.0	−15.4	−0.1	−0.1	6.4
Exports of goods and non-factor services	32.7	15.1	−1.7	10.8	1.0
Imports of goods and non-factor services	29.7	−10.2	29.6	1.7	9.1
Gross domestic product		−11.6	−7.0	2.6	3.8
Memorandum item:					
GDP (trn zlotys) [4]		560.3	808.8	1 149.5	1 556.1

1. In prices of 1990.
2. Due to ongoing data revisions growth rates for GDP defined by sources and by uses do not agree. New methodology, which improves price deflators and allows consistent estimates of inventory accumulation, have been used in deriving GDP by use for 1991, 1992 and 1993, but no such estimates are as yet available for sources. The differences are significant: with the old methodology GDP fell by 7.6 per cent in 1991 (−7.0, new methodology) and rose by 1.5 per cent in 1992 (2.6, new methodology). Data for GDP by branches for 1990-1992 estimated according to the old methodology.
3. Central Statistical Office, first estimation.
4. In current prices, new methodology.
Source: Central Statistical Office, *Statistics Yearbook* 1993 and Ministry of Finance.

importance in the economy (still around 37 per cent of GDP), the recovery of industrial production by some 2.6 per cent in 1992 (old methodology)[1] – and by a further 3.5 per cent in 1993 – was particularly significant, reinforcing the positive developments already observed in services and construction during 1991.[2] Slowing the recovery was a sharp drought-induced fall in agricultural value-added during 1992. Sustained industrial growth is generally regarded to have commenced in the second quarter of 1992 when industrial sales reached their lowest level. However, after making some allowance for seasonality it appears that the trough may have already been reached in the third quarter of 1991: the growth of industrial output was quite substantial between August and December 1991 (Diagram 1). In retrospect, the Polish economy displayed surprising resilience in responding to systemic changes, stabilisation and the loss of the CMEA market.

After contracting in 1991 in the wake of a budget crisis, public consumption grew strongly in both 1992 and 1993. The growth in public consumption in 1992 was in part due to the rebound in budget sector salaries following a substantial squeeze during 1991. However, it also reflects the substantial pressure on the

Diagram 1. **INDUSTRIAL PRODUCTION**
(three-month moving averages)

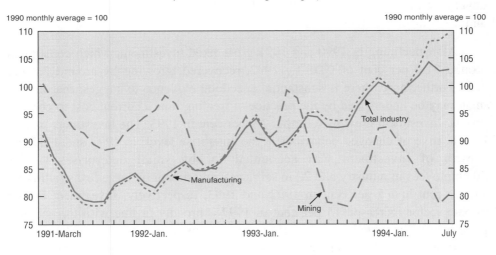

Source: Central Statistical Office, *Statistical Bulletin* and OECD Secretariat calculations.

authorities to maintain public services and the comparative lack of success in improving the efficiency of public expenditures. Private consumption began to expand in late 1992, reinforcing the demand impulse from public consumption, and grew by 5.3 per cent in 1993.

The forces underlying the development of private consumption are particularly difficult to ascertain. On the income side, real consumer wages and employment declined in both years (real consumer net wages by 2.7 and 1.0 per cent respectively and the number of employees by 8 and 4 per cent). Strong anecdotal evidence suggests that wages may be substantially understated because of efforts to avoid high social security contributions. Real income from social security benefits, including unemployment benefits, increased by 8.7 per cent in 1993. Entrepreneurial earnings are difficult to estimate. There is some evidence to suggest that they increased strongly between 1991 and 1992, accounting for most of the growth in consumption, but decelerated in 1993 despite an improvement in corporate profitability. In 1992 a surge in completions of co-operative housing and widespread defaults by households on repayments to the housing co-operatives substantially increased household cash flow, enabling a weak increase in both consumption and savings. In 1993 forces governing the increase in consumption – and decline in household saving – included: the introduction of an import surcharge in December 1992 and a VAT in July 1993; an expected devaluation of the zloty in the first half of 1993; reduced deposit interest rates; and a boom in the stock market.

After declining in 1990 and 1991 gross fixed investment, which constituted around 21.0 per cent of GDP by 1992, recovered, growing by around 2.8 per cent. Furthermore, there is substantial anecdotal evidence to suggest that investment may be understated by the practice of treating it as a current cost to conceal profits. Investment grew by a further 2.9 per cent in 1993. The investment pattern is indicative of changed behaviour at the enterprise level: in 1992 and 1993 the growth of investment was accounted for by small enterprises (under 50 employees in industry and 20 in services), investment by large firms falling by 11 per cent and 5 per cent in 1992 and 1993, respectively. Investment by the private sector increased 15 per cent in 1992 – broadly in line with the sector's growth of value-added – while that by the state-owned sector fell by 8 per cent. The decumulation of inventories, which was quite marked in 1992, continued in 1993, though at a reduced rate. The ratio of inventories of inputs and intermediate

Table 2. **Sources of household income** [1]

	1990	1991	1992	1993	Share of total income 1993
	Year-on-year percentage growth				Percentage
Real (net) income of households					100.0
Using GDP deflator	−5.3	17.6	9.2	4.8	−
Using CPI deflator	−19.9	4.1	−0.4	1.6	−
Social benefits in kind	0.4	−12.4	−9.9	−4.3	11.0
Personal income of households	−22.8	7.1	1.0	2.4	89.0
From observable sources	−	5.6	−6.3	−0.2	44.1
Wages [2]	−34.3	−4.7	−10.0	−6.1	24.7
Money social benefits	−14.3	28.3	−0.2	8.7	19.4
From non-observable sources	−	9.1	9.7	5.0	44.9
Work on private farms	−60.6	−32.4	20.1	7.6	4.7
Work outside agriculture [3]	47.4	−2.8	42.1	5.5	15.1
Additional activity [4]	0.2	−11.5	−17.3	−2.6	1.0
Other income [5]	0.1	29.3	−4.1	4.4	24.1

1. Unrevised figures, not consistent with recent CSO revisions to 1991/1992 national income accounts.
2. From the CSO Statistical Bulletin.
3. Non-agricultural jobs held by farmers.
4. Contract work.
5. Including imputed rents.
Source: Ministry of Finance estimates, Central Statistical Office.

goods to industrial sales began falling in July 1991, followed several months later by the ratio of finished goods inventories to sales. These began to stabilise in the second half of 1993.

Exports, predominantly to the OECD area, grew by 10 per cent in 1992, making a strong contribution to growth of GDP. In 1993, exports grew by only 1 per cent but the slowdown was concentrated in the first half; after August 1993, following a widely anticipated devaluation, they recovered strongly. Coming in the midst of a recession in western Europe the performance of exports must be viewed as good, and may be attributable to improvements on the supply side which are discussed below. In particular, although the real effective exchange rate has fluctuated over the period, showing some tendency to appreciate, labour productivity has increased more rapidly than wages, thereby lowering relative unit labour costs.

15

Production increases have become more widespread

In 1992 industrial output growth was unevenly distributed across branches. This changed in 1993 when industrial growth accelerated: the coefficient of variation of output growth fell from 2.39 in 1992 to 0.84 in 1993.[3] In 1992 industries suffering from the collapse of ex-CMEA markets and defense contracts continued to decline: many of these industries also suffered from the switch of consumer and capital good demand towards imports.[4] With the exception of leather, non-ferrous metallurgy, power and coal, all sectors grew in 1993.

Reflecting the differing growth rates of sectoral output, some changes in the productive structure of the economy have become apparent. The share of heavy industries – mining, metallurgy and engineering products – declined while transport equipment, fuel and food grew. Overall, the share of industry – initially very large in comparison to countries with similar per capita GDP – declined by 4 percentage points between 1990 and 1992, with construction and trade increasing proportionately. The share of employment in the service sector increased from 35.4 per cent in 1989 to 43.6 per cent in 1993, while the proportion in industry fell from 35.3 to 30.7 (Annex IV).

Inflation has fallen and relative prices stabilised

Consumer and producer price inflation has continued to decline although the deceleration appears to be slowing. Year-on-year consumer price inflation fell from 70 per cent in 1991 to 43 per cent in 1992 and 35 per cent in 1993. The development of inflation in both years was strongly influenced by changes in administered or policy-influenced prices. The government has pursued a policy of slowly adjusting household energy prices to world levels, and public transport prices and state-controlled rents to levels which will eventually cover costs. Together with tax changes, such price increases contributed some 7 percentage points to inflation in 1992 but only around 1 or 2 percentage points in 1993. Removing the effects of energy prices and tax increases, inflation for the rest of the consumer basket did not differ greatly between the two years.

The gap between consumer and producer prices has been declining. Producer price inflation fell from 48 per cent in 1991 to 29 per cent in 1992 but rebounded to 32 per cent in 1993 following the introduction of VAT, which contributed about 5 percentage points to the increase (Diagram 2). Policy-

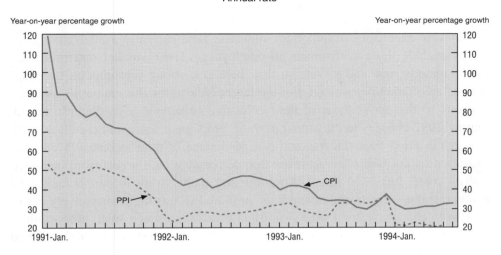

Diagram 2. **FALLING INFLATION**
Annual rate

Year-on-year percentage growth

Year-on-year percentage growth

CPI

PPI

1991-Jan.   1992-Jan.   1993-Jan.   1994-Jan.

Source: Central Statistical Office, *Statistical Bulletin.*

induced changes in industrial organisation led to a substantial increase in coal prices in the second half of 1993. Relative producer prices have finally started to stabilise even though the relative price of energy continued to increase through 1993. As noted in the first *Economic Survey,* the variation of relative prices was high in 1990/1991 and this increased still further in 1992: the standard deviation of annual price changes across industrial branches increased from 25 to 29. However, in 1993 the standard deviation fell to 6 points.[5]

There is evidence of changing behaviour and resource reallocation

The behaviour of exports, fixed investment and inventories, as well as the changing sectoral structure of production, suggest that improved supply-side behaviour has been a driving force in the recovery. This interpretation is supported by the changes which have occurred in the ownership structure of the economy, improved financial discipline, inter-sectoral resource flows, and a decline in the level of losses incurred by enterprises. For important segments of the economy wage setting is not yet subject to market forces, and enterprise balance sheets and profitability remain weak.

17

Reallocation of resources

The changing branch structure of industry in 1992 indicates that market forces were exercising an important influence. Data currently available on enterprises exclude those with under 50 employees.[6] These smaller enterprises are predominantly new and private so that there is a strong presumption that their actions are market-determined. For the larger older firms this cannot be assumed *a priori* so that an analysis of their collective behaviour is particularly useful. During 1992 changes in the output of these firms were positively correlated with changes in gross financial returns (as a percentage of total income).[7] Moreover, increased output was often achieved despite pressure on margins from increased energy costs. Increased financial returns and output were in part achieved by economising on inputs and inventories: profitability was highly negatively correlated with changes in total stocks (finished goods represent a small proportion of total stocks) so that sectors which economised on inputs were more profitable and also more inclined to increase output. In 1993 some of these statistical relationships weakened, particularly the relationship of profits and inventories, as demand factors may have played a more important role.

Although statistics must be treated with caution, an important reallocation of capital appears to be taking place through both investment and the sale of existing assets. As noted above, investment by smaller enterprises has increased substantially. For the larger enterprises, investment, though declining in aggregate, shifted during the review period away from heavy industries toward light industries, communications and trade. A significant proportion of investment appears to be directed toward renovations and small, low-cost, modifications with very high rates of return and short pay-back periods.[8] Moreover, sectoral investment has been correlated with profitability: in 1992 relative profitability explained around 70 per cent of the variance of investment across sectors, although this relationship weakened to 30 per cent in 1993.

The private sector, which now accounts for over 50 per cent of GDP and around 57 per cent for the labour force, has been the driving force behind economic growth. Along with the rapid creation of new businesses and growing investment, much of its expansion has occurred through a reallocation of the capital stock. This has occurred via asset sales from state-owned enterprises, particularly in 1991 when asset sales could have accounted for around 30 per cent of their income. Another method has also been important: around 1 000 enterprises have been liquidated under Article 19 of the Law on State-Owned Enterprises (this is different from the bankruptcy procedure) and assets sold to the highest bidders.[9] Private-sector industrial production grew at annual rates of 23.4 and 34.7 per cent in 1992 and 1993 respectively, its share of total production increasing 7 percentage points to 37 per cent (Table 3). In 1993 private industrial enterprises reported profit margins of only 1.7 per cent, which would appear to be

Table 3. **Development of the private sector**

	1989	1990	1991 [1]	1992	1993	1990	1991 [1]	1992	1993
	Share in percentage					Year-on-year percentage growth			
GDP [2]	28.4	35.0	45.3	49.7	50.0+	–	33.3	11.3	10.0
Employment [3]									
Including private agriculture [4]	43.9	45.1	50.2	53.7	57.5	–1.6	4.8	2.4	6.5
Excluding private agriculture [5]	29.6	30.9	36.6	40.4	45.2	–0.4	9.9	4.7	10.5
External trade									
Total	–	8.6	36.2	47.2	53.0	–	–	–	–
Exports	–	4.9	21.9	38.4	44.0	–	–	–	–
Imports	–	14.4	49.9	54.5	59.8	–	–	–	–
Investment [6]	35.3	41.3	40.8	44.0	42.8	0.1	–8.6	15.2	–
Sales [7]									
Industry	16.2	18.3	27.0	30.8	37.4	–27.2	25.2	23.4	34.7
Construction [8]	33.4	41.7	63.1	78.7	86.8	–	63.2	35.0	19.5
Trade [9]	59.5	63.7	82.8	86.4	88.9	15.4	39.6	12.5	12.3
Transport [10]	11.5	14.2	26.5	38.1	44.1	–	34.5	39.1	18.5
Unincorporated businesses (number in millions)	–	1.135	1.420	1.630	1.784	39.6	25.1	14.8	9.4
Incorporated businesses	–	33 239	47 690	58 218	66 391	153.6	43.5	22.1	14.2

1. New definition of private sector: including co-operative sector. In 1990 legal changes created a true co-operative sector, so that from 1991 it has been classified as part of the private sector.
2. In constant prices of 1984 for 1989-90; prices of 1990 for 1991-93.
3. Average for year.
4. As share of total employment.
5. As share of non-agricultural employment.
6. In current prices.
7. Share of private-sector sold production on total sales, in current prices.
8. Building and construction.
9. Retail sales.
10. Sold services.
Source: Central Statistical Office and Central Planning Office.

inconsistent with the efficient allocation of capital, but this result is difficult to reconcile with the high observed levels of growth.[10] In other sectors such as construction and trade, private ownership is already dominant. These profound changes in ownership have been associated with an equally important change in enterprise structure: whereas in 1991, 91 per cent of output was accounted for by firms with above 50 employees (20 in services) by 1993 this proportion had fallen to 86 per cent.

Underlying these ownership and sectoral changes, and contributing to their overall efficiency, has been an improvement in financial and especially payments discipline. This is a difficult concept to measure but a number of indicators point in a similar direction. First, actions between debtors and creditors have increased. The number of Chapter 11-type actions (under the Law on the Mutual Settlement of Debts) increased from 76 in 1991 to 688 in 1992 and 665 in 1993, and the number of petitions for bankruptcy increased from 1 250 to 3 661 and 5 249 respectively, even though the cost and uncertainty of this latter procedure discourages petitions.[11] Second, inter-enterprise credit, which had been growing rapidly in 1991 – and had been noted with concern in the last *Economic Survey* – stabilised in 1992/1993: the ratio of payables to total income has remained constant and the ratio of payables to receivables has increased only modestly. Third, over the same period real bank credit has declined substantially. Nevertheless, payments discipline, while substantially improved, still has some way to go: all enterprises complain of slow payment and excessive legal barriers to debt collection.

Productivity, profits and wages

A striking feature of the economic recovery has been the growth of aggregate labour productivity: labour productivity in industry (measured in terms of gross output) increased by 13 per cent in 1992 and by a further 9.6 per cent in 1993. Productivity gains were widespread although variable across industrial branches (Annex IV); no comparable figures are yet available for the service sectors.

Despite the marked improvement in labour productivity, reported gross profit margins – at least in those larger firms covered by the statistics currently available – fell in 1992 by some 2.5 percentage points. The deterioration was fairly widespread, including several service sectors such as trade. A great deal of the deterioration was driven by cuts in subsidies and especially by the decline in income from sales of assets. Profitable enterprises bore the brunt of the decline in profit margins while large losses were concentrated in a few branches: mining, ferrous metallurgy and transport equipment. Aggregate profits recovered in 1993 by 1.5 percentage points but this was mainly due to declining losses rather than rising profitability: gross losses in relation to income declined from 17.7 per cent to 11.8 per cent while the gross profit margin for profitable firms, which had declined in 1992, remained constant at 8.4 per cent.

The balance sheet for the enterprise sector as a whole – at least that part covered by the statistics – has deteriorated, reflecting the fact that in aggregate it has been earning negative net profits for several years. Accordingly, the ratio of current assets to liabilities has fallen steadily from 1.6 in January 1991 to 0.9 in January 1994 while the ratio of current liabilities to total income has doubled over the same period. The losses have not been financed through increased inter-enterprise credit which, as a share of new additional financing, has fallen from 41 per cent in 1991 to 26 per cent in 1994, nor from bank financing, which declined from 36 per cent in 1991 to 28 per cent in 1992 before recovering to 37 per cent in 1993. Rather liabilities to the budget have increased rapidly, particularly in the form of lease payments and arrears to the social security fund (FUS); liabilities to the FUS, amongst others, increased from 15 per cent of current liabilities to 23 per cent in January 1994. Tax arrears are, however, highly concentrated in a few large firms and sectors. Enterprises with high tax arrears often have large indebtedness to banks: the bulk of enterprises have no or very little debt to the banking system. The enterprise sector in Poland is thus extremely dualistic even though this feature diminished somewhat in the course of 1993.

Although increased labour productivity has been accompanied by an increase in producer real wages, the latter has been insufficient to account for the reported changes in profitability. Producer real wages (excluding profit-related bonuses) increased by some 7 per cent in 1992, thereby continuing the strong growth which characterised 1991. The increase decelerated in 1993 to some 3.5 per cent, and, excluding the effects of VAT, would have remained essentially unchanged. With industrial labour productivity increasing by some 13 per cent in 1992 unit labour costs fell, but at the same time recorded profitability declined, both in absolute terms and in relation to income. One explanation for this is the increased price of energy and the continuing burden of debt service. However, measurement error may also be important: tax returns lodged in 1993 indicate that profits in 1992 were substantially higher than statistics based on large enterprises would indicate. In 1993 the further improvement in unit labour costs was reflected in somewhat higher profits and reduced losses, as would be expected.

Over the review period the growth of producer real wages at the sectoral level has varied quite widely, due mainly to different price behaviour. Considering the larger enterprises reported in the currently available statistics, two groupings may be distinguished. In the first group are traditional high-wage branches of Polish industry such as fuel and energy, and metallurgy. Over the period since 1991 these sectors have been able to maintain their relative wage *vis-à-vis* other branches. For this group, 1992 increases in nominal wages were negatively related to labour productivity implying non-market behaviour and sharing of monopoly rents. (This relationship appeared to weaken in 1993.) These sectors are characterised not only by strong political influence and large indebtedness but also by a greater incidence of regulated (or quasi-regulated) prices. Changes in such prices were a major factor in 1993 when real wages declined in coal, fuel and mining – as did losses. In the second group, covering most other industrial sectors of the economy, relative wage costs exhibited a consistent and very strong relationship to productivity suggesting stronger financial discipline.

There are indications that the malfunctioning of the labour market is inhibiting growth and the creation of employment in sizable sectors of the economy. With the exception of highly educated manpower, there appears to be no tendency for occupational wages to converge across sectors of the economy. Wage rigidity in traditional high-wage sectors of the economy has slowed the realignment of relative wages, and has probably contributed to unemployment and the stickiness of inflation. While the appropriate relationship between sectoral productivity changes and wages in economies with fully-developed markets is still an object of discussion, in Poland the close relationship between the two has restricted the pass-through of productivity growth into lower prices and higher output. In the private sector, competitive forces in the labour markets may be becoming more significant, although newly privatised firms also appear, at least initially, to be concerned with preservation of employment and wages.

Unemployment

Unemployment[12] continued to increase in 1992 and 1993, but its rate of growth slowed. Whereas over one million people were added to the register in 1991, only an additional 350 000 and 380 000, respectively, were added in the following two years. Nonetheless this growth pushed the unemployment rate steadily higher; it reached 16 per cent in early 1994. Regional disparities in unemployment, particularly urban-rural, have widened substantially. In 1993 unemployment in rural, administrative areas (voivods) increased to 30.3 per cent as opposed to 7.6 per cent in other voivods.[13] Thus the large urban, industrial centres of Warsaw, Cracow, Poznan and Katowice[14] exhibit the lowest unemployment rates, while the less urbanised voivods of northern Poland, characterised by large state farms and poor-quality soil, suffer from the highest rates of unemployment, with many having rates well over 20 per cent.

The slower growth of unemployment during 1992-1993 was due to a significant increase in the outflow from the pool of the registered unemployed (Table 4). By itself, this does not constitute an improvement in the labour market. Although the outflow to employment has steadily increased in absolute terms since 1991, it has fallen relative to the level of unemployment. The monthly rate of outflow into employment was under 2 per cent of the unemployed labour force in 1992-1993.[15] Nearly a third of the outflow constituted persons removed from the register because they did not confirm their availability to work or because they gave up their unemployment status. One reason for this appears to be that

Table 4. **Unemployment: inflows and outflows**[1]

Thousands

Increment of unemployment		Inflow		Outflow	
		Total	Previously worked	Total	To work
1990	1 126	1 595	1 140	469	319
1991	1 030	1 720	1 277	690	501
1992	354	1 560	1 237	1 206	656
1993	380	1 970	1 582	1 590	763
1994[2]	92	1 214	n.a.	1 121	600

1. Registered unemployment.
2. First seven months of year.
Source: "Registered unemployment in Poland", I-IV Quarter 1993 Cenral Statistical Office, Warsaw 1994.

many workers fail to re-register when their unemployment benefits terminate after one year. Even so the percentage of registered unemployed no longer receiving benefits increased from 21 per cent in 1991 to over 50 per cent in 1993, most of this growth taking place in late 1992. In 1990-1991 a high proportion of the outflow had been accounted for by early retirements but in 1992-1993 this was only marginal. Inflows into unemployment have remained at a high level, reflecting continuing restructuring, even though mass layoffs have declined.[16] New entrants into the labour force have risen, lifting the proportion of the unemployed who are first-job seekers from 17 per cent to 20 per cent.

The typical unemployed is young, female, and has only a basic vocational education. This stereotype has changed only slowly since 1990. In many state-owned industrial firms, women were often employed in the internalised service sector in clerical positions, or as part of the associated social, educational and cultural institutions. With restructuring, these jobs were the first to be eliminated. In 1993, as restructuring affected the work place more fully, the increase in male unemployment exceeded (slightly) that for females for the first time since the transition began. Unemployment rates tend to decrease with age and education. Continued reliance by enterprises on natural attrition of the work force has made it difficult for new job entrants to find work. The cohort aged under 25 accounts for over one-third of total unemployment,[17] and that under 34 for over 60 per cent, though school-leavers *per se* account for only a small proportion of total unemployment – some 7 per cent. Unemployment among older workers is quite low, possibly due to the policy, pursued especially in 1991, of promoting early retirements following mass layoffs. This may also explain why unemployment among workers with only a primary education is lower than among those with vocational training; many older workers were the least-educated, so that their retirement has altered the profile.

Trade performance

After growing dynamically during the first two years of transition, the growth of exports slowed from about mid-1992 to late 1993. Indeed, on a payments basis they declined by 3.0 per cent in 1993. At the same time imports have continued to grow steadily, with a surge in the last months of 1992 and the first half of 1993; during 1993 imports increased by 17.7 per cent (Diagram 3). As a result, the registered trade balance on a payments basis deteriorated by some

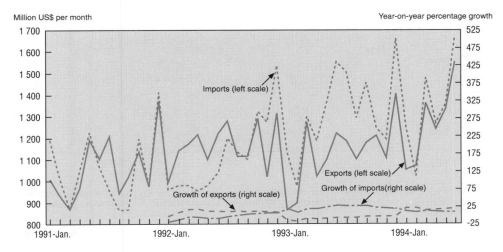

Diagram 3. **THE DEVELOPMENT OF EXPORTS AND IMPORTS**
(Payments basis)

Source: National Bank of Poland.

$1.8 billion in 1993[18] giving rise to concerns about the competitiveness of Polish exports, and the openness of both domestic and foreign markets.

The slowdown in exports between mid-1992 and mid-1993 does not appear to be adequately explained by declining competitiveness. Measured in terms of real effective exchange rates (using producer prices) competitiveness began to decline in mid-1992 through year-end, and then improved following the August devaluation (Diagram 4).[19] However, the level of competitiveness over this period was not greatly different from 1991 when export performance was reasonable. Measured in terms of unit labour costs, competitiveness improved during the course of 1991-1992 while the zloty remains devalued in comparison to estimates of its purchasing power parity exchange rate. Competitiveness may have been a problem for particular products and markets: bilateral trade with the six countries which devalued in late 1992 or early 1993 (Italy, United Kingdom, Finland, Sweden, Norway and Spain) declined by some 10 per cent in 1992. Exports to Germany, which account for some 32 per cent of all exports, declined by around 1 per cent as German GDP fell by 1.3 per cent. Apart from particular

Diagram 4. **INDICATORS OF COMPETITIVENESS**

Real effective exchange rates

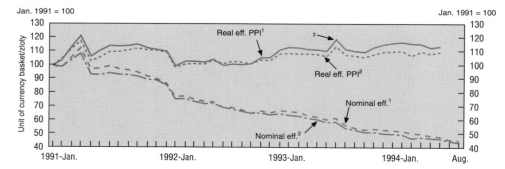

1. Currency basket comprises Poland's six major trading partners, with weights assigned as the average of import and export weights for 1992: (Germany: .52, Italy: .12, United Kingdom: .1, Netherlands: .1, France: .08, Austria: .07).
2. Currency basket comprises ECU and US$, at weights of .7 and .3, respectively.
3. The sudden increase in the real effective exchange rate in July 1993 (arrow) is due to the introduction of VAT, which increased prices by some 5 per cent. As exports are zero-rated, there has in fact been no decline in actual competitiveness of Polish producers.
Source: OECD Secretariat statistics and calculations.

products, there is no evidence that trade barriers increased – quite the contrary (see Chapter II). For certain products, higher domestic demand and internal prices, together with limited capacity, crowded-out exports, but it is not likely that this was an important factor overall: there is no evidence of a build-up in unfilled orders.

The rapid rise in imports appears to reflect three influences: the changing structure of the economy, expectations of tax and exchange rate changes, and excess demand. The Polish economy is characterised by a comparatively low level of imports relative to GDP, which will undoubtedly increase in the course of restructuring. Although there is reason to be cautious in aggregating trade data, imports are dominated by intermediate inputs which accounted for around 61 per cent of total imports (on a customs basis) in 1992 and 1993. Investment and consumer goods comprised 17 and 22 per cent respectively. The increase in consumer imports may have been a one-time level adjustment. A large rebound in durables purchases followed increased consumer confidence as the recovery took hold, and may have been reinforced by long-deferred demand for imported goods. Within the intermediate goods category, energy imports declined from 20 per cent of the total in 1990 to 12.6 per cent in 1993 – largely as a result of the decline in world energy prices by 27 per cent since 1990.[20] It is worth stressing that increased imports of intermediate products contribute to the competitiveness and productivity of the Polish economy. The rapid surge in imports over the period was also related to the introduction of an import surcharge in late 1992, the expectation of a devaluation in mid-1993, and the introduction of the VAT in July 1993, although the former two factors will ultimately lower the demand for imports, *ceteris paribus*. The fact that nearly all categories of imports increased also suggests a role for generalised excess demand.

Balance of payments and external debt

The structure of the balance of payments has been importantly influenced by debt-related flows. Following the Paris Club agreement signed in April 1991, interest due has been partly offset through interest cancellation. For the period 1991 to 1994, of total interest payments due to all creditors were $13.6 billion, of which $3.2 billion was paid, $6.2 billion to the Paris Club cancelled, and in the absence of an agreement with the London Club until March 1994, interest arrears increased by $3.5 billion. In addition, $500 million were rescheduled, and principal arrears accumulated by $5.4 billion. With respect to the capital account, developments were mixed. Foreign direct investment, at least from the balance of payments perspective, has remained modest and did not cover repayments of medium and long-term debt. Short-term capital inflows were quite strong in 1993 with the bulk of this likely coming from cross-border sales, in effect unrecorded exports. Net sales by the foreign exchange offices (kantors) and the public to the banking system of $1.7 billion, classified as short-term capital inflows, are thought to represent revenue from foreign shoppers and from tourism.[21] Official reserves after a $473 million decrease in 1992, continued to decline in the first half of 1993 by $680 million, but were unchanged for 1993 as a whole. In early 1994 they amounted to around 4.5 months of average imports (Table 5 and Table 6).

The second stage of the Paris Club Agreement, providing for an additional 20 per cent debt reduction, came into force in April 1994 after Poland successfully completed the IMF stand-by programme. The first stage of the debt reduction[22] was valuable for Poland: in addition to interest cancellation, six countries

Table 5. Balance of payments in convertible currency [1]
Million US$

		1990	1991 [2]	1992	1993	1994 [3]
A.	**Current account**	716	−1 359	−269	−2 329	−527
	Merchandise exports	10 863	12 760	13 997	13 585	7 621
	Merchandise imports	8 649	12 709	13 485	15 878	8 055
	Trade balance	2 214	51	512	−2 293	−434
	Services: credit	1 327	1 577	1 612	1 846	918
	Services: debit	1 477	1 341	1 268	1 477	900
	Services: net	−150	236	344	369	18
	Interest income: net	–	–	85	100	35
	Interest: receipts	581	541	527	400	118
	Interest: payments	3 910	3 404	4 666	3 924	1 567
	Interest: net	−3 329	−2 863	−4 139	−3 524	−1 449
	Unrequited transfers: credit	6 320	7 153	8 319	7 874	3 813
	Private	6 015	6 244	5 620	5 676	2 920
	Official	305	909	2 699	2 198	893
	Unrequited transfers: debit	4 339	5 936	5 390	4 855	2 510
	Private	4 339	5 936	5 390	4 855	2 510
	Official	0	0	0	0	0
	Unrequited transfers: net	1 981	1 217	2 929	3 019	1 303
	Private	1 676	308	230	821	410
	Official	305	909	2 699	2 198	893
B.	**Medium and long-term capital**	−4 153	−4 472	−984	120	166
	Credits received	−4 205	−4 632	−1 289	−471	−120
	Drawings	428	786	562	922	173
	Repayments	4 633	5 418	1 851	1 393	293
	Credits extended	42	43	21	11	−5
	Drawings	22	49	10	6	14
	Repayments	64	92	31	17	9
	Direct investment: net	10	117	284	580	291
C.	**Short-term capital**	−451	−1 254	−570	1 152	1 198
	Credits received	−339	8	–	−74	−30
	Credits extended	7	−46	–	21	−6
	Buying and selling foreign currency	−119	−620	–	1 750	1 582
	Other financial operations	–	−596	–	−545	−348
D.	**Errors and omissions**	360	−699	50	17	368
E.	**Exceptional financing**	7 755	6 569	2 500	1 376	471
	Rescheduled obligations	6 572	2 091	0	0	3
	Changes in arrears	−2 930	4 478	2 500	1 376	468
	– increase	1 183	4 587	2 533	1 387	468
	– decrease (paid)	−4 113	−109	−33	−11	0
F.	**Valuation changes in:**	0	−58	−254	217	−307
	– Official reserves	0	−29	−149	106	−179
	– other assets and liabilities	0	−29	−105	111	−128
Total (A-F)		4 227	−1 273	473	553	1 369
G.	**Changes in reserves:**	−4 227	1 273	–	−553	−1 369
	Changes in official reserves	−1 938	1 188	−473	6	−916
	Changes in gross official reserves	−2 417	866	−367	128	−1 295
	Credits from IMF	479	322	−106	−122	379
	Changes in other dues and liabilities	−2 289	85	–	−559	−832

1. On a cash basis, excluding credit transactions for 1993 (to become available later).
2. Since 1991 all settlements abroad have been in convertible currency.
3. First six months.
Source: National Bank of Poland.

28

Table 6.   Debt servicing

Million US$

	1990	1991 [1]	1992	1993	1994 [2]
A. Current account					
Interest: payments	3 910	3 404	4 666	3 924	1 567
Due and paid	430	888	1 095	870	385
Due but not paid	3 480	2 516	3 571	3 054	1 182
Rescheduled	2 487	579	0	0	1
Cancelled	0	864	2 041	2 090	841
Converted	8	7	6	5	1
Arrears	985	1 066	1 164	959	339
Unrequited transfers: credit					
Official	305	909	2 699	2 198	893
Foundations	–	–	253	61	47
Food aid	257	0	0	0	
Debt converted	48	45	45	47	5
Debt forgiveness	0	864	2 401	2 090	841
B. Medium and long-term capital	–4 205	–4 632	–1 289	–471	
Credits received	428	786	562	922	173
Repayments	4 633	5 418	1 851	1 393	293
Due and paid	310	347	443	923	158
Due but not paid	4 323	5 071	1 408	470	135
Rescheduled	4 085	1 512	0	0	2
Converted	40	38	39	42	4
Arrears	198	3 521	1 369	428	129

1.   Since 1991 all settlements abroad have been in convertible currency.
2.   First six months.
Source: National Bank of Poland.

chose option "A" (a 30 per cent reduction of capital) reducing the stock of debt by $2.9 billion. With the second stage now in effect, interest liabilities in 1994 and 1995 have been reduced from $984 million and $1.4 billion to $540 and $670 million respectively, and until the turn of the century annual interest payments on Paris Club debt will remain at around $660 million. Principal repayments increase rapidly after the year 2002, peaking in 2008.

In September 1994 an agreement was signed with the London Club to reduce the country's $14 billion debt by 49.2 per cent in conformity with Brady plan rules. The reduction comprises all components of the debt, including accrued interest. Poland will buy back around 26 per cent of the total debt including unpaid interest at 41 cents to the dollar, 55 per cent will be converted to

30-year Brady bonds, 11 per cent to fixed rate par bonds, and the remainder (around 8 per cent) will comprise new money conversion bonds. The time profile of cash flow has been timed to avoid the peaks associated with Paris Club repayments. Interest payments will be on average $400 million during the first five years and $500 million after this as Paris Club payments decline: capital repayments will increase only after 2009 when Paris Club commitments reach their peak. The government's medium-term strategy document, "Strategy for Poland", expresses the intention to reduce substantially foreign debt through debt/equity swaps, but specific plans have still to be formulated.

The London Club agreement has immediate implications for the balance of payments. The monthly servicing commitment has been raised from 15 per cent to 30 per cent of interest due and instalments on revolving credit from 20 to 30 per cent, resulting in payments in 1994 of some $405 million. The initial costs of the agreement, due to debt buy-backs from creditors choosing that option (around 25 per cent by value), and the purchase of zero-coupon US Treasury bonds for collateral, are reported to be $1.9 billion. Budgetary implications are discussed below.

After both London and Paris Club agreements Poland's external debt indicators have improved substantially. It will nevertheless remain a moderately indebted country for some time to come (Table 7). The way is now clear for

Table 7.   **External debt indicators, end-1993** [1]

	GNP per capita (US$) 1992	Interest accrued/exports	Debt/exports	Debt/GDP	Interest accrued/GDP
Poland [1]	1 960	13	346	64	1.2
After London and Paris Clubs	1 960	9	287	53	1.6
Argentina	6 050	22	436	36	1.8
Mexico	3 470	12	233	35	1.8
Philippines	770	9	164	62	3.4
Venezuela	2 900	13	218	60	3.6
Morocco	1 040	18	343	78	4.1
Hungary	3 010	14	303	59	2.8

1.   After first stage of Paris Club. Interest included arreas. With interest actually paid the interest/export ratio in 1993 was 6.4 per cent and in relation to GDP 1.6 per cent.
Source: Poland and Hungary: national source and OECD Secretariat; Morgan Grenfell, Developing Country Research, 26 April 1994. GNP per capita: *World Bank Atlas* 1994.

Poland to return to the international capital markets and for an eventual reduction in the cost of credit to it.[23]

Income Distribution

The social cost of the transition in Poland has become a major source of debate, but the lack of reliable and consistent statistics makes it difficult to assess accurately the relative burden. The Central Statistical Office (GUS) collects statistics on household incomes, expenditures, consumer durable stocks, and on wages. As part of its overall strategy to bring Polish statistics up to OECD standards, beginning with 1993 GUS substantially revised its household surveys; the GUS increased its sample size, and broadened its coverage from four to six household groups – now including the self-employed. While these changes are to be welcomed and augur well for future analysis of Polish incomes, they have the unfortunate consequence of precluding comparisons with earlier years.

It appears that the burden of the transition has fallen hardest on the unemployed, particularly small farmer-employee households. Farmer-employees accounted for a relatively large proportion of job-losers. Farmers (or their spouses) with more than two hectares are not counted as unemployed when they lose their non-farm jobs, and are not eligible for unemployment benefits. The effect on incomes of non-farm job loss is substantial, *e.g.* in 1992 farmers with 5-7 hectares of land receive 58 per cent of their income from non-farm work. Unemployment compensation has been fixed at 36 per cent of the average wage, and expires in 12 months, when it may be replaced with other income support. For former workers in high-wage heavy industries like mining and metallurgy, the drop in income has been large.

The beneficiaries have been the self-employed, with pension recipients and those workers who have retained their jobs in traditional high-wage industries. Estimates from personal income figures indicate that real earnings of the self-employed and contract employees[24] grew at very rapid rates through 1992, and probably accounted for all of the increase in consumption that year. Preliminary estimates indicate that the real income growth for these groups was relatively lower in 1993, probably slightly above the growth rate of GDP. While the relative position of pension recipients has improved – between 1989 and 1993 average pensions grew 18 per cent more than average wages – it is difficult to discern the relative level of pensioners. On the one hand, average pensions are

31

still only 70 per cent of average wages, on the other hand, 1993 expenditure data indicate that pension household expenditures were 115 per cent of employee households.[25]

Finally, there is some evidence that the social cost of transition has been less than could be inferred from declining real wages and pensions, and rising unemployment. Indicative of this are data on consumer durables. While not directly comparable because of the sampling changes mentioned earlier, the increase in consumer durables' holdings between 1990 and 1993 has been so substantial as to be difficult to attribute to changes in sampling technique alone. Thus for farmer-employee households, car ownership per 100 households rose from 35.1 to 53.4, not accounting for quality changes provided by greater access to convertible-currency trade.[26]

Fiscal and monetary policy

Maintaining control of the deficit

In an economy with a relatively simple financial structure such as Poland's, fiscal and monetary policy are intimately linked via the need to finance the deficit. The level of money and credit in the Polish economy is relatively low and the growth of demand for money has appeared to be only moderate. The increase of credit compatible with sustained deflation has thus been limited in both real and nominal terms thereby restricting the room for manœuvre for fiscal policy. On the one hand, a smaller deficit would increase the credit potentially available for the economy but, on the other hand, limited fiscal revenues and spiralling needs, especially social ones, push for a higher share of financing for the deficit. To this simple schema should be added a third factor: the fiscal policy instruments utilised in achieving any given deficit target. Some fiscal policy actions may result in a lower deficit but be so distortionary as to discourage growth and encourage inflation – and *vice versa*.

Fiscal policy in 1992/1993 had to be formulated under these difficult conditions. The deficit has, *ex post*, absorbed a large share of credit expansion (44 and 25 per cent in 1992 and 1993 respectively) while the record on fiscal policy instruments is mixed: against important reforms of the tax system, social security contributions remain very high and there has been little progress in improving the efficiency of expenditures. Moreover, the share of general government expenditures has increased in relation to 1990 and is high by international standards.

Fiscal policy goals and outcomes

The fiscal situation was exceptionally difficult in 1991 with the state budget deficit threatening to deteriorate rapidly in the second half of the year. Exceptional measures and a revised budget were introduced in October 1991 and these succeeded in holding the deficit to 3.8 per cent of GDP. However, it was clear at the time that the measures did not address the fundamental problems and that expenditure programmes – particularly those relating to social security payments and debt service – contained powerful expansionary pressures which had to be dealt with. Tax revenues were particularly weak, illustrating vividly that too much time had been wasted in installing a tax system which would be responsive to wage incomes in particular. These two issues – improving the tax system while maintaining controls over expenditures – dominated fiscal policy in 1992/1993.

The formulation of fiscal policy in 1992 was made difficult by the delay in installing a new government after the elections in 1991: the budget was not passed by the Parliament until June 5. The budget deficit for the year was set at Zl 65 trillion, equivalent to 5 per cent of GDP, and the budget's share of credit expansion was to be around 46 per cent. The deficit was viewed by the government as about the maximum possible, while expenditure – even though expected to rise as a share of GDP by 1.5 percentage points (from 33 to 34.5 per cent) – was regarded as the minimum politically acceptable following the cuts which were made in late 1991. Revenues were projected to rise by 2.4 percentage points, from 26.5 to 28.9 per cent of GDP, reflecting higher turnover taxes and the newly introduced personal income tax.

The outcome for 1992 was a deficit of Zl 69 trillion (around 6 per cent of GDP), despite the budget amendment in November 1992 authorising a deficit of some Zl 81 trillion or around 7.2 per cent of GDP (6.9 per cent for general government). The reason for not using the legislative room to increase the deficit still further was the lack of finance. The increased borrowing limits were only approved at the end of November, and, although the NBP bought all the bills it was committed to by the budget law, there was no time to arrange sales to commercial banks. Revenues were Zl 25 trillion less than expected, the receipts from turnover and corporate taxes being especially weak. Expenditures were

33

Zl 21 trillion lower, mainly on account of smaller-than-planned subsidies to the social insurance fund and payments on foreign debt (together amounting to some Zl 9.5 trillion).

The state budget for 1993 was intended to stabilise the deficit in nominal terms at the level authorised for 1992 – Zl 81 trillion – which would have represented a decline as a share of GDP by around half a percentage point. To this end a large number of measures, mainly on the income side, were put in place. The most important included a 6 per cent surcharge on imports from December 1992, the replacement of the narrowly based turnover tax with a VAT in July 1993, and a 9 per cent cut in pension indexation from March 1993. The share of revenues in GDP was expected to stabilise at around 27.5 per cent but expenditures were expected to fall by some 1.5 percentage points. While fiscal consolidation was an important objective, it was nevertheless a limited one: the share of the deficit in the increase of net domestic assets was still expected to be in the range of 68 per cent as compared to the actual outturn in 1992 of 66 per cent.

The outcome for the state budget deficit for 1993 was considerably better than expected: about Zl 43 trillion on a cash basis or 2.8 per cent as a proportion of GDP. On a commitment basis it would have been higher as the arrears of budgetary units increased by around Zl 4 trillion in the course of the year. Revenues were 6 per cent higher than projected while expenditures were Zl 12 trillion less than budgeted although no budget cuts were necessary: as in 1992, subsidies to the Social Insurance Fund (ZUS) and foreign debt service were less than budgeted (by some Zl 13 trillion).

The success on the budget revenue side was due to personal income tax and the VAT: the revenue from these two taxes was about Zl 13 trillion higher than budgeted. Particularly important was the personal income tax, with revenues about Zl 10 trillion above expectations. Significantly, this was due to an under-estimation of self-employed income in 1992 which led to back taxes being paid in 1993. With respect to the VAT, it was assumed that monthly revenue would be nearly the same as the widened turnover tax; in fact monthly inflows towards the end of the year were around Zl 2 trillion higher.

Although there were undoubted successes in widening the tax base and in improving enforcement, the budget outcome does not adequately reflect the underlying fiscal stance which was more expansionary for most of the year.

Revenues surged in December,[27] while the moderate increase in wages until the end of the year meant that the subsidy to the ZUS was substantially lower than expected. The expenses associated with increased wages, such as subsidies to the social insurance fund, will become evident from the second quarter of 1994 when a revaluation of the pension base will be made. Despite a much lower-than-anticipated budget deficit, real credit to the enterprise sector fell by 5.6 per cent measured in terms of producer prices.

The budget for 1994 provides for a deficit of Zl 83 trillion, or around 4.1 per cent of projected GDP. Both expenditures and revenues will increase as a share of GDP. Outlays on social welfare are set to rise, which means that the role of the state budget in redistributing incomes will increase in 1994. Debt servicing will also increase as a share of total expenditures. The 1994 budget will not permit the ratio of debt/GDP to stabilise; for that a deficit of around 2 per cent of GDP would be necessary. As in 1993, the accompanying monetary plan envisages very little real increase in credit to the enterprise sector: 1.5 per cent in real terms. Consequently budget financing will be tight: the banking sector will have to more than double its purchases of bonds in comparison with 1993 – from Zl 38 trillion to Zl 89 trillion.

The scale of general government is substantially greater than the state budget, with general government expenditure reaching nearly 50 per cent of GDP (Table 8). The general government sector includes eleven extra-budgetary funds (the most important being the two social insurance funds for non-agricultural and agricultural sectors and the Labour Fund which covers unemployment benefits,[28] around 2 000 municipalities and many extra-budgetary units (such as high schools, kindergartens, and economic units) at both central and local levels. About 25 per cent of the Social Insurance Fund's expenditures, 94 per cent of the Farmers Pensions Fund's revenue and 60 per cent of the Labour Fund's revenue represent transfers from the state budget. Without such transfers, the state budget itself would run a surplus and the extra-budgetary funds would be in large deficit.

General government employs close to 2.2 million people or about 17 per cent of the labour force. Of these, 1.1 million work in the education system, 0.8 million in health care and social welfare and 270 000 in the central administration. With this level of employment the budget is significantly affected by wage developments and indeed over the review period public-sector salaries bore the brunt of expenditure control, especially in 1992. The sensitivity of fiscal

35

Table 8. General government expenditures and revenues

	1990	1991	1992	1993	1994	1990	1991	1992	1993	1994
	Trillion zlotys					As percentage of GDP				
Total revenue[1]	268.3	354.7	518.8	742.1	940.8	45.4	43.9	45.1	47.7	46.2
State budget										
Including transfers	196.2	210.9	312.8	459.0	613.0	33.2	26.1	27.1	28.9	30.1
Excluding transfers	195.1	209.6	311.4	450.3	612.4	33.0	25.9	27.2	29.5	30.1
Local budgets	..	37.5	44.5	69.4	88.9	0.0	4.6	3.9	4.5	4.4
Extra-budgetary funds	63.2	84.5	125.0	163.8	218.5	10.7	10.4	10.9	10.5	10.7
State extra-budgetary units	10.0	15.7	18.2	23.0	21.0	1.7	1.9	1.6	1.5	1.0
Local extra-budgetary units	..	7.4	19.7	27.9	..	..	0.9	1.7	1.8	..
Total expenditure[1]	252.6	370.6	575.0	778.0	1 018.6	42.7	45.8	50.0	50.0	50.0
State budget										
Including inter-govt. transfers	193.8	241.9	381.9	502.4	696.0	32.8	29.9	33.2	32.3	34.2
Excluding inter-govt. transfers	150.6	165.7	244.9	324.4	465.6	25.5	20.5	21.3	20.8	22.9
Local budgets	..	35.0	48.1	71.7	106.3	..	4.3	4.2	4.6	5.2
Extra-budgetary units	91.0	144.7	239.0	322.0	422.4	15.4	17.9	20.8	20.7	20.7
State extra-budgetary units	11.0	13.0	15.0	21.2	24.3	1.9	1.6	1.3	1.4	1.2
Local extra-budgetary units	..	12.2	28.0	40.3	..	..	1.5	2.4	2.6	..
Total deficit[1]	15.7	-15.9	-56.2	-35.9	-77.8	2.7	-1.9	-4.9	-2.3	-3.8
State budget										
Including transfers	2.4	-31.0	-69.1	-43.4	-83.0	0.4	-3.8	-6.0	-2.8	-4.1
Excluding transfers	44.5	43.9	66.5	125.9	146.8	7.5	5.4	5.8	8.1	7.2
Local budgets	..	2.5	-3.6	-2.3	-17.4	..	0.3	-0.3	-0.1	-0.9
Extra-budgetary funds	-27.8	-60.2	-114.0	-158.2	-203.9	-4.7	-7.4	-9.9	-10.2	-10.0
State extra-budgetary units	-1.0	2.7	3.2	1.8	-3.3	-0.2	0.3	0.3	0.1	-0.2
Local extra-budgetary units	..	-4.8	-8.3	-12.4	..	..	-0.6	-0.7	-0.8	..

1. Excluding inter-sectoral transfers between its elements, *i.e.* state budget, local budgets, extra-budgetary funds and extra-budgetary units.
Source: Ministry of Finance.

policy outcomes to wage developments is further increased by the indexing of many social benefits to the average level of wages in the economy.

The changing composition of incomes and expenditures

As a result of continuing changes to the tax system, the structure of state budget revenues has shifted steadily in the direction of that usual in a market economy: indirect and personal taxes accounted in 1993 for around 65 per cent of state budget revenue (it was about half of this in 1990) while the role of corporate taxes has fallen from 43 per cent to 14 per cent (Diagram 5). The structural weakness of the budget *vis-à-vis* enterprise profitability, which was painfully apparent in 1991, has thus been substantially diminished and tax revenues are now more responsive to both prices and wages. Three general issues however, remain to be solved. First, a number of marginal tax rates are too high and this is especially true of the social security contributions. Second, the share of tax payments by the private sector remains disproportionately low: they amounted to 8 per cent of profits taxes over the last two years even though the private sector's

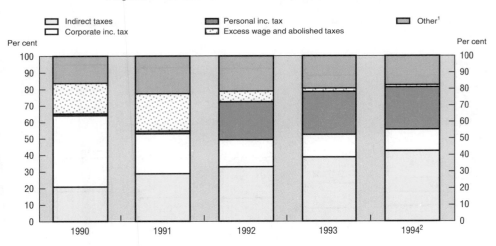

Diagram 5. **STRUCTURE OF STATE BUDGET REVENUE**

1. Non-tax, privatisation and foreign revenue.
2. Budget Act projection.
Source: Ministry of Finance.

37

share of total sales has risen from 7 per cent at the end of 1991 to 23 per cent in September 1993. Third, tax enforcement clearly needs to be improved and separated from questions of industrial policy which needs to be placed on a more transparent footing (Chapter II).

Over the period the structure of government expenditures has shifted away from subsidies and investment, as observed in 1990/1991, toward debt service and social expenditure, and this is expected to continue. These latter two expenditures are substantially under-represented in Diagram 6. Interest payments are on a cash basis and will therefore rise as Poland becomes current on its foreign debt. The item "social insurance" only represents state budget subsidies to the pension funds. Taking expenditures by these funds into account shows that Poland is now characterised by about the same level of social security expenditures in relation to GDP (around 20 per cent) as countries in western Europe which have substantially higher levels of national income.

The growth of social security transfers in relation to GDP was arrested in 1992 and 1993 by a number of measures which reduced the level and frequency

Diagram 6. **STRUCTURE OF STATE BUDGET EXPENDITURE**

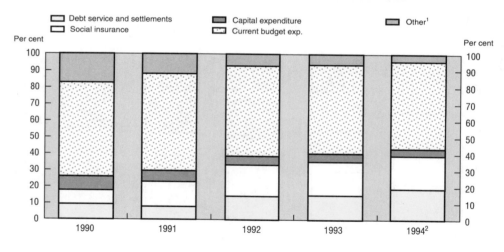

1. Subsidies and reserves of the Council of Ministers.
2. Budget Act projection.
Source: Ministry of Finance.

38

of indexation of benefits. The budget measures of late 1991 reduced some pensions and removed branch benefits. However, these measures were overturned by the Constitutional Tribunal in 1992 and branch benefits were reinstated in 1993. The liability for back payments amounts to some Zl 20 trillion and the expectation is that this will be settled by the issue of mass privatisation vouchers (in the National Investment Funds) to claimants. Large savings were made in 1993 when the revaluation of benefits was lowered from 100 per cent to 91 per cent of the average wage. Taken together the measures reduced the replacement ratio from 65.3 to 60.7 per cent of average wage, in 1991 and 1993, respectively (Diagram 7). However the number of pensioners has continued to increase, though at a smaller rate than in 1991, while the number of contributors has steadily declined. As a result, the proportion of the social insurance and labour funds financed by the state budget has increased from 12.9 per cent in 1989 to around 30 per cent in 1993.

In 1994 social security payments will increase both in relation to the budget and GDP: in real terms they will grow by some 6.4 per cent with the bulk of the

Diagram 7. **FACTORS UNDERLYING PENSION EXPENDITURES**

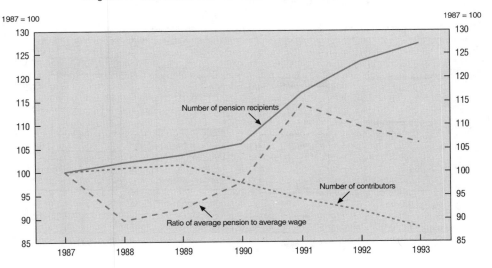

Source: Ministry of Labour and Social Affairs.

increment accruing to the farmers' pension fund (KRUS). This growth is only partly due to demographic factors[29] and more to a policy decision to increase the replacement rates: normal pensions will rise by 3.5 per cent in real terms and farmers' pensions by 11 per cent, from 63 per cent to 67 per cent of the wage earners' pension.

Financing the deficit and the growth of public debt

The financial aspects of fiscal policy have changed markedly over the period in response to a steadily increasing public sector borrowing requirement.[30] Long-term and short-term marketable debt instruments have been introduced, although the banking sector still accounts for about 90 per cent of budgetary finance. With the repayment of foreign liabilities and the assumption of responsibility by the budget for numerous domestic debts, the borrowing requirement has increased steadily: in 1994 it will be around Zl 115 trillion, Zl 30 trillion higher than the prospective deficit.[31] The conduct of fiscal policy is being increasingly restricted by the build-up of debt and the need to service it fully (Diagram 8).

Diagram 8. **STRUCTURE OF STATE BUDGET DEFICIT FINANCING**

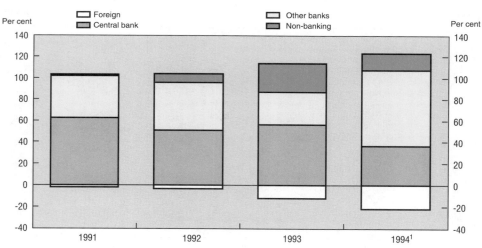

1.   Budget Act projection.
Source: Ministry of Finance.

The most rapidly growing component of debt is domestic and it is responsible for a large increase in the debt servicing expenditures of the budget. Domestic debt was 19.3 per cent of the total at the end of 1991 (15.4 per cent of GDP), 24.7 per cent at the end of 1992 and 26 per cent at the end of 1993 (23 per cent of GDP). About 20 per cent of domestic debt is at non-market interest rates and 25 per cent is denominated in dollars, increasing the sensitivity of the budget to exchange rate changes. Outstanding external liabilities from the 1970s amounted to about $47 billion (not including the second tranche of the Paris Club debt reduction) at the end of 1993: around Zl 995 trillion at the current exchange rate or about 64 per cent of GDP. The share of Paris Club debt is about 62 per cent of the total.

The share of debt service in budget expenditure increased from 4 per cent in 1991 to 8 per cent in 1992; it increased further to 12 per cent in 1993, or 3.9 per cent of GDP. Debt service in 1994 is expected to reach Zl 103 trillion while the whole budget deficit will be about Zl 83 trillion. As a result of the London and Paris Club agreements Poland will start to fully service its (reduced) foreign debt, and interest payments in the next several years will amount to some $1.2 billion annually ($660 million for the Paris Club and $400 million for the London Club). The 1994 budget plan foresees foreign interest payments more than doubling, whereas total expenditure will rise by 38.5 per cent. The immediate impact of the London Club agreement will be a surge in interest payments, but in 1994 part of these will be accounted off-budget.

Monetary and exchange rate policy

During the first phase of the transition in 1990 the objectives for monetary policy were as clear-cut as the instruments were limited: to defend convertibility of the zloty and to bring down quickly the very high levels of inflation. For this purpose, until October 1991 the exchange rate was used as a nominal, though from time to time variable, anchor and it was central to the formulation of monetary policy. However the deceleration of inflation proved to be slower than expected, leading to a real appreciation which was regarded as impairing Poland's growth prospects. In order to minimise any further real appreciation, a pre-announced crawling exchange rate regime was introduced and has remained in effect throughout the review period.

The importance attached to the maintenance of substantial current account convertibility[32] has remained but with respect to inflation the objective is now to bring inflation down gradually. In combination with the move to a crawling exchange rate system, the impression has been given that monetary policy has more room for manœuvre than in the past. As a result, conflicting demands on the authorities have proliferated and policy constraints have multiplied, making the conduct of monetary policy even more difficult. Three specific points might be cited in this regard. First, growing public debt and relatively high fiscal deficits have led to pressures to keep interest rates low and on a downward track. Moreover because so many fiscal arrangements are linked to the refinance rate of interest it has become very difficult to use it as a policy instrument. Second, pressures on the NBP to sustain growth and not to do anything that would threaten recovery have increased markedly. This has included demands to increase the growth of credit to the enterprise sector, lower real and nominal interest rates, and help finance comparatively large fiscal deficits. At the same time systemic weakness in the banking system necessitated tightening prudential regulations, resulting in a ''credit crunch'', as banks have sought to improve their balance sheets. Third, the need to maintain and to increase official reserves, together with concerns about growth and the balance of payments, has resulted in demands on the NBP to target the real exchange rate – with all the ambiguities that this brings for controlling inflation – rather than to use the exchange rate as a nominal anchor, even adjustable.

Monetary developments 1992-1993

Monetary conditions over the period present a conflicting picture. From the perspective of credit to economic units, monetary conditions tightened considerably. Real credit fell in 1992 and again in 1993, though some of the latter resulted from a one-off increase in the PPI of around 5 per cent following the introduction of the VAT in July. By contrast, credit to the budget increased strongly over the period.[33] When viewed in terms of the quantity of money, conditions have been quite accommodating. Real money supply increased by 8 and 18 per cent (CPI- and PPI-deflated, respectively) over the period and income velocity fell steadily from 3.6 in 1991 to 3.2 in 1993. The bulk of the increase in money supply occurred in the second half of 1992 and in December 1993; for 1993 it was relatively stable for the year as a whole (Table 9 and Diagram 9).

Table 9. **Consolidated banking system**

End-of-quarter, current trillion zlotys

	Q4 1991	Q4 1992	Q4 1993	Q2 1994
Total money	261.0	411.1	559.2	630.4
Domestic currency	196.5	309.2	398.3	449.9
Cash circulation (excl. cash in bank vaults)	56.2	78.0	99.8	121.6
Cash issue	–	–	–	–
Cash in bank vaults	–	–	–	–
Individuals' savings deposits, *of which:*	68.6	121.7	162.7	185.6
Demand	10.5	16.7	25.5	30.8
Enterprise funds (deposits)	71.8	109.5	135.9	142.7
Foreign exchange accounts	64.5	101.9	160.9	180.5
Individuals' accounts	61.2	98.3	154.3	171.9
Enterprise accounts	3.2	3.6	6.6	8.6
Assets	261.0	411.1	559.2	630.4
Net foreign reserves	77.8	132.1	186.9	226.0
in bn US $	7.1	8.4	8.8	10.0
Domestic assets, net	183.2	279.0	372.4	404.4
Credit for non-financial sector	193.6	248.9	332.0	369.8
Credit for the budgetary sector, net[1]	88.3	190.0	300.3	331.7
Balance of other items	−98.7	−159.9	−259.9	−297.1
Memorandum item:				
Official exchange rate	10 957.0	15 767.0	21 344.0	22 626.0

1.   Including municipalities, extrabudgetary funds and units.
Source: National Bank of Poland and Central Statistical Office.

Tightened prudential regulations and more cautious lending behaviour by banks contributed to a decline in real credit to economic units and increasing adverse selection during 1992 and 1993. In 1992 the NBP introduced new regulations which increased substantially the amount banks had to set aside for provisioning against non-performing loans, tightened capital-adequacy ratios (see Chapter III), required banks to establish bad-debt workout departments, and prohibited fresh loans to enterprises with non-performing loans. In combination with the change in management responsibilities following bank incorporation in 1991, banks' lending policy became increasingly risk-averse and high collateral was demanded for new loans. At the same time, the demand for credit by enterprises was said to be low, the high level of interest rates being often cited as a reason. Another reason may have been that, with the threat of bankruptcy

Diagram 9. **GROWTH OF REAL MONEY AND CREDIT**
En-of-quarter

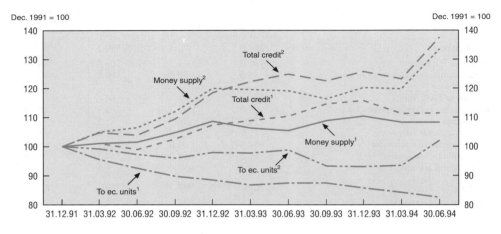

Dec. 1991 = 100

1. CPI-deflated.
2. PPI-deflated.
Source: National Bank of Poland.

increasing, many Polish firms became more risk-averse, avoiding borrowing and repaying debts when they could in an effort to become debt-free. Bank credits remain highly concentrated both by sector and by enterprise.[34]

The sharp decline in credit was not foreseen in the policy framework for 1992 and the contraction may have been even greater than aggregate figures would indicate. The monetary plan for 1992 foresaw an increase in credit of Zl 80 trillion which would have amounted to a real increase of some 3.6 per cent. To achieve such an objective the NBP continued credit controls on the 14 major banks but the shortfall from these ceilings increased throughout the year.[35] Aggregate figures mask important changes in the credit process: out of a nominal increase of Zl 58 trillion some Zl 10 trillion was due to interest capitalisation, and directed credits to agriculture and construction amounted to around Zl 10 trillion. For a large segment of the economy nominal credit may have actually declined. During 1993 the value of credits to the non-financial sector increased 32 per cent in nominal terms as banks started lending again.

44

The changes in prudential regulations and in bank behaviour have had important implications for the conduct of monetary policy by increasing bank liquidity and the money multiplier. Rising bank liquidity has resulted from the "flight to security" as banks have reduced their exposure to the enterprise sector (*i.e.* loans) and increased their holdings of government securities, mainly of a short-term nature. It also reflected regulatory changes limiting banks' maximal foreign currency position in relation to all currencies to be no greater than 40 per cent of own funds (they had until August 1993 to achieve this). The money multiplier at the same time increased steadily from around 2.8 to 3.3. The increased multiplier in part reflected the steady decline in reserve requirements over the period as the NBP sought to lower the cost of reserves for banks and to improve their profitability, as well as improvements to the payments system which have reduced the need for banks to maintain large current account balances (see Chapter III). Taken together the two developments have meant that the NBP has had to be increasingly careful in managing the supply of reserve money and has needed new monetary instruments to do this (Diagram 10 and Diagram 11).

Diagram 10. **MONEY MULTIPLIER**[1]

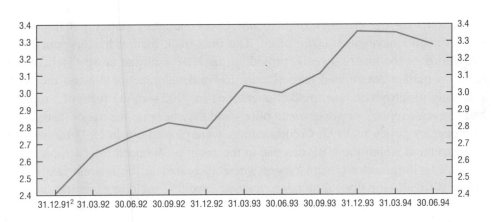

1. Total nominal money supply/(liabilities of the NBP to the banking sector + cash in circulation (including bank's vaults) + non-financial sector foreign currency deposits at the NBP).
2. Definition of money supply revised at end-1991.
Source: National Bank of Poland.

Diagram 11. **INDICATORS OF BANK LIQUIDITY**

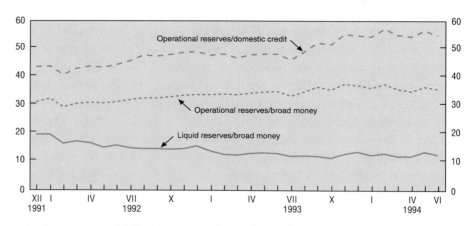

Note: Liquid reserves = cash in banks' vaults + receivables of the NBP.
Operational reserves = liquid reserves + receivables of banks, exchange houses and the post + Treasury bills + NBP bills.
Source: National Bank of Poland.

The previous *Economic Survey* stressed that the NBP lacked adequate instruments for the effective implementation of monetary policy but important improvements have since taken place. The inter-bank market has deepened and matured over the last two years, providing the NBP with the closest indicator it has of a market-determined interest rate. These developments allowed the NBP gradually to introduce open market operations in 1992 – in the form of ''repos'' and ''reverse repos'' of government bills – and they became the major instrument of monetary policy in 1993. Credit ceilings were phased out in 1993 but remain an instrument which the NBP can use in the event of the need to control a surge in bank lending under circumstances where increases in the interest rate might prove difficult. Finally, although refinance credit – including central investments – has decreased in relation to money supply from 13 per cent in 1991 to 8.4 per cent in 1993, the refinance rate still appears to exercise an important signalling role for banks in making major changes in interest rates – and this despite the development of the interbank market. The predominant role of refinance credit and some other credit lines is the provision of credit at low interest rates. These are subsidised by the budget and go to certain sectors and activities, such as agriculture, or to balance a maturity mismatch as with central investments which are a carry-over from the past.

In seeking to develop operational targets for the money supply, the NBP has had to balance the inflationary and balance of payments risks of an excess money supply with the contractionary effects that an excess demand for money might bring. In 1992 it erred on the side of expansion but this has been carefully corrected in the course of 1993. Following a 12 per cent devaluation of the zloty against the basket of currencies in February 1992, the NBP was relatively free to focus on domestic objectives. The original intention, which was ambitious, was to allow the real money supply in CPI terms to increase by some 6 per cent, which would have meant a small remonetisation of the economy. The latter was expected to follow the substantial deceleration of inflation in 1991. In the event, high financing requirements of the budget meant that by October the NBP had bought all of the bills it was required to do by law. The budget correction introduced in November increased the amount it was required to buy still further and led to an expansion of the real money supply for the year by around 9 per cent (CPI terms).

A number of considerations led the authorities to accept an overshooting of the monetary targets and not to begin tightening immediately. With the exception of November 1992, the free market exchange rate had remained close to the official rate, net foreign reserves of the banking system had continued to increase and there had been no systematic tendency for households to switch to foreign exchange accounts. The balance of trade had deteriorated in the second half of 1992 but it was unclear how much this had to do with the long-awaited introduction of a 6 per cent surcharge on imports and a new tariff schedule, and would therefore be self-correcting. Moreover, at the end of the year industrial sales slowed, making the NBP unwilling to risk inhibiting the recovery which might have been entailed by a rise in bond interest rates to finance the budget. Indeed the NBP had allowed inter-bank rates to decline steadily in the course of 1992 and had followed these with decreases in the policy rates: the rediscount, Lombard and refinance rates (Diagram 12).

By early 1993 it was evident that monetary policy had erred on the expansionary side and that there was an excess supply of money. Bank excess liquidity was high – the current accounts with the NBP had surged from Zl 5 trillion to

Diagram 12. **INTEREST RATES**

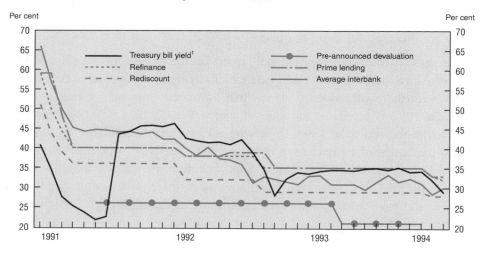

1. As of January 1993, there is a change in the weighting system used to calculate the average yield.
Source: National Bank of Poland.

Zl 19 trillion, only in part due to deferred income tax payments and other seasonal factors; domestic demand was expanding rapidly; the current account had moved further into deficit; official reserves were declining; and the positive contribution of foreign assets to the growth of money supply had disappeared (Diagram 13). The sentiment that a devaluation was in the offing had increased and was probably a factor behind an increase in foreign currency accounts of households. In addition, the 1993 monetary programme called for a further increase in the real money supply of around 3.6 per cent.

In such a situation the usual policy response would have been to restrict the growth of reserve money and to increase interest rates. This course of action was rejected by the authorities who felt that, with the instruments of monetary policy available, any tightening would have led to a decline in new credits to enterprises and therefore to a decline in growth. Given the impossibility of changing the budget, the expectation that credits to enterprises would have been disproportionately affected was probably reasonable although the linking of credit to growth was dubious: in 1992 growth was achieved without an increase of bank credit. The initial response of the NBP was, however, to cut the policy interest rates in

48

Diagram 13. **CONTRIBUTION TO CHANGE IN MONEY SUPPLY**

Percentage of money supply[1]

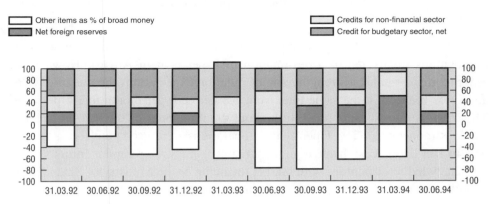

1. In the monetary survey the item "other", which includes among other things the payments float, is negative, complicating a simple interpretation of percentage contributions. The item "other" has been deducted from the money supply and the percentage contribution of the remaining components refers to this net aggregate.
Source: National Bank of Poland.

February by some three percentage points. This was ostensibly to follow the decline in interbank rates and treasury bill yields, but was widely seen as a response to a tighter budget, which was only passed by the Parliament with some difficulty in February; one of its assumptions was that the refinance rate would fall substantially throughout the year. The impact of the cut was that banks immediately lowered deposit interest rates by some 3-8 percentage points, further reducing the return from holding zloty assets. This effect was compounded in March by a change from quarterly to yearly capitalisation of interest which reduced returns from holding zloty assets still further.

Faced with such a situation, monetary policy was tightened with the only instrument the NBP had available: it started aggressive open market operations to drain banks of excess reserves. By April the level of commercial bank current accounts at the NBP had been reduced from its peak of Zl 19 trillion back to Zl 5 trillion. The yield on Treasury bills was driven up by some five percentage points to above the interbank rate, which also increased. Nevertheless, banks showed little interest in purchasing Treasury securities, so that the NBP had to monetise the budget deficit. For the first half of the year the NBP did not seek to maintain the growth of money supply at the rate which had been foreseen in the monetary plan for 1993: the real money supply was allowed to decline by around 2.5 per cent.

The decline of official reserves by $680 million up to June and a build-up of expectations finally led to a devaluation of 8 per cent in August. However in order to guard against a strengthening of inflation expectations the rate of devaluation was reduced at the same time from 1.8 per cent per month to 1.6 per cent. The devaluation was supported throughout the remainder of the year by a fairly cautious monetary policy. Open-market operations were used actively in the last half to sterilise excess bank liquidity arising from strong capital inflows. This ultimately led to difficulties with budget financing as the Ministry of Finance was unwilling to raise the interest rate on primary issues to reflect the market rate. Up until May 1994 the NBP showed great caution and refrained from lowering the refinance rate although it sought at the same time to decrease interest rates on foreign currency accounts – reserve requirements were introduced in February 1994 on these accounts at the rate of 0.75 per cent on demand deposits and 0.5 per cent on time deposits, payable in zlotys. In May 1994, in response to a lower-than-expected first-quarter rate of inflation, the refinance rate was lowered by two percentage points to 33 per cent. In the absence of wage controls, the NBP has stressed it will take a cautious approach to any further reductions.

The monetary programme for 1994 is fairly cautious although it is still difficult to identify clearly the demand for money by economic agents: the real supply of money is projected to increase at the same rate as GDP so that velocity is expected to remain constant in 1994. At the same time, inflation is assumed to decelerate further from 37 per cent in 1993 to 23 per cent (December-on-December) and from 35 per cent to 27 per cent measured as a period average. Official reserves are projected to decline marginally in the course of the year. Even though interest rate policy is not restricted by the provisions of the budget law, the room for manœuvre for the NBP to defend the exchange rate is nevertheless limited: the 1994 budget is based on the assumption that the refinance rate will decline substantially in the course of 1994 and there is a strong sentiment in the Parliament that the recovery should not be threatened by interest rate policy. For its part, the NBP has made it clear that the monetary programme need not be maintained throughout the year if circumstances were to change, particularly increased inflation and an upsurge in wages.

Assessment

Although the money/GDP ratio has steadily declined over the period, a striking feature of the monetary situation in Poland remains the low level of monetisation. With the decline in inflation from above 100 per cent at the start of 1991 to the 30-40 per cent range in 1993, a greater remonetisation might have been expected. Rather, attempts, as in 1992, to increase the money supply more rapidly led to a rapid spillover into a widening current account deficit and to expectations of a devaluation; a switch to foreign currency holdings and to a decline in official reserves ensued. In assessing monetary policy over the period a pertinent question is how it might have contributed to these developments.

There are two key inter-related channels by which monetary policy might have directly influenced the demand for money: interest rates and the exchange rate. A frequent criticism of the NBP is that it has maintained nominal and real interest rates at high levels thereby lowering the demand for credit. The same critics overlook the fact that lower real interest rates will, in the conditions characteristic of Poland (*i.e.* few non-money financial assets), lower the demand for money. Real interest rates are based on expectations and are therefore unobservable. Diagram 14 however presents some indicators which enable a tentative judgement to be formed. Particularly striking is the fact that for holders of domestic money the real rate of interest might have been negative over much of the period. Positive real interest rates were only available for longer term deposits. From the viewpoint of holders of domestic money, interest rates may have been too low, rather than too high. From the viewpoint of borrowers the real interest rate on debts was around 10 per cent and declining over the period (see Annex III for estimates of the effective lending rate). While high, much of this can be attributed to high costs of intermediation, reserve requirements and levels of bad debts.

With respect to the exchange rate the NBP has attempted to reduce inflation expectations by setting the pre-announced crawl close to the target rate of inflation. The pre-announced rate of devaluation has in turn set the floor for nominal interest rates. While this policy has a lot to recommend it, conflicting policy objectives have substantially reduced its effectiveness. In particular concern with the real exchange rate and competitiveness has led to step devaluations as in August 1993 and the possibility of such devaluations probably plays a significant role in the decisions by economic actors. Thus the exchange rate policy has

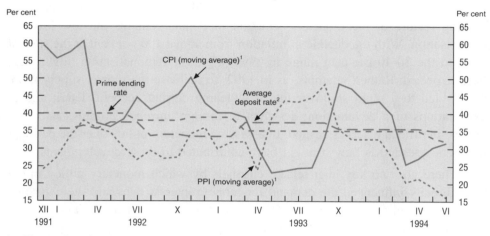

Diagram 14. **INDICATORS OF REAL INTEREST RATES**

Per annum

1. Five-month moving average of monthly rates, annualised.
2. Three-month zloty commercial deposit rate.
Source: National Bank of Poland, Central Statistical Office, OECD Secretariat calculations.

probably not succeeded in keeping inflation expectations on a rate of decline which would be compatible with an increased demand for money.

In sum, neither the riskiness nor the tax on holding money has been reduced sufficiently to cause a substantial re-monetisation. For this to take place nominal interest rates would have to be higher and inflation expectations kept on a greater rate of decline. The shift in the exchange rate regime has not really given monetary policy more room for manœuvre but rather increased the need to balance competing objectives.

Short-term prospects and risks

Recent developments

Developments in the first half of 1994 confirm that the growth momentum is continuing and has probably strengthened: GDP is estimated to have grown in the first half by 4.5 per cent (year-on-year). Industrial sales increased by around 11 per cent in the first half and growth resumed in August after the usual seasonal decline in July. In terms of value added, initial estimates point to growth in the range of 7.0-7.5 per cent. Other sectors are also exhibiting strong performance. Sales by the industrial construction sector increased by some 7.4 per cent while in industries producing consumer goods and food products output has grown by around 10-15 per cent. Value added in the trade sector may thus have grown at an impressive pace. The exceptions to these positive developments are agriculture and housing construction. Poor weather conditions in July have certainly led to a fall in value added though the magnitude is unclear at the time of writing. However, given the relative size of agriculture in the economy the decline would have to be quite large to have an appreciable affect on GDP: a fall of some 5 per cent would only translate into a decline of GDP by some 0.3 percentage points. In housing construction the declines are concentrated in the co-operative sector. All indications point to a continuing though unrecorded increase in private housing.

The private sector has continued to be the driving force in the recovery. Industrial sales by private companies have grown by 37 per cent (year-on-year) while those by the public sector have declined somewhat; the private sector's share of industrial sales has increased from 27 to 33 per cent. Differing behaviour is also becoming apparent between the two groups of enterprises in other ways. State-owned firms have managed to increase labour productivity by 11 per cent almost wholly by decreasing employment by some 10 per cent, but in the private sector labour productivity has increased by around 20 per cent at the same time that employment has increased by 13 per cent. In the enterprise sector more generally, the tendency for financial performance to improve, which was evident in 1993, has continued with gross profits increasing by some 30 per cent and losses declining by 7 per cent. Net profits have accordingly increased strongly, reinforced by lower taxes on state-owned firms and new investment allowances for all enterprises which came into force in 1994.

There are some signs that growth might be starting to have a positive impact on the labour market. The official unemployment rate has stabilised at around 16.7 per cent and the quarterly inflow into unemployment has fallen considerably in comparison to 1993. However, the official measure of unemployment may have become increasingly misleading. The quarterly survey of the labour force, which utilises an internationally acceptable definition of unemployment, closely followed the development of registered unemployment in 1993. However, from the first to the second quarters of 1994 the rate of unemployment declined by

1.9 percentage points to 13.5 per cent, a development not reflected in the registered unemployment statistics.

In contrast with the underlying continuity on the supply side, 1994 has been characterised by marked changes with respect to aggregate demand with both exports and investment growing strongly. Exports measured on a payments basis increased by around 20 per cent in the first half, continuing the growth which was first observed at the end of 1993. The devaluation in August 1993 may have exercised an influence on this development, but rapid growth in the German market in particular is likely to have been equally important. On a customs basis exports have increased by some 15 per cent. Excluding housing cooperatives, investment has increased by 11 per cent with growth rates being particularly impressive in the private sector where expenditures increased by 86 per cent. Public sector investment has also increased by 23 per cent, even though output is stagnating in this sector. An increase in profits has undoubtedly contributed to both making investment attractive as well as contributing to financing: in the first half, bank credit to enterprises increased by 11 per cent which was only a little above the rate of producer price inflation. The growth of investment may be overstated to the extent that, following changes in the tax system, expenditures previously classified as operating costs are now correctly coming to be treated as investment. Private consumption has also continued to grow, but in contrast to 1993, by less than GDP. Fiscal policy has been tighter than planned: expenditures have remained on target but revenues have been much stronger than expected. Pressures to increase expenditures further have been resisted.

Imports (on a payments basis) have increased by 8 per cent in the seven months – on a customs basis they have even declined. As a result, the trade balance has improved markedly, from a deficit of $1.4 billion in the first seven months of 1993 to a deficit of only $300 million in 1994. The current account has also improved significantly showing a deficit of only $170 million, although some $670 million in interest payments will fall due in the last quarter of the year. Short term capital inflows, probably associated with cross-border shopping, have also remained exceptionally strong, amounting to some $1.5 billion in the first six months, practically the same as in the whole of 1993. In consequence, official reserves have increased substantially (by $1.2 billion) but will decline later in the year with the implementation of the London Club agreement.

Strong capital inflows and an accumulation of reserves, especially in July and August, have necessitated changes in the implementation of monetary policy. An increase in net foreign assets during the summer threatened to raise money supply above the NBP's target. The initial response was to sell treasury bills outright (*i.e.* without a repurchase agreement) and in September to lower the returns to the foreign currency component of the money supply by lowering the monthly rate of devaluation from 1.6 per cent to 1.5 per cent. At the same time, NBP interest rates were maintained at current levels so as not to provide a stimulus to credit expansion. In principle this could stimulate further capital inflow. However, in a country such as Poland with underdeveloped financial markets, demand for money appears to be positively related to interest rates and the capital flow appears to be more related to informal trade than to interest arbitrage.

Real wages in the enterprise sector have increased by 3.4 per cent in comparison with the first half of 1993, but wages and salaries as a whole declined by 1.4 per cent. Wage increases have given rise to concern when controls lapsed from April to July 1994. In March wages surged by some 15 per cent in relation to February (by 8.8 per cent excluding bonuses) and again in June they rose by some 4 per cent. However, after each episode they have quickly returned to low monthly growth rates. It appears that wage increases have been confined mainly to profitable enterprises. This provides additional evidence supporting the judgement that the Polish labour market is highly segmented, and that it might be difficult to maintain high levels of profitability over the medium run. During the first half of 1994, consumer prices were, on average, 31 per cent above their 1993 levels, and in comparison with December they had increased by around 12 per cent. Until September consumer price inflation appeared to be settling at around 2 per cent per month (around 27 per cent per annum). Producer price inflation was significantly lower running at around 20 per cent per annum.

Projections

Throughout the projection period the major forces influencing macroeconomic developments are expected to be restructuring at the enterprise level, and rapid growth in the principal export markets. It is reasonable to assume that in 1994 the supply side is capable of sustaining growth of at least 4 per cent – more if the drought is less severe than expected – with modest levels of investment:

there is still room for large efficiency gains through high yielding, but small, investments and by reallocating the existing capital stock through both privatisation and asset sales. Growth should accelerate in both 1995 and 1996 to around 5 per cent although the level of investment required to support this will start to rise (Table 10). Such levels of growth will start to influence the labour market though this may not be fully apparent for some time: the projections refer to registered unemployment which is not expected to change quickly. However, the actual situation is probably more accurately reflected in the labour force survey which should start to reveal a steady fall in joblessness over the period, despite a steady re-entry of small farmers onto the labour market.

Buoyant supply conditions are projected to underpin a rapid growth of exports. Exports could grow by some 17 per cent in 1994, reflecting in part a rebound from the low growth achieved in 1992/1993. Thereafter more moderate, though still high, growth is projected of around 8 per cent. With export markets growing by around 6.5 per cent this will represent a modest gain in market share. The projection assumes that economic policy will be oriented to support such an export drive not only through exchange rate policy and structural measures, but also through managing domestic demand in order to avoid any crowding-out of exports. To this end the projection assumes that the authorities will be able to

Table 10. **Summary of projections**

Percentage, except where noted

	Budget assumptions	OECD		
	1994	1994	1995	1996
Inflation, CPI				
Average	27	30	23	18
Dec./dec.	23	–	–	–
GDP	4.5	4.0	5.0	5.0
Exports (in foreign currency)	6	17	8.0	8.0
Imports (in foreign currency)	2.5	6.0	8.0	10.0
State budget deficit	4.1	4.0	3.5	2.5
Registered unemployment (end-year)	17.3	16.5[1]	16.0	15.0
Current account (bn US$)	−1.8	−1.3	−1.5	−1.9
External interest paid (bn US$)	–	1.3	1.2	1.4

1. In May 1994, the quarterly labour force survey indicated an unemployment rate of 14 per cent.
Source: National sources and OECD Secretariat.

56

maintain their intention to lower the state budget deficit to 2.5 per cent of GDP in 1996. Imports are also expected to grow rapidly in line with structural changes in the economy – the ratio of imports to GDP is still comparatively low. The current account is projected to remain quite modest, financed in equal measure by long-term and short-term capital flows. The latter comprise unregistered cross border trade and the authorities will have to remain vigilant that legal or taxation changes do not substantially reduce this source of funding and of demand.

There are a number of risks to this central projection, the most important arising from excess domestic demand – lack of domestic savings – and the way in which foreign savings could be mobilised. Private consumption has already shown signs of strength and if this were to continue could result in a considerably higher current account deficit than projected and higher inflation. More importantly, to the extent that buoyant domestic consumption were to be based on excessive real wage growth, profitability would be reduced and with it the ability of enterprises to finance investment. Under these conditions overheating could quickly occur requiring a significant tightening of macroeconomic policy – and in particular fiscal policy. Such risks would increase if, as the government hopes, foreign direct investment were to increase rapidly. Mobilisation of foreign savings often requires a real appreciation of the exchange rate which, depending on the policy package, might be reached at the expense of inflation targets.

Slow disinflation is projected over the projection period with significant upside risks. The announced policy to avoid a significant real appreciation of the exchange rate will reinforce inflation momentum and is expected to result in slippage from official projections. Wages are expected to rise following the lapse in wage controls, but, if financial discipline is maintained, a wage explosion, although clearly a risk, is not likely. Especially in 1995, the rate of inflation might be held down by a deliberate policy to limit the growth of administered prices. Such a policy measure would be damaging in other ways and it is assumed that it will not be pursued throughout the projection horizon.

Looking beyond the projection period, the base line scenario points to the need to alter policy settings, if growth is to be sustained and indeed increased to the levels which are required for convergence over a realistic period with the OECD area. These issues are discussed in Chapter IV.

II. Furthering structural adjustment

Introduction

The fundamental legal and institutional reforms facilitating market activity were introduced quickly in Poland: price and trade liberalisation, the ability to acquire and dispose of property, and freedom of entry into most activities were all established by the end of 1990. In consequence, the private sector has grown dynamically and is leading the recovery. Additional reform measures to change the behaviour and organisation of pre-existing institutions – in particular state-owned and self-managed enterprises – have proven much more difficult to implement. Interest groups have been well-organised and effective, and the political consensus in such key policy areas as governance and privatisation has been fragile. As a result, policy measures impinging on the behaviour and structure of these enterprises (including state-owned farms) have only evolved slowly since 1990, and implementation has been gradual and partial. A question sometimes asked is whether it matters, since the role of the state sector is set to decline. The position taken in this report is that, indeed, it does matter. Some enterprises currently state-owned (self-managed) will have to contract still further – or even cease to exist – but it is important that this process does not disrupt the spontaneous growth of other parts of the economy. The risk is that, either directly or indirectly, such firms could slow overall growth. The problem of non-performing inter-enterprise debt and loans by the banking system are pertinent examples. On the other hand, some enterprises could normally expect to expand, but in the face of poor incentives for individuals and groups it is not evident that this will take place.

This chapter focuses on policies which affect the behaviour and ability to adjust of state-owned and self-managed enterprises: issues broadly relating to governance and to establishing an appropriate competitive operating environment. This is a complex task for in Poland a multi-track, pragmatic approach to solving problems has been the rule. For example, corporate governance and financial discipline have been influenced by measures to strengthen banks, wages and taxation policy, changes in industrial relations and steps towards privatisation, which is itself multi-track. These policy measures are discussed in the first section, which also touches on some of the issues that are being encountered in reorganising agriculture. Privatisation policy, which has been a point of contention between successive governments, is discussed in the second section. Trade and competition measures are considered in the final section. While they impinge importantly on the new private sector, policy in both areas has often had to address questions about the likely impact on the state sector.

Improving the structure and performance of state-owned firms

Over the review period pressures mounted to alter policy toward state-owned enterprises (SOEs), and these are likely to remain – albeit in an attenuated form – in the immediate future. First, non-performing loans posed increasing difficulties for the banking sector. It was evident that a solution would involve simultaneous action with respect to both banks and enterprises if the problem was not to quickly reappear. Second, privatisation became increasingly controversial while at the same time many enterprises appeared quite content to remain self-managed and not even to become incorporated. However, uncertainty about their future ownership status appeared to be contributing to either lethargy or short termism, evident in some cases through increased wages. Third, resistance to formal wage controls continued to increase, fuelled by sentiments of unequal treatment between the private and state sectors of the economy. More generally, self-managed enterprises were widely regarded as not conducive to growth and a barrier to restructuring of the economy. Piece by piece, over the course of 1992/1993 a wide ranging policy package was developed. Reflecting the highly contentious nature of the issues, there were long negotiations between the government and social partners, culminating in 1993 with the Pact on State Owned Enterprises. Before the most important elements of the Pact had been implemented elections intervened. The new government, which came to power in September 1993, presented its policy intentions in these areas in June 1994 in the Strategy for Poland, but at the time of writing it is unclear whether all the proposals will become government policy. In several important respects the new proposals represent a departure from the Pact and from the previous policy framework.

Establishing financial discipline and improving governance

In developing policy for SOEs – whether those nominally owned by 65 state founding organs, but under the effective control of employees' councils, or those incorporated as joint stock companies and wholly owned by the "Treasury" – the authorities have had to address two interrelated issues, which bear directly on economic performance: financial discipline and corporate governance.[36] By and large, they have been successful in establishing financial discipline, but improvements in corporate governance – ensuring that enterprises act in a rational "owner's" interests in seeking to increase net wealth and corporate profitability – have been much more limited.

The improved performance by, in particular, small and medium SOEs has resulted from a marked change in the attitude of government toward SOEs and *vice versa*. Despite some contradictory policy signals, the approach of the government toward the SOEs became firmer in 1992/1993. This was particularly apparent during a wave of strikes in August 1992 when the authorities continually sought to push responsibility for wage formation, and for the future of the firms themselves, back onto the enterprise management and employees. At the same time, the attitude of many enterprises appeared to change. The damaging expectations of a government bail-out engendered by the debate over industrial policy and general debt forgiveness in 1990 and 1991 was apparently replaced by a new spirit of realism as some of the SOEs decided that the future lay in their own hands. As a result, financial discipline steadily improved during the review period, with more and more firms resorting to action against each other to recover debts while reorganisation continued, and might have accelerated, in a number of them.[37] Somewhat in contradiction to these patterns, tax arrears have increased and tax enforcement has been weak especially with respect to the larger firms (see below).

An important initiative influencing both governance and financial discipline was the enterprise and bank debt restructuring programme, described in more detail in Chapter III. The principle of the programme is that enterprise debts will be restructured in a decentralised manner through negotiations between banks and their indebted clients. Banks have been given incentives to increase their governance role in enterprises through both recapitalisation – which allows them more independence in judging enterprises – and tighter prudential regulations. Recognizing the cumbersome nature of the bankruptcy system, banks have been equipped with new legal powers so as to by-pass the court system.

The enterprise and bank debt restructuring programme places the banks in a strong position to monitor closely the business plans and performance of the SOEs and to fulfil some of the functions of an owner. However, the programme does not by itself solve the governance problem: bank monitoring and enforcement of debt repayment and associated "restructuring" only covers a small part of what can be considered suitable governance, which is to structure incentives in such a way as to promote the increase of enterprise wealth. Moreover, the programme applies only to 700 or so of the largest SOEs while many of the remaining 5 000 SOEs are essentially free of bank debt. In the Polish context an improvement in governance requires a clearly defined privatisation path, since uncertainty here has contributed to poor corporate performance. In particular, SOEs currently have little incentive to increase wealth and strong incentives to increase total wages, albeit subject to increased financial discipline.

The linchpin of the transformation of SOE governance was to have been the Pact on State-Owned Enterprises (Pact), which was finalised in early 1993 after long negotiations between the Suchocka government and labour unions. As in many other economies in transition, while the state is the *de jure* owner, SOE control is largely held by enterprise employees. This has taken the form of Employees Councils which appoint the enterprise manager and which have a veto right over any change in ownership – including incorporation as a joint stock company. The goal of the Pact was to give workers sufficient incentives in future privatisation to avoid decapitalisation and wage maximizing behaviour, while compensating for the loss of control by providing for a continued presence in enterprise supervision.

In order to clarify the future of the enterprise, during a period of three months (later increased to six months), the workforce and management would have to decide how to change the operation and ownership of their enterprise. No matter which privatisation method was chosen, the workforce would acquire 15 per cent of voting shares free of charge. This was intended to correct the perverse incentive effects which were inherent in the sale of shares to employees at a preferential price.[38] Moreover, to compensate for the termination of Employees Councils which would accompany legal incorporation, a third of the members of the newly-established Supervisory Board were to be elected by the workforce.[39] If management and employees of large enterprises failed to choose a privatisation method, the enterprise would be commercialised compulsorily. Under such conditions it could also be transferred to the mass privatisation programme or disposed of in any other way seen fit by the Ministry of Privatisation. For firms which were solvent, the four existing paths to privatisation (see below) would all be available. Firms which were insolvent could still choose a privatisation route but this would be subject to agreement with the creditors – and in particular the banks. An insolvent enterprise could also be privatised by means of a management privatisation contract.

Three elements of the Pact have been implemented: changes in the labour codes, collective bargaining, and the Fund for Safeguarding Claims of Workers, established in September 1993. This Fund satisfies trade union demands for guaranteed wage and severance pay in the case of enterprise bankruptcy. It was financed by a 1 per cent contribution based on wages from January to April 1994, and 0.5 per cent thereafter. A Tripartite Commission was created in February 1994 to serve as the forum for central collective bargaining and discussion of related issues.[40] In addition, the Commission – composed of union, enterprise (SOEs and private), and state representatives – will determine indices for wage growth exempt from excess wage taxes. A major component of the Pact was reform of the collective bargaining system. Within the framework of the new government's medium-term strategy the system will be established in 1995. The new law on collective bargaining establishes rules for the recognition of unions and provides for three levels of bargaining – central, sectoral or regional, and enterprise.

Under the Pact legal incorporation of enterprises and the termination of Employees Councils were viewed as an essential step to privatisation and to reorganisation of corporate structure. There was little presumption that the state could be an effective owner. This view appears to have changed in the government's new medium-term policy framework. While final decisions are still pending, it is proposed to incorporate all state-owned firms under the Commercial Code, a move which would eliminate Employees Councils. Ownership will be assumed by around ten regional offices of a newly established State Treasury which will exercise ownership through management contracts. The offices might also be involved in privatisation.

It is impossible to fully assess the plan at this stage since crucial details are still lacking. Nevertheless, initial indications point to some caution. First, experience to date with the Ministry of Privatisation in overseeing around 500 incorporated enterprises does not lend support to claims that simple incorporation leads to improved performance. Appropriate management contracts are not easy to develop and, in the presence of politically powerful firms, could lead to bargaining over non-economic objectives and to a deterioration of performance. The emphasis in the Strategy on non-profit objectives such as employment guarantees would, indeed, point in this direction. Second, in the small and medium-sized SOEs, research points to a delicate balance between interests, which while they may not be particularly dynamic, have nevertheless led to improved financial discipline and some restructuring. It is not clear what the formal subordination of management to the State Treasury would bring in the way of improvement.

Wages and incomes policy

For the 6 000 or so state enterprises which still account for a major proportion of economic activity, ownership functions by the state have been exercised through an excess wages tax (popiwek) and a charge or a lump sum tax on equity (dividenda). Continuous political pressure rather than improved enterprise management has led to a progressive relaxation of wage controls over the period 1992/1993. The highest penalty tax on excess wages was reduced from 500 per cent in 1991 to 400 per cent in 1992 and 300 per cent in 1993, while the number of exemptions has increased. However, to benefit from the various exemptions and allowances an enterprise must remain current on tax payments and social security contributions. Beginning in 1992, exporters were able to decrease their liability for paying the penalty tax by the proportion of exports in their sales: if 50 per cent of sales were accounted for by exports, the tax liability was correspondingly reduced.

From the macroeconomic perspective an important change in wage formation was introduced in September 1992 when permissible wage increases were directly specified by the Council of Ministers. Up till then, the enterprise wage norm was explicitly linked to consumer price inflation via an indexation coefficient which varied between 0.6 and 0.7 throughout 1992. In principle, direct specification of wage increases allows the government to take into account a wide range of macroeconomic indicators and not only the rate of inflation. Over the short time the system was in operation it is difficult to judge whether this occurred. On average the reference wage has been allowed to increase by around 1.5 per cent per month from September 1992 to March 1994;[41] over the same period the average rate of CPI inflation was 2.6 per cent and 2.4 per cent with respect to the PPI. With the new wage controls approved for the remainder of 1994, government policy is to assure an increase of average real wages at half the growth rate of GDP, or 2-2.5 per cent, but how this could be achieved is not evident.

An important step to link the permissible wage increase to economic performance was taken in March 1993. Enterprises which expected that the ratio of gross profits to wages would improve in 1993 in comparison with 1992 could apply to the local tax chamber for an agreement on permissible wage increases. Under this arrangement, companies could increase average wages by 20 per cent without incurring excess wages tax and another 25 per cent proportionate to improvements in profitability, with the penalty tax rate being 100 per cent.[42] However, there were a number of restrictions: the ratio of wages to gross profits calculated on a quarterly basis could not deteriorate in comparison to the same ratio for the whole of the previous year; the firm had to remain current on liabilities to the budget, and if the enterprise failed to meet its agreement it would be subject to the normal excess wages tax. By the end of 1993 over 500 enterprises had entered into such agreements.

The excess wage tax lapsed at the end of March 1994. An Act introducing a new system was finally signed into law by the President in July 1994, but the controls will only run to the end of the year. The authorities still consider it important to control wages in the SOEs, but to make the controls more flexible and to allow more room for bargaining between the social partners. Under the new system in force, enterprises must choose between four options. Three of them are only available for those economic units which are not in arrears on either taxes or social security contributions, or which had settled any arrears by the end of June 1994, including agreements to repay which are discussed below. If an enterprise is not current it must follow option four which amounts to the old "popiwek" system. The four options are:

- Option one sets permissible wage increases through a management contract with the founding body.[43] Wage targets will be linked to specific objectives depending on the situation of the company. Around 100 enterprises are expected to sign such agreements. It will be most important that the objectives reflect normal commercial criteria of profitability rather than quantitative ones like exports;
- Option two requires an agreement with the local tax chamber specifying the wage limits based on criteria will be determined by the Ministry of Finance and the Ministry of Labour;
- Option three is a continuation of the adapted popiwek from 1993 with the exception that agreement with the local tax chamber will not be necessary. Wages are divided between a part which can be treated as a cost and a part which will be subject to excess wage tax, the proportion depending on an improvement in performance. If an enterprises has reduced its workforce by more than 5 per cent over the preceding year it will have to choose another option. This clause was put in at the request of unions which wished to avoid an incentive for ''mass'' layoffs followed by wage increases;
- Option four follows the old system in specifying the permissible increase in wages although the rate of penalty tax has been reduced from on average 220 per cent to 150 per cent. The biggest change is that the allowable wage increase will be determined by the Tripartite Commission. If it fails to make a decision, the Council of Ministers is empowered to take one.

One of the most controversial measures regarding the SOEs has been the ''dividenda'' or lump-sum tax on what amounts to an enterprise's own funds. Rather than being regarded as a normal servicing of capital, enterprises and unions have regarded it as a discriminatory tax; this belief was reinforced by the fact that loss-making firms were also required to pay the tax. Indeed the previous *Economic Survey* argued that it should be more related to profits. In line with commitments made during negotiation of the Pact the government intends to introduce a new instrument in 1995: net profits after payments of any excess wage penalties will be divided equally between retained earnings, the payment of bonuses which would not be considered as wages for purposes of wage controls and a ''dividend'' to the Treasury. Although the new ''tax'' will lower the room for wage growth and provide income to the budget it is not evident that it contributes to resolving the incentive or governance deficiency faced by SOEs.

Restructuring policy for industry

Industrial policy measures in Poland have been largely indicative in nature, despite strong pressures from sensitive sectors and bureaucratic interests for a more activist role for the state. Over 70 sectoral studies have been completed or commissioned which identify targets for employment and capacity reduction, technological investments and industrial reorganization. The state's role in these plans has in fact been modest, except for an active role in industrial reorganization, generally following a strategy of consolidating a number of firms into a few holding companies. This strategy has sometimes avoided the closure of weak firms, relying instead on cross-subsidies from relatively stronger firms, and placing responsibility for allocating capacity and employment cuts with the management of the holding company, rather than with the government. Direct government funding of these programmes has been modest, though some relief of tax arrears and loan guarantees are available. In certain socially-sensitive sectors, extra social safety net support is being provided, in part through a special Intervention Fund set up with World Bank financial support (described below). Evaluation of business plans and financial restructuring for highly indebted SOEs is largely being conducted under the bank debt restructuring programme, though the government participates through the restructuring tax arrears. However, by and large, firms have to rely upon their own resources and access to private financial sources for new investments and technical restructuring. Indicative plans are now being implemented for sugar, coal, steel, and energy, though for the sugar industry regulatory control on output has been introduced.

Preferential credits, channelled primarily through the Industrial Development Agency (IDA),[44] have been the primary instrument of active industrial policy. The IDA co-ordinates restructuring programmes for nearly insolvent, politically sensitive industries, and where necessary carries out liquidations for the Ministry of Industry. As part of this mandate, the IDA extended preferential credits to troubled enterprises, based on its initial 1991 capitalization of Zl 800 billion. No new budgetary funds have been allocated since nor has the IDA been recapitalised. Given its target clientele, it is not surprising that a substantial proportion of the IDA portfolio has become non-performing.[45] Debt arrears are causing the agency to be decapitalised, so that the IDA finds itself increasingly limited to small projects. In order to facilitate adjustment, in June 1993 the IDA began a policy of debt writeoffs and converting debt into equity for viable firms.[46] So far, conversions have taken place in 21 large industrial enterprises and 11 smaller ones. Discussions have been ongoing about recapitalizing the IDA, and it is now involved in screening enterprises for the Intervention Fund.

Implicit industrial policy has become much more pronounced since 1991, through the tolerance of the build-up of tax and social security fund (ZUS) payment arrears. As noted in Chapter I, tax arrears have been the largest source for financing current losses. Tax arrears are not distributed randomly, but are largely confined to large, loss-making SOEs in strategic sectors. In 1993 electronics firms accounted for 34 per cent of tax arrears, followed by fuel and energy (19 per cent), food processing (15 per cent), and light industry (13 per cent).[47] ZUS arrears are also heavily concentrated in state firms in certain sectors, though the distribution is slightly different: coal mining, steel, and shipyards account for the preponderance. Enterprises accumulate arrears without any specific policy or approval of the government. Decisions on whether to enforce collection appear to be *ad hoc*: "... the procedures of granting tax credits are not standardised and decisions are made at various levels of state administration. Fragmentary information shows that delays were applied mostly in relation to the enterprises which had developed rehabilitation plans ..."[48] At the time of writing, explicit postponement of arrears has occurred in only 50 per cent of cases.

The authorities are now attempting to regularise the situation without actually tightening enforcement *per se*. First, some of the large debtors will be dealt with as part of the bank-led conciliation agreements. Second, the new wage policy, linking wage increases to being current on budget payments, gives firms incentives to come to an agreement. Third, there is an attempt to collect some proceeds from old taxes. This latter measure came into force in March 1994 and covers liabilities resulting from repealed taxes which arose before January 1993 in the case of the excess wage tax, and 30 June 1993 in the case of the turnover tax and the "dividenda". An enterprise may repay 10 per cent of its debt to the budget (excluding interest) and prepare a plan of paying off its total tax liabilities. This plan should be accepted by the relevant tax office and there must be no current liabilities to the budget and to the ZUS. If the enterprise meets these

Table 11. The development of tax arrears

Trillion zlotys

	31/12/1990		31/12/1991		31/12/1992		31/12/1993		30/06/94	
	Total	Postponed	Total	Postponed	Total	Postponed	Total	Postponed	Total	Postponed
Turnover tax	0.7	0.3	2.7	0.5	6.6	2.7	8.7	2.7	7.4	1.9
Corporated tax	2.0	0.5	3.7	1.8	4.7	2.2	9.1	1.3	7.5	1.6
Dividenda	0.5	0.1	5.5	1.2	6.6	2.0	6.3	1.6	5.8	1.5
Wage tax	0.1	0	1.9	0.2	1.3	0.2	1.1	0.2	1.0	0.2
Excess wage tax	2.5	0	12.1	8.5	10.7	6.8	15.4	7.7	16.3	8.4
Excise	..	..	..	..	..	..	..	..	0.4	0.1
VAT	..	..	..	..	..	..	..	..	3.4	0.4
Social security, *of which:*	..	..	..	..	14.6	..	30.3	..	37.4	..
Public sector[1]	..	..	..	..	12.4	..	25.9	..	30.6	..
Private sector	..	..	..	..	2.2	..	4.3	..	6.8	..
Total	5.8	1.1	26.1	12.2	44.5	13.9	70.8	13.5	79.2	14.1
Percentage of general government revenue	2	..	7.3	..	8.5	..	10	..	n.a.	n.a.

1.   Public sector is the old definition and therefore includes co-operatives. In January 1994 co-operatives had arrears to social security of Zl 1.2 trillion.
Source: Ministry of Finance.

conditions the liability would be further reduced by the amount of its prepayment and the remainder would be repaid in instalments over five years. At the end of the repayment the firm would receive a refund up to 15 per cent of the original debt.

An Intervention Fund was created in December 1993 for enterprises whose restructuring would be socially sensitive: either very large firms or those which are the dominant employer in a region. Funds will be available to support restructuring and liquidations, either as loans or subsidies.[49] Funds can be used for providing for severance pay and a social safety net for workers, options not available under bank restructuring, The fund is financed through the budget, based on the domestic currency counterpart funds of most of a World Bank EFSAL loan – $350 million spread over three years. Criteria for acceptance are intended to be sufficiently tough so that the Fund is not regarded as a bail-out.[50] To date, four applications have been recommended and submitted to the Council of Ministers for approval.[51]

Restructuring programmes have begun in coal, steel, energy and agriculture, and others are planned for shipbuilding, defence industries and heavy chemistry. Two examples – coal and steel – illustrate the general nature of these programmes. Hard coal mining was a high-wage, high-prestige industry under the old regime and the basis for the old energy-intensive economy.[52] Despite a decline of 25 per cent in employment since 1989,[53] losses had become serious by 1992. The causes of this were three-fold: high wages, excess capacity, and low prices. Wage developments in coal mining are politically sensitive, given the dependence of Polish power on coal, and the fact that wages account for roughly half of coal extraction costs. Workers have successfully maintained their high wages relative to all other sectors, despite declining productivity and demand. Demand has declined with the fall in GDP and shift in industrial output to less energy-intensive industries, creating overcapacity. Continued production from high-cost producers created conditions of oversupply, putting downward pressure on prices. Coal prices were liberalised in 1992, and subsequently were set by negotiation between the mines and their major consumer, the power generating industry. Faced with the monopsonistic position of the power industry and a state of excess supply brought about by lack of financial discipline, mines accepted prices below costs and ran large losses.[54]

The government is pursuing a restructuring programme in three stages. The first stage, primarily involving reorganisation, began in the first half of 1993. Mines were converted to joint-stock companies in March 1993. Recommendations of the sectoral study were to make coal mines into independent units, allowing loss-making mines to go bankrupt. The authorities chose to pursue an opposite strategy: 63 independent mines were combined into seven holding companies, merging profitable and marginal companies, with the holding companies left to allocate production cuts internally. In 1994-95 five loss-making mines will be closed and four more will be liquidated over the next few years supported by a World Bank loan for this purpose. Following the consolidation of the industry, new negotiations between coal mines and the power industry took place in August 1993. With a more unified bargaining position, the results were much higher coal prices, approaching import parity. As a result of these changes (beginning in September 1993), operating losses fell significantly and the net financial result for the industry as a whole became positive for the rest of that year. However, tax arrears have continued to mount and the rate of profit remains unacceptable for the industry as a whole – though not for some mines.

The steel industry in Poland comprises 26 mills with capacity of 15 million tons annually. It is characterised by obsolete technology, distorted product mix, high raw materials and energy consumption, excessive employment, and high pollution. The goals of the government in restructuring the steel industry are to re-establish profitability and international competitiveness, and to reorient production toward higher value-added products.

As part of its Association Agreement with the EC, Poland has been granted ten years to restructure the sector, with essential activities to be restructured within six years. A restructuring strategy designed by Canadian consultants in 1992 has largely been adopted: it targeted a 40 per cent reduction in capacity, which will include liquidation of all or part of eight mills and departments. Currently the government has two mills under liquidation, with another likely. The estimated total cost of restructuring is $4.45 billion over the ten-year period for financial restructuring, new investments, environmental protection, and employment-reduction schemes. Most of these funds will have to come from internal or private financial sources; for 1994 the government agreed to provide up to Zl 2 trillion (around $90 million) in loan guarantees for three mills. A major part of this will be spent on total liquidation of obsolete open-hearth furnaces and broad implementation of continuous casting technology. Again the authorities chose to ignore the recommendations of the sectoral study, which advocated concentrating continuous casting in one mill, and is pursuing its introduction in several mills. As part of restructuring, those steel mills not already commercial-ised will be transformed into joint-stock companies; there are no short-term plans for full privatisation and for industrial reorganisation. The process will be managed by a co-ordinating council, which will include representatives from the relevant ministries and regions, led by the Ministry of Industry. The restructuring of the industry is expected to result in a decrease of employment by 80 000 jobs to 43 000 workers. Only about half of this change will result in net job loss, the rest is associated with spinning-off non-core operations and associated social, cultural and educational institutions. The restructuring plans have yet to be implemented and the coordinating agency established. It appears that the primary constraint is a lack of funding for the restructuring programme.

Labour market policies

Active labour market policies in Poland affect a small fraction of the unemployed population: the maximum level in any given month during 1992/1993 was around 5 per cent of the unemployed population. These policies include public works, "intervention works" and retraining, and are financed from contributions to the Labour Fund. In 1993 spending on active policies accounted for Zl 3.5 trillion or 11.1 per cent of Labour Fund expenditures: three-quarters was spent on creating jobs, involving a total of 296 000 people, and Zl 450 billion spent on vocational training and retraining, and 93 000 finished some form of training.[55] The 1994 budget included a 67 per cent increase in spending, and aimed at reaching 10-20 per cent more people. Training is available free of charge to anyone registered as unemployed; those receiving unemployment benefits are entitled to a 15 per cent premium on their benefits. Training courses are short term – three-quarters run for less than three months – and the period spent in training is counted towards the total period of eligibility for unemployment. Training courses are tailored to local labour demand. Intervention works – government wage subsidies to employers – provide a maximum subsidy equivalent to 30 per cent of the average wage of the previous quarter.[56] The duration is limited to the period of recipient's rights to unemployment benefits, a maximum of 12 months.

The mix between the three forms of support is decided by local labour offices in accordance with local conditions; choices are periodically reviewed by the Ministry to assure cost-effectiveness. In general public works are viewed by the authorities as being the most expensive and least-effective, since they hold little prospect of long-term employment. By contrast, intervention works are much less costly and have had a 30 per cent retention rate, with training being more costly but having a slightly higher placement rate of 34 per cent.

In addition to the active labour policies described above, efforts are being made to soften the impact of high unemployment in crisis regions.[57] To this end the government has instituted a loan programme using money from the Labour Fund for job creation. Loans are made to qualifying enterprises, with the maximum loan set at 20 times the average monthly salary and a maturity of four years.[58] Loans are available at three times these levels in high-unemployment regions. Interest rates range from 60 to 100 per cent of the refinancing rate, depending on the type of investment activity. In 1993 loans totalling Zl 530 billion were extended for the creation of 12 000 jobs. Special tax benefits are also extended for investment in crisis regions, including accelerated depreciation and deductions for training. Finally, retirement may also be taken three years earlier than in other regions.

Assessment

As noted in Chapter I, financial discipline has clearly improved in SOEs. Perhaps central to this change was the decision by the authorities to avoid engaging in an activist restructuring policy, and to pursue a decentralised process with responsibility resting with the banks and the enterprises themselves. With respect to non-performing loans, many inherited from 1990/1991, a similar approach has been pursued. The authorities rejected across-the-board debt forgiveness, letting the process of financial restructuring proceed exclusively via the courts and bankruptcy laws, and also rejected dealing with the problem in a centralised way such as by creating a new debt restructuring agency. There were a number of practical reasons for this strategic decision. As one policy-maker put it ''... we did not believe that a centralised, government sponsored agency can vigorously and effectively recover bad debts. We did not believe in our ability to create, within a reasonable time period, a strong institution in terms of high quality of its staff and internal organisation. Neither did we believe in the possibility of devising an adequate incentive system that would ensure that institution's active approach toward the indebted enterprises. We also did not believe that such an institution could be made to resist the political pressure. ... By painlessly removing the burden of bad debt from the banks, the centralised approach creates a danger that the bad loan portfolio will re-emerge in the future''.[59] These decisions signalled to most SOEs that they would largely be left to their own resources.

The evidence on governance is less clear. Heavily-indebted firms with bank conciliation agreements will now be under bank surveillance, and there are strong incentives for state-owned banks to pursue firm governance aggressively. However this still leaves around 5 200 firms mostly controlled by employees' councils. While excess wages have declined since 1991 (Diagram 15) and popiwek receipts fell, arrears have increased, suggesting either that enforcement has been lax, credibility lacking or both. The surge in wages in the last two months of 1993 as popiwek was expiring, and again in the spring of 1994 when it did expire, suggests that a number of firms are still pursuing wage-maximisation

Diagram 15. **THE OPERATION OF WAGE CONTROLS**

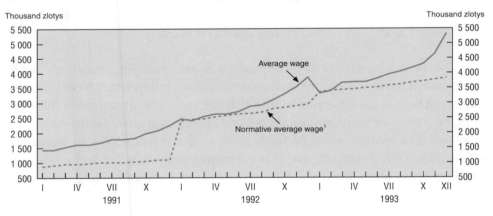

1. Wage controls are based at the enterprise level so that the normative wage for the whole economy should only be regarded as indicative. Normative wages are rebased each year on some components of December wages. As these are unobservable, the OECD Secretariat has approximated the rebasing by using October wages which are relatively free of bonuses, etc. Adjustment for January 1992 following the introduction of a personal income tax was done at a net rate of 17%.
Source: OECD Secretariat calculations.

strategies, albeit now subject to more financial discipline. Corporate governance is particularly problematic in certain sectors. In sectors like energy, the monopoly rents from rising energy prices have been passed on as wage increases. In politically powerful sectors, wages are determined by union strength. These sectors – railways, mining and certain light industries – are mainly responsible for the majority of popiwek arrears. In enterprises facing substantial restructuring or liquidation, it appears that workers are pursuing an end-game strategy, maximising the wage share of earnings at the expense of tax payments to the owner, the state, and of replacement of depreciating assets.

Restructuring policy seems to be generally driven by budgetary priorities, with mixed results. The decision to provide indicative plans seems well-based. In limiting actual government financing to some loan guarantees, it not only protects the budget's limited resources, but places the onus on firms themselves to improve profitability in order to generate resources for new investment. The exceptions are enterprises with access to the limited resources of the IDA, or the new Intervention Fund. In these cases the amount of resources committed is relatively small and probably necessary in the light of alleviating social costs, even if the principle of stringent conditionality may slip somewhat in practice. The weakness of the overall approach is that incentives for the enterprises to achieve economic profitability – not just to generate a positive cash flow – are not provided at the same time, raising questions about its efficacy.

The same imperatives to restructure without expending budgetary funds have resulted in some decisions on industrial reorganization which have been less salutary. There is no reason to believe that the industrial organisation inherited from the past in coal mining, metallurgy and energy is at all suitable to a market economy. The owners would normally have a clear responsibility to reorganise such holdings. However, the state is not a normal owner but in effect a monopolist, leading to clear conflicts of interest between forming holding companies under protected conditions or promoting competition. Industrial restructuring policy in Poland in key areas has represented an uneasy compromise between these two position. Government decisions to create monopolistic holding companies, such as coal and power generation, have avoided burdening the budget and the authorities with the political cost of closing weak firms. The cost has been one of efficiency – forcing stronger firms to cross-subsidise weaker firms, and creating monopolistic structures with the attendant consequences for pricing and competition.

Restructuring agriculture

The share of the population in rural areas has remained constant since 1988, as has the share of agricultural employment,[60] while the share of agricultural GDP has dropped from 12 to 7 per cent over the same period. The majority of the over 2 million private farms are quite small, with an average size of 6.3 hectares – over 65 per cent have less than 7 hectares. Many of these small farms are not viable, and have had to rely heavily on earnings from outside agriculture to supplement their incomes;[61] the decline of industrial employment has thus affected their incomes quite significantly. Relocation out of rural areas has been discouraged by the low probability of finding work, and rising commuting and urban housing costs. With easier access to food, lower taxes and relatively good housing, rural areas have become a reservoir of underemployed labour.

The objectives of agricultural policy have evolved since prices were liberalised in 1990, and an underlying intention is now to move towards the EC's Common Agricultural Policy, as part of the aim of joining the Union.[62] The principal goal of agricultural policy is now finding markets for agricultural products and improving competitiveness through better product quality and promotion. The authorities are particularly concerned with what they perceive as unfair import competition from subsidised EC foodstuffs. The principal tools of active agricultural policy have been tax concessions, import protection, and preferential credit support. Direct subsidies have been nearly eliminated in agriculture: they exist only on calcium fertilisers and fuel, and amounted to Zl 2.5 trillion in 1993.[63]

Agricultural producers benefit from a number of tax exemptions, which constitutes the most important support measure. Farmers pay land taxes rather than income taxes. Land taxes are low, and set in terms of rye equivalents by local municipalities, depending on land quality. Exemptions from the land tax are numerous, including complete exemptions for poor quality land, exemptions of five years on newly acquired or fallow land, and three years on land taken out of cultivation. Farmers make only low contributions for social benefits, so that in 1993 agricultural pensions were 90 per cent subsidised (as a share of expenditures) by the state budget. Agricultural inputs are exempt from turnover and VAT; food products also benefit from a reduced VAT rate of 7 per cent.

Low-interest loans, with the balance paid by the budget, are the most important explicit form of government support for agriculture. This has taken the form of credits for purchases of seeds, fertilisers and pesticides, purchases of land and machinery, and debt rescheduling. Preferential credits are also extended to processing plants for purchase of raw materials and there is a small lending programme for SMEs in rural areas. Debt rescheduling has been conducted by the Fund for Agricultural Restructuring which undertook a programme of purchasing farmers' debts to banks and rescheduling them on more favourable terms, at 5 per cent interest over seven years. The Fund also offered modernisation credits at 20 per cent over seven years. This programme, in existence from 1992 through March 1993, allocated Zl 2.5 trillion, split 70-30 between private farmers and agro-industries. Since July 1993 the Fund's activities have been suspended because of financial irregularities. A new agency, the Agricultural Restructuring and Modernisation Agency (ARMOR), was established in January 1994 to continue with a revised programme. Under the new system, commercial banks will be responsible for evaluating and extending credits, and clear, formal application procedures have been designed to avoid past problems, with ARMOR subsidising the difference between market and preferential interest rates. With the decline in the level of compulsory bank reserves beneath 10 per cent of total deposits, interest earnings on the reserve will no longer accrue to ARMOR. Remittances from the NBP have been increased correspondingly and a similar amount will be transferred to ARMOR directly from the budget. The budgetary allocation for interest subsidies, Zl 1.5 trillion in 1993, has been raised to Zl 2.5 trillion in 1994.

The Agency for Agricultural Marketing (AAR) is charged with running the government's price stabilisation programme. It is empowered to intervene in support of most basic commodities, including grains, meat and dairy products, sugar. A system of intervention purchasing, begun in 1990 for most grains and dairy products, was converted to a minimum price system in 1992, with prices negotiated between farmers, the government and the AAR based on market prices and production costs. Intervention purchasing continues for some items, mostly grains.

The AAR's principal method of market intervention is through low-interest loans to purchasers who agree to hold grain after the harvest. These future purchases involve payment of 50 per cent up front; at the end of the contract the AAR either takes delivery and pays the remainder or receives the money back. This approach proved to be problematic in 1993, as many recipients, mostly state farms and storage companies in bad financial condition, found it necessary to sell the crops which were the underlying security, effectively defaulting.[64] To recoup some of these losses, the AAR has engaged in debt-for-equity swaps with granaries; AAR accounts receivable from this process totalled about Zl 3 trillion at the end of 1993, compared with overall capital of Zl 7 trillion. Budgetary resources for 1994 were set at Zl 2.6 trillion and explicitly earmarked for state reserves, with only Zl 800 billion for private intervention.

Tariff policy has also been a source of agricultural support. Agricultural tariffs in 1991 averaged 26.2 per cent, and ranged from 18.4 to 32.0 per cent, increasing with processing. Tariff revisions in March 1992, October 1992, May and July 1993 served to generally raise tariffs on agricultural products, with some agricultural tariffs fixed in ECU terms to counteract the affects of devaluation in neighbouring countries. In 1992 a three-tier import tax was imposed, ranging from 6 to 40 per cent; this was unified at 6 per cent in July 1993. In October 1992 a variable import levy was announced and finally introduced in June 1994 on 28 products. These temporary levies, which have been imposed on essential agro-food products, are set to cover the difference between world prices and Polish domestic prices, after accounting for tariffs and border taxes. Estimates of the minimum inflationary impact are around 1 percentage point, depending on assumptions.

In addition to agricultural support, the government has been involved in restructuring state farms through the Agricultural Property Agency (ASWRP). State farms accounted for 18.1 per cent of land under cultivation in 1992 – down to 13 per cent in 1993 – before the transition. By the spring of 1994, all of the 1 640 state farms, had been transferred to the ASWRP. Associated with this were several hundred thousand apartments, over 1 000 processing plants, and numerous social and cultural institutions. Most state farms are in the process of selling machines and equipment, cutting employment, and reducing crop acreage and livestock herds. Debts to the budget are automatically forgiven, but estimates are that state farms have outstanding debts of Zl 10 trillion to the banking sector and around Zl 1 trillion in inter-enterprise debts. Privatisation of state farms has proceeded slowly despite favourable instalment plans for purchasers; interest rates are only one-quarter of the commercial rate. New farmers often lack collateral to obtain loans. Structurally, privatisation is hindered by the fact that most small private farmers who would be willing to purchase land are located in the south and east, whereas most state farms are located in the north and west. Generally, farmers prefer to purchase small plots contiguous to their existing holdings, whereas the ASWRP is reluctant to break up large tracts to preserve economies of scale. Pricing remains an issue; often the minimum land prices set by the State do not fully take into account the level of indebtedness of the farms. In some areas, lack of clarity with respect to restitution claims has deterred purchases. As a result of these considerations, only two per cent of total land has been sold. Two-thirds is under temporary management contracts, generally five years in duration, with the remainder, about one-third, under lease.

Privatising state property

Although over 1 000 enterprises were privatised during 1992/1993, the process has remained a sensitive political issue. As a result, the tempo of privatisation has varied greatly over the period: privatisation by direct sales and by flotation (capital privatisation) practically ceased through most of 1992 but accelerated rapidly in 1993 until the fourth quarter. Disputes about privatisation modalities have continually delayed the mass privatisation programme which is expected to finally become operative in late 1994. Regardless of the privatisation path, techniques have evolved over the review period to meet not only the criticisms but also to adapt to changing circumstances and policy issues. Sales proceeds to date have been modest, re-igniting a major unresolved issue: the trade-off between selling price on the one hand, and the creation of effective governance of former SOEs on the other.

Privatisation has been voluntary and pursued through a multi-track approach, but if the proposals in the medium-term strategy are implemented this will change radically; after compulsory corporatisation, privatisation would no longer be voluntary with the initiative to be taken by the owner, rather than firms. The modalities will also change, but in a way which is not yet clear. As noted above, the State Treasury will assume ownership from the current 65 founding bodies and this could lead to a simplification of the privatisation process and concentration of decision-making. Whether it will in fact do so will depend on the relation between the Ministry of Privatisation and the State Treasury, and whether privatisation will be accorded priority. At the time of writing, this is unclear. The medium-term strategy also notes that employment guarantees will be introduced and that, in the presence of a trade-off between efficiency and owner-ship change, priority will be given to the former. While privatisation could well accelerate, the bureaucratic grounds would also be in place which might slow it down.

Small and medium privatisation

From the perspective of numbers of enterprises, the focus of the privatisa-tion programme has remained the so-called "liquidation" sales by which a new private firm takes over either the assets and liabilities of an existing SOE which is then struck off the list of SOEs (Article 37), or acquires the assets or parts of an enterprise which is being wound up on account of poor financial performance (Article 19) (Table 12). The more important path concerns Article 37 privatisa-tions: of the 917 firms privatised in this manner by the end of 1993, 674 employ-ing 220 000 people had been leased (most with a transfer of ownership at the end of the contract), and 138 disposed of by direct sale. The number of enterprises applying for privatisation via this route has been declining for several reasons. In 1992 and 1993 expectations were generated that the conditions of sale would be improved, leading to a wait-and-see attitude, but the number of suitable firms has also declined. Nevertheless it is estimated that a further 1 200 enterprises represent qualified candidates for privatisation via this route.

Liquidation via Article 19 mainly involves the sale of assets or parts of an enterprise rather than sales of the whole operation. Experience seems to have been positive in the case of asset sales, with capital often becoming immediately profitable. In the case of Article 37 privatisations (leasing sales), encumbrances from the past have often continued to weigh down the new enterprise.[65] An important barrier to the sale of state property by this method is concern by the liquidators not to sell below valuation which is often reported to be unrealistic.

Privatisation by leasing (one of the options under Article 37) has proved popular since it comes closest to legitimising the worker/management control which exists in most small and medium-sized firms, but it has also inevitably led

Table 12. **Summary of progress in privatisation**

	Cumulative stance at:				
	31.12.90	31.12.91	31.12.92	31.12.93	30.06.94
Total number of state-owned enterprises	8 453	8 228	7 245	5 924	5 258
Small/medium enterprises privatised by liquidation under:	49	989	1 576	1 999	2 132
Article 19	18	540	857	1 082	1 171
Article 37	31	449	719	917	961
Companies converted to joint-stock companies awaiting privatisation	38	260	480	522	579
Capital privatisation, *of which:*	1	30	52	98	119
Leverage buy-outs	1	3	3	3	3
Public flotation	0	12	13	16	17
Trade sales	0	11	34	79	99
Other [1]	0	4	2	0	0
		1991	1992	1993 [2]	1994 [3]
Income from privatisation (tm zlotys)		1.7	5.2	8.0	12.3
Capital privatisation		1.6	3.2	4.4	4.5
Leasing and sale of liquidated assets (Articles 19 and 37)		n.a.	1.6	3.3	3.5
Bank privatisations		0	0.4	0.8	4.3

1. At end-1993, this classification was discontinued.
2. Provisional.
3. Budget Act.
Source: "Dynamika Prywatyzacji", Ministry of Ownership Changes, Warsaw, No. 19, 1993.

to proposals to make the terms increasingly concessional. Proposals discussed in the context of the Pact have included allowing the new owners up to two years to contribute their required capital to the new company (20 per cent of the own funds of the old SOE), lowering the interest rate used to compute repayments and granting ownership of the assets before the final instalment payment. This last proposal has arisen in the light of experience which suggests that the new enterprises lack collateral to obtain bank loans. While it is certainly sound to give companies some tradeable property right to pledge in line with the instalments they have made, postponement of the capital contribution by the new owners would seem to work in the other direction: lowering the ability of the company to raise loans and reducing its resources still further. The policy question is, however, whether an acceleration of insider privatisation through reduced down-payments would create a better governance structure than the original worker/

manager-controlled SOE. Pending the introduction of some of these ideas via new legislation, the Ministry of Finance has introduced a number of concessions: the interest rate has been lowered to 17.5 per cent and the lump sum payment due after the first three years[66] of the contract may either be spread over the whole period of the lease or waived altogether.

On the basis of limited survey information it would appear that employee/manager buyouts have resulted in operational improvements – though at the price of an initial wage increase – and may have initiated a process which will eventually lead to improved economic performance and growth. Some studies indicate that 90 per cent of companies privatised in this manner have changed their production profile and 75 per cent have improved productivity significantly.[67] About 10 per cent of firms in 1993 had trouble in meeting lease payments. Increased internal flexibility may have been one source for these improvements for it would appear that in many cases the monitoring of management did not change significantly.[68] Looking ahead, it appears that the structure of shareholding in many of these enterprises will have to become more consolidated, and the role of employee/shareholders correspondingly reduced, if the enterprises are to undertake deeper restructuring. Attempts to accelerate privatisation via this route through lower down-payments, may be ineffective unless restrictions on transferring shares are liberalised.

Capital privatisation

The most difficult issues with privatisation have concerned the larger firms and so-called "capital privatisation". After slowing to a trickle in 1992 following governmental changes and negotiation of the Pact, 46 enterprises were sold during 1993 and 21 in the first semester of 1994. The majority of these sales were made by tender (trade sales) with preference being given to sales where a "strategic investor" was involved. Frequently this was a foreign investor. Of the 119 enterprises privatised, until the end of June 1994, domestic investors purchased 45, and 49 were sold to foreign investors; in eight cases a joint domestic/foreign entity was involved. The sales have involved increasingly complex deals as the authorities have sought to achieve political support for privatisation while at the same time achieving economic and environmental objectives.

Despite a booming stock market throughout most of 1993 – the share index rose from 1 299 in March 1993 to 18 000 in February 1994 – only three companies were privatised by public flotation (one was in process at the end of the year – Bank Slaski). The inability to use the opportunity of a bull market to increase privatisation was due to several factors. The length of time required to prepare a prospectus is one of them, but it does not explain why there was no attempt to sell some of the Treasury's 30 per cent holding in already-privatised companies. The major reason appeared to be a concern by the authorities to avoid losses by individual investors once the price turned downward, which was widely expected at the same time. Thus rather than auction shares on the exchange the authorities chose to set a "realistic" issue price and to accept an excess of demand; in the case of Bank Slaski the over-subscription was around 7:1. While it is prudent to protect and enhance the reputation of new financial markets, losses were in any case expected once the "bubble" burst so that the question remains whether a valuable opportunity was missed: after reaching a record value in March 1994 of 20 000 points, the index collapsed to 8 000 in June.

Given the opposition which may arise during the privatisation of large firms, the authorities have increasingly sought to establish contractual commitments with respect to employment, wages and investment. Employment guarantees of 18-36 months have been obtained for 115 000 workers in newly privatised enterprises, and in several cases involving foreign investors substantial wage increases have also been agreed as part of the sales contract. Contractual investment commitments for some Zl 10 trillion have also been obtained.

Although major polluting industries such as oil, chemistry and metallurgy have not yet been affected by privatisation, a start has been made in dealing with environmental standards and in clarifying owner liability. For this purpose a joint Interministerial Environmental Unit was set up in February 1993 and to date around 40 environmental assessments of enterprises to be privatised have been completed. In some of the early sales a contract price was first established and an Escrow account established to deal with specific environmental clean-up commitments. In the light of experience, this approach appears to be inefficient and not conducive to privatisation so that specific contractual commitments with penalty clauses are now being introduced.

Foreign direct investment

Registration of large foreign direct investments by the PAIZ, the government agency grounded to promote foreign investment, indicates a cumulative investment, of some \$3.7 billion from 1989 to June 1994. Nearly 60 per cent of this occurred in 1993. Ten large investments account for about 40 per cent of the total, but foreign activity has been much broader than this would indicate: by the end of 1993 some 16 000 commercial law companies with foreign participation were registered, with 5 200 in industry and 6 800 in trade.[69] For the larger projects, activity has been concentrated in the food, electronics, telecommunications and automotive sectors. At the start, most foreign investment, and almost all the largest projects, represented acquisitions of privatised firms, but in 1993 greenfield investments became equally important. The balance of payments figures are substantially lower, cumulative flows since 1989 amounting to only around \$1 billion. There are several reasons for this large discrepancy: in the case of privatisation, part of the purchase price will include a takeover of enterprise debt, which counts as foreign investment, but does not involve a capital inflow from the balance of payments perspective. Moreover, investors are only usually required to make a downpayment of 20 per cent, the remainder being contributed over a period of time.

An experimental survey of foreign investment indicates that more than half of firms with foreign participation are involved in exports.[70] Foreign exporters are primarily located in the clothing, metallurgy, construction and building services sectors, mirroring the growth areas of Polish exports. The survey reported that building materials, clothing and electronics were the most profitable for foreign firms. Their major business concerns were increases in taxes and continuing changes in customs duties. About a third of respondents reported that they suffer from anti-competitive behaviour, both by suppliers and competitors. A complaint frequently expressed by investors is the difficulty in acquiring land. Foreigners still require the permission of the Ministry of the Interior and often the Ministry of Defence to acquire all types of land. Although still time-consuming,[71] the number of approved transactions has increased rapidly. Other surveys have confirmed the importance of FDI in providing new market opportunities for exports and a more aggressive approach in restructuring an enterprise.

Several policy instruments have been used to promote FDI although generally Poland ensures national treatment. Tax incentives, which were provided in 1990/1992, have been phased out although some possibilities for exemptions remain. Trade policy has been actively used. A duty-free export quota to the EC was initially instrumental in attracting investment in the automotive industry.[72]

The policy environment is fairly liberal. Foreign investors are free to remit profits and capital gains, and Poland has concluded a network of double taxation agreements. Protection of intellectual property has improved; a new copyright law went into effect in 1994 and pirating has become less common. Licensing policy is largely open, with permission required only in strictly defined exceptions of banking, insurance, telecommunications and wholesale trade in imported goods. The new law on public procurement offers national treatment, although only companies manufacturing in Poland qualify for public procurement contracts.

Joint stock companies awaiting privatisation

As part of the capital privatisation route, 522 enterprises had been converted into joint stock companies owned by the Treasury (in effect the Ministry of Privatisation) as of the end of 1993; around 350 of these are intended for privatisation via the mass privatisation programme (MPP) and the remainder for sale, mainly by tender. According to the Privatisation Law the enterprises may only remain in this legal form for two years. Following delays in the MPP and in privatisation more generally, the status of 20-30 enterprises has now had to be extended. To manage the enterprises in the meantime, the Ministry of Privatisation has established supervisory boards requiring recruitment and training of some 3 500 board members.

The motivation for enterprises agreeing to be incorporated has varied over time – many have refused to embark upon this path to privatisation. An important motive at first was probably to avoid or minimise the special taxes on SOEs – popiwek and dividenda – but there is no clear evidence that these firms have taken advantage of such possibilities. However, neither is there evidence that they have undertaken extraordinary restructuring measures. To the extent that restructuring and changed behaviour is clearly correlated with systematic factors it is with the size of the enterprise: regardless of legal form, small and medium-sized SOEs appear to have been more effective at adjusting to new market opportunities.[73]

Mass privatisation: National Investment Funds

The broad outline of the mass privatisation programme remains essentially unchanged since the previous *Economic Survey,* but many issues have now been settled and the implementation phase will hopefully begin before the end of 1994. The enabling legislation governing the structure and operation of the National Investment Funds (NIF) became law in 1993. By December more than 100 foreign and domestic enterprises – including international investment banks – forming 33 consortia had submitted bids to run a fund. A selection committee has been assessing the applications since December 1993 and has also been considering applications for membership of the Funds' supervisory boards. The number of funds which will be established depends on the number of companies which will participate in the programme. By May 1994 367 had been approved for participation and another 100 applications were still under consideration in September 1994. With each fund responsible for 30 companies, a participation by 450 firms would require 15 funds.

The distribution of share certificates is planned for the beginning of 1995. All Polish citizens 18 years and over are eligible to receive share certificates and the cost of participation is to be 10 per cent of monthly average salary (*i.e.* around Zl 500 000). The share certificates will represent claims in all of the NIFs and will be in the form of tradeable paper securities, though initially only large packets will be tradeable on the stock exchange. As holdings of share certificates become more concentrated via over-the-counter trading, the possibility will be created for holders who have opened investment accounts with brokers to request the issue of paperless shares in the individual funds. These could then be traded on the stock exchange.

Other methods of privatisation

As part of the moves to restructure and to privatise state enterprises, the government in early 1994 initialled a ''Stabilisation-Privatisation-Restructuring'' programme with the EBRD. The programme is targeted at companies in poor condition but potentially viable, needing financial stabilisation and then restructuring. During 1994 the EBRD, in combination with the government, proposes to establish three or four investment companies each with a major domestic commercial bank as a partner. The banks will contribute shares of enterprises in which they have taken equity stakes as part of the conciliation programme and the Treasury the remainder, so that the enterprises will become fully-owned by the funds. It is envisaged that around 40 enterprises will enter the scheme initially as a pilot project; if successful the programme will be enlarged in the future. The

SRP funds will be responsible for restructuring and privatising the enterprises. It is intended that they will introduce new management and capital into the firms. There will be a success fee at the time the companies are privatised and the capital gains distributed. A waiver from double taxation of dividends will be necessary to make the scheme viable.

Restitution

An important unresolved issue concerns restitution: reprivatisation. Under current law, restitution claims can only be executed if property had been nationalised illegally. If the property is still in the possession of the state, it should be returned to the former owner, but if it has been disposed of, compensation should be paid. Over 9 000 claims have been received since 1990 but the state, lacking finance, has adopted a policy of suspending decisions on claims. This is actually illegal. Several hundred affirmative decisions have nevertheless been issued but only three compensations have been paid. This is an undesirable state of affairs, compounded by the uncertainty which has arisen because many former owners cannot file their claims under existing law. For example, no claim may be lodged if the nationalisation act itself provided for compensation, even if this was never paid. In response to a request for intentions made in September 1993 by the Ministry of Privatisation, 3 000 claims were submitted by April 1994 (nearly half for agricultural property) and estimates for compensation for all claims has been put in the range of Zl 150-350 trillion. While the problem is nowhere as severe as occurred in the new states of Germany, it is nevertheless an issue which, four years into the transition, must finally be resolved.

At present there are two legislative proposals to settle the situation: a government draft and a deputies' bill. The government bill proposes compensation, mainly in the form of privatisation bonds which would be issued for this purpose by the Ministry of Finance. A former owner would acquire bonds of a lesser value than the nationalised property and could use them for the purchase of shares at auctions, or for purchasing a 5 per cent reserve of shares in each privatised enterprise, which is already being set aside by the Ministry of Finance.[74] The government and the deputies' bills differ in several respects. In the latter, the coverage both in terms of time and nationalisation measures is wider, and there is more room for restitution rather than compensation. Experience in other countries suggests that restitution should be avoided unless absolutely necessary, even if compensation in the form of bonds has to be increased.

Creating a competitive framework

Trade and competition policy impact on the entire economy and have an important influence on the establishment and development of new enterprises. In Poland the need to restructure existing state enterprises has been an increasingly important consideration for trade policy formation. This has constrained the scope for the enforcement of competition policy although the two are becoming increasingly intertwined through formal trade arrangements.

Trade policy

Fundamental restructuring of Poland's trade regime took place in 1990/1991. Nevertheless over the period 1992/1993 the institutional arrangements governing trade have continued to develop, further strengthening its integration with the world economy. At the same time trade policy instruments have been used quite actively by both Poland and its trading partners.

Changing institutional arrangements

• Association Agreement with the European Community

The Association Agreement between Poland and the European Community was signed in December 1991 and is described at length in the previous *Economic Survey*. An Interim Agreement governing only trade questions became effective in March 1992 and the full agreement covering a wide range of issues including questions of movement of labour and capital, trade in services, convergence of legislation and competition policy entered into force in February 1994. In the meantime the preamble was strengthened by the Copenhagen Summit in June 1993 which affirmed that ''the associated countries in Central and Eastern Europe that so desire shall become members of the European Union'' as soon as they meet ''the economic and political conditions required''. The implementation of the Agreement is governed by the Association Council comprising Poland and the European Commission with European Community members as observers. The Agreement is still to be scrutinised by the GATT.

The objective of the Agreement, at least its trade aspects, is to achieve free trade for industrial products in ten years, but no such commitments are made for agricultural goods. The time profile of liberalisation is asymmetric: the agreed liberalisation will be introduced over five years by the EC and over seven years by Poland. Non-agricultural goods are classified into three groups. As from March 1992 non-sensitive industrial products have enjoyed free access to EC markets. For semi-sensitive goods duties either were eliminated in two annual steps of 50 per cent beginning in March 1992 or are being phased out over a four-year period as from that date. Trade in sensitive products – textiles, coal and steel, furniture, cars and some chemicals – is covered by separate protocols. For textiles and clothing, duties will be phased out over six years and quotas dismantled before 1998; steel and coal duties are being phased out over four years and quantitative restrictions on steel will finish in January 1996.

The agreement is more restrictive with respect to food and agriculture, and is fixed within the general framework of the CAP: concessions are given in the form of lists of exclusions to the CAP rules which predominate over any concession resulting from the agreement. For some of these products, EC import duties and levies will be cut by 20 per cent a year over three years and tariff quotas will be increased from an agreed quantity by 10 per cent a year for five years. Unlimited Polish exports beyond any agreed quantitative limits are permitted on the payment of full EC import levies and duties. For its side, Poland made a one-time reduction in some agricultural import tariffs by 10 percentage points.

The agreement specifies safeguard clauses for market disruption, infant industries, industries undergoing restructuring, industries facing important social problems, balance of payments problems, etc. Anti-dumping actions are permitted in accordance with GATT articles.

Poland will have ten years to open its services, financial and insurance markets to EC companies. Provisions with respect to competition policy – and in particular the regulation of state aid – are discussed in the following section.

• Agreement with EFTA

In December 1992 Poland signed an agreement with EFTA under which a free trade area is to be created over ten years. Pending ratification by the Polish Parliament the agreement has been provisionally applied since November 1993. The agreement is similar to those with the EC and involves asymmetrically phased reductions of tariffs and non-tariff barriers and certain provisions for temporary safeguards. Industrial and processed agricultural goods are covered in the multilateral agreement and agricultural goods in separate bilateral protocols. Most EFTA countries have barriers to agricultural trade that are often more protective than those of the EC. It is very difficult to categorise the liberalisation of agricultural goods but in general concessions are not limited by quotas.

- Central European Free Trade Agreement (CEFTA)

In December 1992, an agreement was concluded with the Czech and Slovak Republics and Hungary (CEFTA) to establish a free trade zone by January 2001, although all countries expressed their willingness to shorten this period to five years; in April 1994 the target date was brought forward to 1997. The agreement has not yet been ratified by all countries but its trade provisions entered into force on 1 March 1993.

The mechanisms specified by the agreement are similar to those negotiated with both the EC and EFTA: the progressive removal of tariffs and non-tariff barriers with a series of transitional safeguards allowing industries temporary protection to adjust. A major difference is that concessions are symmetrical: the value of benefits resulting from concessions had to be the same for each side. This led in practice to difficult negotiations and limited liberalisation. For industrial goods the timetable for tariff reductions was advanced by three years in April 1994 with fresh cuts of between a quarter and a third taking effect in effect from July 1994. Full liberalisation for sensitive products has also been brought forward to the beginning of 1998 but the tariff schedule for the ''most sensitive'' products will remain in force until 2001. The proportion of trade in agricultural and manufactured products covered is small and tariff reductions concern only a limited number of products usually within fixed quotas.

- GATT

Although the tariff schedules introduced in Poland since January 1990 have met GATT rules they were not presented to the Working Group for renegotiation of its accession protocol. The main reason for this was the government's desire to combine the offer to the Working Group with that for the Uruguay Round, but it also left the tariff schedule unbound. After negotiations the offer was accepted by both the interested parties of the Uruguay Round and by the Working Group. In April 1994 Poland signed both the final document of the Round and the Declaration on the World Trade Organisation. Consequently, it will become an original member of the WTO with all rights and obligations when the WTO is created.

With the exception of cars, linen and petroleum, all industrial tariffs are now bound at a level not higher than at 1 January 1994.[75] The list of commitments put forward fulfils the requirements of the Round, including progressive liberalisation of trade and tariffication of non-tariff measures in the case of agricultural products.

Although the GATT Agreement on Subsidies and Countervailing Measures is not yet ratified by the Polish Parliament it is *de facto* in force through the Association Agreement with the EC. The Uruguay Round final document modifies the Subsidies Code by providing a waiver for seven years on state aid rules for economies in transition (Article 29). However, the Association Agreement has different, and potentially stricter, conditions. For a period of five years (from February 1994) any public aid shall be assessed as if Poland were in its entirety a region of the EC with abnormal conditions (high relative unemployment levels and low income) and this provision may be extended for a further five years. The rules governing the distribution of state aid to regions in the EC are quite strict. State aid for coal mining and steel are covered by separate agreements with the Coal and Steel Community and, in the case of steel, linked to global rationalisation and reduction of capacity.

• NIS

Trade with the NIS has revived strongly in the first semester of 1994 and has become an important contribution to export growth. Trade relations with the Russian Federation were consolidated with the Treaty on Trade and Co-operation which was signed in August 1993 (still awaiting ratification by the Russian Parliament). Poland has extended to Russia – and other NIS – MFN status but retains the right to implement selective bilateral safeguard measures. Indeed such measures have already been applied. The major barrier to trade remains the Russian payments system but the fluid tariff laws have now become an important additional restraint. Nevertheless private Polish enterprises are adapting to the difficult and undefined trading rules still predominating in the NIS; up to 40 per cent of trade has been is on a barter basis.[76]

Little progress has been made in implementing the various proposals for triangular trade (*i.e.* linking aid to the NIS with purchases from CEECs). However, in August 1992 a new EC direct credit line for ECU 1.25 billion became operational for some NIS countries, and half of the credit can be used for products originating in the CEECs or the Baltics. As is usual under EC regulations, requests from NIS countries must be filled by tender. In the field of agriculture Polish supplies have been uncompetitive due to export subsidies extended to EC producers. Bureaucratic delays and the limited coverage of products has meant that no meaningful transaction has been reported under the scheme.

The use of trade policy instruments by Poland and its trade partners

Although a wide-ranging set of agreements are now in place with the object of promoting trade liberalisation, the instruments of trade policy have continued to be actively deployed by both Poland and its trading partners.

- Polish commercial policy

The Polish tariff schedule continues to be subject to alteration and businessmen frequently cite it as a source of uncertainty in surveys. The agreements with the EC, EFTA and CEFTA have all necessitated changes but there have also been technical reasons: Poland follows the EC's Common Nomenclature whose detailed classifications are changed annually. The binding of the tariff has reduced some of the uncertainty – since tariffs may only be reduced – but the uneven course of liberalisation still leaves residual uncertainty about the tariff structure (*i.e.* the relative tariff of different goods). In order to stabilise the tariff structure, in December 1993 the Government decided that in the future, new tariffs will be introduced only once a year as is the case in the EC.

The last major revision in July 1993 lowered the average tariff rate, excluding agriculture, from 16.3 to 14.6 per cent but the protective element might have increased for two reasons. First, lower duties are charged on imported raw materials and semi-finished products than on finished products. Second, tariff quotas have been increasingly used to relieve manufactures of duties on inputs: in 1994, 24 tariff quotas were in force favouring final users, the most important category being electronic goods. Taken together, cascading tariffs and tariff quotas have certainly increased the effective rate of protection for a number of producers including automobile manufacturers. As no calculations exist for effective rates of protection the exact incidence of the tariff system remains unclear for

Table 13. **The structure of customs tariffs**

	1991 [1]	1992 [2]	1993 [3] Basic	1993 [3] Effective	1994 [3] Basic	1994 [3] Effective
Harmonised System trade categories [4]						
Agricultural	26.2	21.1	21.9	18.5	21.9	18.3
Mineral	8.9	1.8	2.0	1.3	2.0	1.3
Chemical	14.1	12.4	..	..	..	..
Chemical products	..	..	13.0	9.6	13.0	9.5
Plastic	15.0	..	14.9	14.4	14.9	14.4
Fur, leather, wood and paper	..	10.4	..	..	..	..
Fur and leather	25.7	..	14.6	13.2	14.6	15.5
Wood and paper	13.4	..	..	..	..	..
Wood	..	..	14.0	11.6	14.0	11.6
Paper	..	..	10.8	7.6	10.8	8.2
Textile, footwear and clothing	20.6	18.8	..	..	..	..
Textiles	..	..	18.2	16.9	18.2	16.9
Footwear and clothing	..	..	20.3	20.2	20.3	20.3
Industrial mineral and metal	14.7	..	..	..	..	..
Industrial mineral	..	..	14.9	13.5	14.9	13.5
Industrial metal	..	17.9	17.5	13.2	17.5	13.1
Machinery, transport equipment and precision instruments	16.1	..	..	..	..	..
Machinery	..	..	15.5	7.0	15.7	7.4
Transport equipment	..	24.0	27.5	26.0	27.5	24.3
Precision instruments	..	..	15.5	8.7	15.5	8.8
Jewelry, arms, arts objects, miscellaneous	19.1	..	..	..	..	..
Jewelry	..	..	18.3	16.8	18.3	16.8
Arms	..	..	35.0	34.3	35.0	34.3
Miscellaneous	..	19.0	18.3	17.3	18.3	17.3
Total categories	18.4	12.0	15.5	11.7	15.5	11.6
Memorandum items:						
Average rate incl. agriculture	18.4	12.0	15.5	11.7	15.5	11.6
Average rate excl. agriculture	16.3	10.7	14.6	10.7	14.6	10.7
Variance	84.6	..	..	..	..	..

1. As of August.
2. Average new cutoms tariffs taking into account tariffs resulting from the transition agreement with the EC.
3. Weighted by import structure in the first eight months of 1993.
4. Overall categories: averages calculated on a frequency-weighted basis.
Source: Polish Ministry of Foreign Economic Relations and OECD Secretariat calculations.

policy-makers. If the experience of other countries is a guide, the tariff structure may be taxing some export activities and industries still to be established such as component suppliers.[77]

Other instruments of commercial policy include the 6 per cent surcharge which was imposed on imports for balance of payments purposes in December 1992. Although it is fairly non-discriminatory with respect to imports, the ultimate effect of the surcharge could be to tax exports. VAT and import tax are refundable for exports: they are zero-rated.

Up till now lack of sufficient staff and budgetary resources has meant that anti-dumping, countervailing and safeguard measures have not been used to any great extent; several safeguards are, however, in place against imports from the NIS. This situation is now changing and about 40 applications are at present being processed. The criteria for undertaking measures is not yet known, but as in many other countries there may be an administrative bias against broader consumer interests in favour of specific producers. With respect to agriculture, commercial policy has been particularly active, including variable import levies imposed in 1994.

• Trade partners

In industrial trade with the EC export restrictions have only been considered a problem by the authorities for some textile products, indicating a liberal interpretation of contractual commitments: of 89 ceilings faced by Polish goods in 1992 including 68 on sensitive products, 42 were breached but levies were only imposed in five cases. Of 13 quotas facing Polish goods, only six were used. For textiles and clothing none of the 20 quotas was binding and utilisation rates were low.[78]

In the case of agricultural exports to the EC the situation is different and rather complex. According to the authorities the main constraints have taken the form of minimum prices, variable levies and transportation conditions. However, preferential quotas have been under-utilised. In 1992 Polish exporters managed to utilise fully the quotas for only 23 out of 76 products and in 29 cases the degree of quota utilisation did not exceed 20 per cent. The weighted average utilisation rate for agricultural and food products was 77 per cent. In 1993 the quota was used in full for only four products and for another 20 the quotas were utilised by 10 per cent or less.

Table 14. **Selected protection measures introduced by trading partners, March 1992-December 1993**

Product	Measure	Sub-measure or effect on trade	Description	Introduction date
EC				
Ferrosilicon	Dumping	Provisional duties Final ruling Residual duties imposed	EC imposed provisional duties of 32% on imports after Commission determined that dumping up to 61.5% had occurred	14.12.92
Frozen strawberries and blackcurrants	Subsidies	Final ruling	EC Commission decided to impose countervailing duties in amount of the difference between Polish prices and EC minimum import prices on imports of frozen strawberries and blackcurrants	10.1.92
Seamless steel tubes and pipes	Dumping	Final ruling Residual duties imposed and quantity undertaking	EC imposed provisional anti-dumping duties on imports of seamless steel tubes (11.8%). They were imposed initially for four months pending an enquiry. Now extended third-country market price – Croatia	12.12.91 14.05.93
Hematite pig iron	Dumping	Provisional variable duty in form of minimum price	Constructed value based on production costs in Poland	9.12.92
Frozen blackcurrants, strawberries	Minimum prices	Final ruling	EC amended a regulation imposing minimum prices on imports of frozen blackcurrants and strawberries	4.1.92
Live animals and fresh meat	Imports prohibition	Introduction	EC imposed import prohibition on animals and fresh meat because of cases of foot-and-mouth disease in Italy	5.10.93
Urea ammonium nitrate	Dumping	Provisional duty	The EC initiated a dumping investigation. Provisional duty in form of minimum price	13.5.93
Cherries	Minimum import	Introduction	The EC Council agreed to introduce minimum port prices on cherries	19.7.93
USA				
Carbon steel plate	Dumping	Final ruling	Dumping margin 61.98% at a time when Poland classed as non-market. Now reviewed but anti-dumping margin remains in place. Damage not proven	March 1992

Table 14. **Selected protection measures introduced by trading partners, March 1992-December 1993** *(cont.)*

Product	Measure	Sub-measure or effect on trade	Description	Introduction date
Canada				
Electric motors	Dumping	Final ruling	Anti-dumping duty 100%. Next review in June 1994	October 90
Austria				
Fertilizers	Import quota	Introduction	Austria introduced 60 thousand tons quota for imports of fertilizers from Central European Countries	April 1993 till April 1994
Cement	Import quota	Introduction	Austria introduced 400 tons limit for cement imports from countries outside of EC and EFTA	April 1993 till April 1994

Source: Ministry of International Economic Relations, Warsaw.

Climatic reasons may have played some role in this under-utilisation but procedural protection by the EC is also certainly an important factor. This arises from tariff quota management.[79] Within the EC importers lodge a guarantee which they lose if they do not use the quota awarded. Moreover, the full duty is paid at the time of import and is only reimbursed some months later. Taken together, no EC importer has applied for the tendered amount. Thus Polish exporters have, to date, delivered to the EC without using the concession, and this may explain why some agricultural product exports were much greater than the amount of quota used. Full duties are payable on exports outside the quota.

Anti-dumping procedures in force in a number of OECD countries appear to be restricting access by Polish producers to world markets either directly, or indirectly via increased uncertainty as, for example, when news of an investigation is leaked. Several practices in particular appear to be quite damaging. First, in addition to imposing anti-dumping duties, "residual" duties have also been applied on all other existing or future exporters in order to prevent circumvention. While this practice is damaging at any time, it is particularly so given the structural adjustments which many enterprises are having to undertake which requires them to find new goods and markets.

Second, a number of countries – the EC in particular – have chosen to calculate dumping margins on the basis of constructed value. This approach comes into play as the basis for determining normal value when there are no, or inadequate, domestic sales of the product concerned. Under such conditions anti-dumping authorities have been able to incorporate pricing assumptions which seem extraordinary, and which reduce the value of Poland's GATT status as a market economy rather than a state trader. Three practices stand out: the inclusion of higher depreciation costs in the dumping margin than the authorities allow, imputing a "reasonable profit" in cases where profitability is low, and increasing energy prices under conditions where transactions are at arm's length (*i.e.* the enterprise is not being signalled out for a subsidy).

Assessment

The integration of Poland in the world economy has deepened during 1992/1993, both institutionally – via agreements with the EC, EFTA and GATT, and through increasing trade and foreign direct and portfolio investment. The trading framework which Poland has negotiated with its trading partners appears to be quite liberal and to increase market access. Notwithstanding this, disappointment has often been expressed in Poland – particularly with respect to the EC. While many factors are at play, the trade balance is often cited: the bilateral trade deficit with the EC is often taken *a priori* as an indicator that the trade agreements are against Poland's interests, and that exports have been restricted.

In a world of convertible currencies and multilateral relations a bilateral imbalance is neither a cause for concern in itself nor an indicator of ''unfair'' trade practices. But export barriers will lower the growth potential of Poland, whatever the trade imbalance. What then is the state of market access? With respect to industrial goods access appears to have improved markedly, even for sensitive goods. A number of quotas remain unfilled but it is nevertheless difficult to clearly interpret this as deficient supply; in some cases, *e.g.* US textiles, quotas have been allocated on goods for which Polish firms were clearly not competitive. However, arbitrary and damaging anti-dumping actions have detracted from the market opening and contributed to uncertainty, thereby magnifying the effects far beyond the level of trade directly involved.

The situation is different in agriculture. Although climatic factors are important, barriers to market access are binding and liberalisation of the Polish market may have contributed to the feeling of disappointment. Subsidies by the EC on agricultural exports to Poland and third countries have increased the loss and directly stimulated a protectionist lobby in Poland. The tentative proposal by the European Commission to withdraw subsidies on agricultural exports to the CEECs is welcome and needs to be implemented.

Turning to Polish trade policy, it appears that objectives and supporting administrative procedures might still require further development, although stability needs to be achieved quickly. The binding of tariffs is in this respect important, but is only a necessary and not a sufficient condition. After the period of exceptionally liberal trade policy in 1990 the authorities now appear to be searching cautiously for ways to actively support industrial and agricultural adjustment, but there are clear problems with this. Not every industry can be protected and it is not evident that producers of final goods, or existing producers, are the most suitable candidates – the more so as the tax incidence of tariffs and other protective measures such as tariff quotas is unclear.

Enforcing competition rules

Competition policy and trade policy are becoming increasingly intertwined. Under the terms of the Association Agreement with the EC, Poland has five years to adopt EC regulations. Particularly important in this respect will be the rules governing state aid which have still to be discussed with the EC in the Association Council. Issues will include subsidised loans, forgiveness of taxation arrears and debt write-offs. However, even if Poland has five years in which to fully comply it does not imply that distortions to competition can be neglected in the meantime. This also appears to be the opinion of the Anti-Monopoly Office (AMO), but where government policy is involved it can act only in an advisory capacity. This it has done in assessing restructuring plans over the review period.

The AMO has been active in seeking to influence industrial organisation so as to promote competition.[80] With respect to the mass privatisation programme it refused permission for 96 enterprises with a dominant market position to participate, although it is not clear whether competition will be enhanced by maintaining the present the *status quo*. Moreover, on the initiative of the AMO a National Investment Fund may hold no more than 30 per cent of its assets in one branch. A list of individual companies that may not be held by one NIF has also been prepared by the AMO, at the request of the Ministry of Privatisation. Whether this will avoid the possibility of a single NIF being in a position to control two competitors is unclear. In addition the AMO has ordered the division of 20 regional state enterprises with a dominant position on local markets, and in 11 instances has prohibited the incorporation of state enterprises. Enterprises with a domestic market share over 80 per cent have been closely monitored and their number reduced from nearly 200 at the start of the transformation to 74 at the end of 1993.

The AMO has also been active in seeking to influence government plans for industrial restructuring where – as has sometimes been the case – competition has been treated as a marginal issue. For example, the Ministry of Agriculture's initial proposal for the sugar industry foresaw a monopoly. This was successfully opposed by the AMO even though the final outcome is still flawed. The Office also registered reservations about the formation of coal holding companies, fearing cartel-like behaviour. When this did in fact occur, the office could not act because the Ministry of Industry was the initiating party. Finally, the AMO has been active in warning against the anti-competitive effects of tariff protection.

III.   Establishing an efficient banking system

Overview

As a result of near hyper-inflation in late 1989/1990, Poland is characterised by a low level of monetisation and financial intermediation: bank credit and money relative to GDP are around 20 and 30 per cent respectively, about half the levels characteristic of other economies in transition such as the Czech Republic or Hungary. At the same time, the banking system is by far the most important financial intermediary in Poland; at the end of 1993 assets amounted to Zl 934 trillion compared with a stock market valuation at that time of Zl 56 trillion, and even lower levels of activity by other institutions.[81] It is thus all the more important that the banking sector be in a position to take on a substantially increased intermediation role in the future so as to support sustained recovery. Over the last two years a great deal of progress has been made in establishing a banking system suitable to this task although several large banks and a number of smaller ones remain fragile and are a cause for concern. Affecting nearly all banks has been the high level of non-performing loans which have bankrupted some, while distorting and reducing financial intermediation in others. Measures have been implemented to deal with the immediate problems including a recapitalisation of state banks. Structural and prudential reforms addressing medium-term systemic issues related to the efficiency and stability of financial intermediation are being put in place. These should ensure that bad debts on the scale which developed between 1990 and 1992 should not recur, despite an external environment which will remain difficult and uncertain for some time to come. The policy response to non-performing loans has not yet served to reduce markedly interest rate spreads, so that taxation of financial intermediation remains significant.

Organisation and performance of the banking system

Bank structure

At the beginning of 1994, the banking sector in Poland comprised 86 banks, most of which are legally if not yet operationally universal banks[82] – in addition to 1 664 co-operative banks. The organisation of the banking system in early 1994 is shown in Table 15. Two features are significant. First, despite the entry of new private and foreign banks since 1990, the state-owned banks still retain a dominant role in the economy – and this remains so even after the privatisation of three banks by early 1994. Second, the specialised state-owned banks constitute a significant part of the system, indicating that the banking sector remains to a degree segmented.

The current structure of the Polish banking system was effectively determined in 1989 at the time of the separation of nine regional departments of the NBP into independent, state-owned, universal commercial banks.[83] These banks were regionally concentrated[84] although they did receive several branches in

Table 15. **Structure of Polish banking**

January 1994

Type of bank	Share of:				
	Number		Assets	Credit	Deposits
	Banks	Branches	Per cent		
State-owned banks:					
Commercial banks	7	420	24	26	20
Specialised banks	6	583	42	31	48
Partly owned (BGZ)	1	107	8	15	6
Co-operative banks	1 664	n.a.	7	8	8
Private:					
Privatised[1]	3	124	8	9	9
Part or fully private	70	490	11	12	9
Total:					
(excluding co-ops)	87	1 724	–	–	–
(including co-ops)	1 751	n.a.	–	–	–

1. Including two commerial banks.
Source: National Bank of Poland.

100

other regions so as to encourage competition. The banks inherited a substantial part of the NBP's loan portfolio including loans which later proved to be non-performing.

The managerial structure of these commercial banks has been changed to meet the demands of a competitive environment and a market economy. The commercial banks were incorporated as Treasury-owned joint stock companies in October and November 1991 and members of their Supervisory Boards selected by the Ministry of Finance.[85] Both the Chairman and the Supervisory Boards are appointed for terms of three years and, even though Ministry of Finance policy up till now has stressed the primacy of professional qualifications, explicit political appointments are not excluded. Moreover, the Ministry of Finance has also issued guidelines to directors instructing them that any requests from Ministries for special treatment should not be fulfilled.[86] Informed observers believe that incorporation reinforced their commitment to banking according to commercial principles. It is the intention to privatise all the major commercial banks eventually; two have already been privatised, Wielkopolski Bank Kredytowy in Poznan in 1993 and Bank Slaski in Katowice in early 1994, and a third is scheduled for late 1994.[87] A small specialised bank was already privatised in 1992.

The nine original commercial banks initially functioned to some extent as coalitions of independent bank branches rather than as single organisational units. All banks therefore set about developing an internal organisational structure including better telecommunications and information networks. This process, which is not yet completed, has been facilitated by the so-called twinning arrangement which came into force at the beginning of 1992. The programme is supported financially by the World Bank and involves agreements between seven Polish and western banks whereby the latter, for a fee, undertake to provide training and practical advice in nine areas of banking operations.[88]

In addition to the creation of nine new commercial banks, four pre-existing ''specialised'' banks were retained, and several new ones have since been established.[89] The original four still account for nearly half of the total assets of the banking system and comprise a savings bank (PKO BP), a bank for foreign trade (Bank Handlowy), a savings bank mainly for foreign currency deposits (PKO SA), and a bank for the food and agricultural sector (BGZ). The savings bank has a nation-wide network of branches (400 in 1994) and other outlets including the post office, and maintains around 1.1 million current accounts, 4 million passbook accounts and 6 million time deposits. In 1992 the bank accounted for around 25 per cent of total bank deposits. Three-quarters of loans by the bank had to be for housing purposes which in part accounts for its importance in terms of credits to the economy: around 27 per cent. The bank is not incorporated but is owned directly by the state; the chairman of the Supervisory Board is appointed by the Prime Minister, and other members by the President of the NBP, Ministry of Finance and the employees (two seats each).

The two specialised banks for foreign currency transactions together account for some 22 per cent of the assets of the banking system. However, the balance sheets and financial condition are quite different. Being an old bank, PKO SA still bears evidence of the foreign debt-crises of the 1970s and 1980s: matching a substantial portion of the foreign currency deposits are dollar-denominated bonds issued by the Ministry of Finance in 1990. The bank makes few loans although it is active on the inter-bank market. Share capital and reserves amounted to 3.5 per cent of total assets at the end of 1992 although this has since improved. Bank Handlowy was in a much better condition with a capital/asset ratio of 14 per cent. This bank also has a significant loan portfolio. Both banks are joint stock companies fully owned by the Treasury.

Excluding the savings bank, the food and agricultural bank (BGZ) is Poland's largest in terms of loans to the economy with a portfolio of Zl 47 trillion: around 17 per cent of the total. Although it is a universal bank like all the others, it remains specialised in the financing of agriculture and agricultural commodity wholesalers. As a result, the bank is still responsible for administering the bulk of directed and subsidised credits for agriculture, making it an important recipient of refinancing credit from the NBP. The BGZ also acts as a bank for 1 245 co-operative banks (April 1994). To this end, it provides refinancing, maintains their membership in the clearance system, and is a depository for their surplus liquidity. Following the new co-operative law in 1990, the status of the BGZ changed. Up until September 1994, the Treasury held 56 per cent of the shares and all co-operative banks owned the remainder. However, because it had a co-operative legal form, the Ministry of Finance had only one vote and therefore was often not successful in having its intentions implemented. The bank has now been incorporated, giving the Ministry of Finance a voting majority of shares.

In early 1994 there were 1 664 co-operative banks, many of which are quite old. They are small and are usually located in rural areas. Until 1990 these banks were limited in their activities and were largely managed by the BGZ; indeed it was hard to describe them as co-operatives. In 1990 the co-operative law was changed granting independence to the individual co-operatives and allowing them in effect to become universal banks. Up until mid-1994, 400 had chosen to break away from the BGZ and to join one of three associations, which are in part regionally based.

The private sector comprises newly established private banks, three privatised banks and seven banks with foreign capital. In addition, three branches of foreign banks have been established and there are 21 representative offices of foreign banks. Nearly 60 private banks emerged during the first two years after 1989 in the wake of a liberal licensing policy and low capital requirements. Since 1992 only around six new licenses have been granted. At the beginning of 1994 there were 72 private banks but of these only 10 could be termed strictly private. Even including the two newly privatised commercial banks, the sector still accounted for only some 20 per cent of banking assets and about 18 per cent of deposits at the end of 1993. However, the larger private banks have now grown to a size equivalent to the smaller state-owned banks.

Evolving bank behaviour: increased competition

Bank behaviour has changed significantly in the period since 1991. Increased competition has been a significant factor, but equally if not more important has been the attitude of the Ministry of Finance. Unlike most other founding bodies in Poland, the Ministry has continuously pressured incorporated banks to improve management and adopt a tough position with respect to non-performing loans. Supporting the continuous pressure has been the prospect of privatisation – including the usual possibility for employees to purchase 20 per cent of shares at a 50 per cent discount – and profit-related bonuses for managers. Without such an active owner – conspicuously absent from the BGZ – it is doubtful whether bank behaviour would have changed to the extent that it has.

Since 1992 competition in the banking sector has increased and banks have increasingly adjusted to the demands of a market economy. During 1990-1991 competition between banks remained restricted because of excess liquidity, banking regulations including credit ceilings, and delayed adaptation to the new commercial environment.[90] However, since 1992 a marked increase in inter-bank competition has been evident for deposits, lending (credit ceilings were eliminated in 1993) and in the provision of services. With respect to deposits a number of banks, including the main commercial ones, have sought to extend their traditionally low deposit base at the expense of the "specialised" banks. For deposits of any maturity there is now a significant spread of interest rate offers depending on such factors as location and riskiness of the bank. One reason for the desire to retain deposits has been the relatively high and volatile cost of funds on the inter-bank market. Interest rate liberalisation and competition do, however, present risks in an environment in which a number of banks are experiencing difficulties. Failing banks – including ones experiencing difficulties with loans – may seek to avoid or delay their demise by outbidding competitors for deposits.[91] Deposit insurance in Poland, which up to the present has been effectively universal, increases the likelihood that such behaviour could occur.

There have been significant advances in the provision of banking services. A number of banks have sought to supply commercial banking products (*e.g.* LOCs, transfers, bill discounting) which were previously the preserve of the specialised banks, while the latter have also sought to expand their activities. Most banks have aimed to become true universal banks and have extended operations into broker and other consumer and producer services. In encouraging competition in banking services, the foreign banks have exercised an influence far beyond the size of their balance sheets. If anything, the process of expanding services has gone too far, and some banks are now reported to be seeking to become niche players and to specialise in certain activities. This would be a welcome sign of a maturing financial market.

There are also indications that banks are responding to the demands of a market economy with respect to new lending activity. Loans are being priced for risk: the difference on interest rates for high and low risk loans is at least 15 percentage points and probably more. More recently there have been signs of competition for good quality industrial borrowers, including a reduction of interest rates to the refinance rate and even below. This is an interesting development since yields on government bonds remain more attractive. A reason for this behaviour might be that banks are establishing long-term strategies which envisage their continuing presence in the corporate market which is at the moment fairly small. Several specialised banks are attempting to expand and to become true universal banks. Bad debt work-out departments under the control of a director were established in early 1992 and are providing banks with valuable experience in assessing restructuring programmes and business plans. This experience will be deepened as part of the enterprise restructuring programme (Chapter II). By and large, banks are seeking to minimise risk which is a sensible strategy given the external environment in which they operate and desirable given their status as universal banks.

There are two important areas where the adjustment to the market economy is lagging and where the banking sector remains subject to administrative decision. Directed credit from the NBP and interest subsidies from the budget remain in agriculture and housing. Taken together these two programmes account for nearly 20 per cent of the stock of credit to the economy (the housing sector alone accounts for around 15 per cent). The issues surrounding policy in these areas are discussed below since they closely concern the financial condition of two major banks.

Bank performance

By early 1994 the banking sector was characterised by highly mixed performance. Fifteen private banks, with deposits of nearly Zl 8 trillion, were performing so badly that, in the words of the President of the NBP, they qualified for bankruptcy while the situation at three large state-owned banks remained extremely difficult.[92] In April 1994 296 co-operative banks were in crisis, with 23 in bankruptcy, and 495 were subject to recovery programmes. The number of commercial banks making losses had also increased from 11 in 1992 to 24 at the end of 1993 (Table 16). At the same time, however, a large number of banks, though operating in a difficult environment, appeared to be performing soundly. In particular, gross profit margins in the major commercial banks were significantly higher than in other banks, while in three banks the solvency ratio was brought above the capital risk weighted asset ratio of 8.0 during 1993. Many co-operative banks were also functioning satisfactorily. Nevertheless, the picture which emerges from Table 16 is one of a banking system under generalised pressure from an increase in non-performing loans, rising costs and declining profits.

Table 16. **Indicators of bank performance**

Excluding co-operative banks

	1991	1992	1993
Solvency			
Number:			
Not at required level/number of banks		18/84	18/87
Negative or very low solvency		8	16
Improved solvency above 8.0			3
Liquidity			
Number with good liquidity		61	34
Three-month liquidity ratio		0.95	0.75
Non-performing credits			
Percentage non performing credits	16.5	26.8	27.4
Required provisions (Zl trillion)[1]		42.0	56.2
Actual provisions (including bank			
recapitalisation of Zl 21 trillion)[1]		14.6	47.2
Profitability			
Number making loss		11	24
Gross proit/income			
– 9 commercial		24.8	25.2
– commercial and specialised banks		20.1	7.2
– private		9.7	3.4

1.   Excluding Bank Handlovo-Kredytowy in 1993.
Source: National Bank of Poland, Department of Banking Supervision.

Structure of costs and incomes

To appreciate the situation of the Polish banking system it is necessary to consider the whole transition period: 1993 was exceptional only because past losses were finally recognised and the implications became better understood. Operating asset ratios for the period point to three important features[93] (Table 17): a low rate of return on capital; declining profitability on intermediation and increased dependency on other sources of income including securities; and rising operating costs.

The rate of return on capital has remained below the inflation rate, although the difference could be narrowing if an adjustment is made for extraordinary losses in 1993. Measuring banking capital is always difficult and this is particularly so in Poland where valuation problems are much more severe. Considering

Table 17. **Operating asset ratios**

Percentage of assets

	1990	1991	1992	1993
Average assets (trillion Zl)	–	577.9	615.5	793
Interest margin [1]	17	5.5	2.8	0.5
(including securities income)	12.69	9.26	5.26	4.25
Other income	1.92	1.74	2.49	2.06
Operating costs	2.15	2.97	2.57	2.73
Provisions	0.00	2.06	0.83	2.18
Rate of return on assets (pre tax)	12.45	5.97	4.35	1.40
Rate of return on capital (after tax) [2]	–	50.6	37.8	–23.9
Costs/total income	60	78	84	97

1. Interest on lending minus interest on deposits divided by total assets.
2. Estimate of own funds (equity and provisions): 1991: Zl 24.5 trillion, 1992: Zl 31.4 trillion, 1993: Zl 50.6 trillion.
Note: For definitions, see *Bank Profitability, Financial Statements of banks, 1983-1992*, OECD, Paris, 1994.
Source: Marta Golajewska, Pawel Wyczanski, *Materialy i Studia*, No. 41, 1994, National Bank of Poland.

only bank equity, the rate of return is high and certainly above the rate of inflation.[94] However, this only reflects the very small equity base of the banks. Including reserves as in done in Table 17 is more appropriate, but still only represents partially the situation: if banks were to be capitalised to levels considered appropriate by the authorities, the measured rate of return would have been still lower. By international standards, the rate of return on assets is not high and once the higher rate of inflation is considered it is clearly inadequate (Table 18).

Interest margins (as a percentage of assets) including incomes from securities – mainly government bonds – have steadily declined to levels characteristic of countries with more stable conditions. The switch in financial operations away from lending to the purchase of government securities is apparent in the increasing divergence between the two measures of margins presented in Table 17. At the same time, banks have become heavily dependent on other sources of income. In 1992 earnings on foreign currency dealings were particularly important while in 1993 brokerage and other securities trading incomes were significant. The policy question is whether these represent a stable base for building a universal banking system.

Operating costs are in the range frequently observed in countries with underdeveloped banking systems and high rates of inflation. Among the reasons which might be given for high operating costs in Poland is the relatively low

Table 18. **International comparisons of operating asset ratios**

Averages 1990-1992, per cent

	Interest margin	Other income	Operating costs	Provisions	Rate of return assets (pre tax)
Poland					
All banks (1992)	2.8	2.5	2.6	0.8	4.4
Germany					
All banks	2.0	0.7	1.7	0.4	0.5
Spain					
All banks	3.8	0.9	2.8	0.6	1.3
Co-operative banks	5.1	0.3	3.4	0.5	1.6
Turkey					
Commercial banks	9.3	0.0	5.0	0.9	3.3
Hungary					
(1989-1991)	4.1	–	–	–	3.2
Portugal					
All banks (1991-1992)	4.5	1.2	2.8	1.7	1.3

Source: Bank Profitability, Financial Statements of Banks, 1983-1992, OECD, Paris, 1994; and Hungarian State Office of Banking Supervision.

level of bank assets relative to GDP. Other factors include high start-up costs for new banks, costly investment in computerisation and telecommunications and increased costs from running the settlements system as non-cash payments have become more important.[95] Increased wages may be another factor although wages only accounted for 7.5 per cent of total costs in 1992 – up from around 6 per cent in 1990.

Non-performing loans have been a major factor driving the decline in interest margins and the rise in provisioning costs. Following audits during 1991 the scale of non-performing loans as a whole became clear: around 25-30 per cent of the loan portfolio to the economy at the end of 1991 had to be considered as non-performing and a significant proportion of these as bad. Even after additional provisioning in the course of 1992/1993 of around Zl 32 trillion, by the end of 1993 the provision for non-performing loans was still only 80 per cent of the amount required while four banks had provisions amounting to only 40 per cent of the required amount. For the banking system, an additional Zl 11 trillion of reserves were needed at the end of 1993. This sum has to be seen in light of the banking sector's total capital of some Zl 63 trillion and gross profits of Zl 4 trillion in 1993 after debt provisions of Zl 25 trillion.

The problem of non-performing loans is even more pressing for some banks since loan concentration appears to be high: 72 banks reported loans exceeding 15 per cent of the bank's capital and in 15 banks "big credits"[96] exceeded 70 per cent of all credit granted.[97] In 1992 "big credits" accounted for 15 per cent of non-performing loans but by 1993 this had increased to 24 per cent. Based on statistical analysis of corporate returns one observer estimates that around 60 per cent of credit to large enterprises – mostly state-owned – could be non-performing.[98] Around a third of these large enterprises are housing co-operatives.

Interest rate spreads: taxation of financial intermediation

On the basis of experience in other comparable countries it is to be expected that a high level of non-performing loans would lead to an increased spread between interest rates on deposits and those charged borrowers, and therefore to a tax on financial intermediation. It is surprisingly difficult to calculate spreads for Poland, but preliminary estimates point to a similar effect. As discussed in Annex III, the effective interest rate on lending is difficult to determine since it is known that banks are willing to trim lending rates quite significantly for good clients. Estimates by the OECD Secretariat point to an interest rate spread of 7 and 9 percentage points for the banking sector as a whole in 1992 and 1993 respectively. For banks dependent on the inter-bank market or for the savings banks (PKO BP), the spreads are considerably smaller. These estimates are substantially lower than those often quoted in public debate which appear to underestimate the cost of funds for banks, and overstate the rate of interest being charged on actual loans.

There are factors other than bad debts serving to tax financial intermediation, one of the most important being the high level of compulsory reserves which do not earn interest for the banks. Since July 1992, compulsory reserves on both current and savings accounts have been 23 per cent, and 10 per cent on time deposits. At the end of 1991 compulsory reserves constituted some 7.5 per cent of the assets of the banking system although this had declined to 3.7 per cent by the end of 1992 (3.1 per cent at the end of 1993). No interest is paid on the basic part of the reserves (10 per cent), but any amount above that earns interest at a rate at least half the rediscount rate. However, due to a decision of the Parliament the interest is not paid to the banks but to the Agricultural Debt Restructuring Agency (see Chapter II).

Using a stylised model of the Polish banking system (Annex V) facilitates a judgement about the importance of the various factors contributing to spreads – and at the same time to illustrate some of the policy choices which were available to the authorities. Calibrating the model for 1992 indicates that non-performing loans accounted for over half the observed spread of 7 percentage points, and compulsory reserves for another 1.5 percentage points (Table 19). Moreover, as many banks were earning close to zero real rates of return, the interest rate spread could even be regarded as on the low side: to earn a 10 per cent real rate of rturn on capital, which might be considered the minimum for longer-term viability, an interest margin of 8 percentage points was necessary. Two major policy alternatives were in principle available: fiscalise the problem by replacing the lost income streams with interest payments from the budget (*i.e.* through issuing bonds), or have banks work out the problem by maintaining high spreads for some time until they had been recapitalised themselves. The difference between the two alternatives in terms of spreads, and therefore the implicit taxation on lenders and borrowers, was significant.

Table 19.   **Decomposition of interest rate spread**

Based on stylised facts at end of 1992

Real rate of return on capital	0%	10%
	Percentage points	
Required spread without minimum reserves and without bad loans	0.7	1.5
Additional margin for reserves (% of deposits 7.7%)	1.5	1.5
Additional margin for bad loans 11% of total assets (30% of loans)	4.6	4.7
Interaction effect	0.5	0.5
Total required spread	7.3	8.2

Source: OECD Secretariat calculations.

Dealing with the issue of non-performing loans

Origin of the problem

The high level of non-performing loans did not result from poor banking decisions during 1992/1993, but unsound practices in the period 1990/1991. The systemic reasons for the build-up are discussed below for each type of bank but it is first appropriate to ask why they did not provision for such loans adequately. Two factors appear to have played a role. First, the fiscal system was unfavourable. Until the beginning of 1994 provisions for bad and doubtful debts were not tax-deductible, thereby increasing the costs of forming a specific reserve. In addition, banks were being steadily decapitalised: until 1992 they were taxed on interest due and not paid. Despite high nominal profits for many banks in 1991 and 1992, only 13 and 11 banks respectively, out of around 80 registered rates of return greater than the rate of inflation.[99]

Second, the usual reluctance of all bankers to accept that a debt is non-performing was reinforced by the lack of bank supervisors and sufficient regulatory powers to force conservative provisioning and lending.[100] The development of sound banking supervision in Poland was held back till 1992 when an amendment to the Banking Act came into operation and a permanent President was appointed for the NBP. Until then the NBP lacked powers to establish mandatory rules for assessing debt quality and establishing specific provisions, or to increase the minimum capital requirements of existing banks. In addition, the NBP also lacked the staff to effectively administer many of the powers it had, leading, for example, to there being no effective, fit and proper person test. This lack of staff was further compounded by a liberal licensing policy with respect to new banks which led to their rapid increase up to 1992: 60 private banks emerged during the two years after 1989, many with the minimum capital base.

The already limited banking supervision powers were weakened unintentionally in 1990 with the passage of the new Co-operative Law. Originally intended to liquidate the co-operative unions of the old regime and to establish genuine co-operatives, the effect on the co-operative banks was far-reaching. Instead of being limited regionally they in effect became universal banks. At the same time, the BGZ, which had regulatory responsibility for these banks, lost it without the NBP gaining the requisite powers.[101] This lacuna has remained up to the present with the NBP having the power to issue recommendations but not regulations in certain crucial areas such as the spread of business activity both geographically and by product. To improve the situation an amendment to the banking and co-operative law is necessary.

Most attention has been devoted to the problems of the nine commercial banks which were created in 1989. Internal audits in 1991 estimated that the share of bad debts ranged between 9 and 79 per cent with the weighted average being 42 per cent.[102] Later audits have shown that the proportion has changed little. The factors behind this development are quite well-known and were described in the 1992 Economic Survey. Some debts were undoubtedly bad before 1990 – and especially those related to central investments – but the high rate of inflation in 1989 and especially in January 1990 effectively wiped out a large proportion of these. The high level of nominal interest rates in 1990/1991, and high real rates in 1991 as inflation decelerated, apparently induced a large number of companies to repay debts to the banks and to increase their security by being essentially debt-free. Other state-owned firms, and invariably the large ones, quickly found themselves in a debt trap: profitability fell strongly, especially in 1991, while low levels of inflation in some of these industries led to very high real interest rates. Moreover these firms were among those expecting most from a government bailout, as part of the widely discussed industrial policy.

The behaviour of the state-owned commercial banks contributed to the situation as they generally failed to change their lending policy. Banks often chose to prolong a credit, usually granted for a three-month period, and to convert the unpaid interest into principal, rather than placing an enterprise which was experiencing payment problems into bankruptcy or subjecting it to other forms of pressure. Since many of these old debtors were large firms and there were no regulatory barriers against exposure, the position of some banks became increasingly difficult. For example, in one large state bank even in 1994 11 state-owned firms account for 90 per cent of non-performing loans.

In some other countries banking crises and bank fragility have often been associated with close ownership relations between banks and commercial companies. At least formally this was not the case in Poland. Informally, however, many banks maintained close relations with the enterprises while being unable to exercise any governance control which it was hoped a universal bank would do. Eventually, as has often happened around the world, the large debtor ''captured'' the creditor.

It is important not to exaggerate the situation. Several commercial banks quite early moved to distance themselves from clients they regarded as risky while in the case of some of the large loans informal debt restructuring agreements appear to have been put into place: accrued interest income in 1991 appears to have little relation with interest rate schedules. More importantly, it is often difficult to see what the banking sector as a whole could have done in 1991 since legal powers and instruments were still very restricted. Bankruptcy was not an effective instrument and the pressure for improvements on the flow side really had to come not only from the owners but also from structural reform more generally. With respect to new loans, bank behaviour certainly altered over the period. The share of banks' assets devoted to risk-free lending to the government increased from 15 per cent to 20 per cent, while collateral requirements for new loans have been stringent. Most of the commercial banks also moved to reduce the problem of adverse selection: the high nominal interest rates attracted the riskiest proposals which, despite the higher income, they wished to avoid.

The systemic factors described above also affected the specialised banks although other factors have been particularly important in the case of both the savings bank (PKO BP) and the agricultural bank (BGZ). Both banks remain in a poor financial condition with bad debts thought to amount to 20 per cent and 45 per cent respectively, while their capital base remains relatively small. Estimates in early 1994 of the recapitalisation required for the PKO BP and the BGZ are Zl 10-15 trillion and Zl 25 trillion respectively.

The problems at the savings bank are directly related to the difficult issue of financing current and past housing investment.[103] At the end of 1993, out of a loan portfolio of Zl 58 trillion, Zl 48.5 trillion was for housing and of this Zl 45 trillion was for old loans (*i.e.* not double indexed mortgages).[104] These loans were extended to building co-operatives (the 500 largest account for 85 per cent of the loans) subject to the condition that the repayments would be limited to 20 per cent of their family member's income. Two problems have arisen. First, in some cases up to 30 per cent of tenants are not paying their dues, leading to increasing insolvency on the part of co-operatives. Under these circumstances the bank has practically no powers of enforcement: in early 1994, 30 000 eviction notices could not be executed. Second, the bank is only permitted to charge 1.1 times the NBP's refinance rate, but must pay high rates of interest on time deposits. Repayments by the housing co-operatives account for only some

20-30 per cent of interest due, the remainder being capitalised. This places the bank in a maturity mismatch position so that the Treasury bought some Zl 29 trillion of capitalised interest over the period 1990-1992 to preserve the bank's liquidity. Legally this is still a debt of the housing co-operatives but its collection is just as unlikely as the capital sum owed to the bank.

The behavioural and economic factors underlying the build-up of non-performing loans are much more severe at the agricultural bank (BGZ) than in the others. The greatest prospective loss arises from the state-owned farms where bad debt at the end of 1993 amounted to Zl 7 trillion from an overall loan portfolio of Zl 46 trillion. This debt has now been consolidated onto the account of the Agricultural Property Agency which was founded in 1992. High inflation and a dramatic decline in the terms of trade in 1990 contributed to a high demand for loans. The BGZ accommodated the demand – and still does – since it views its role as essentially one not of commercial banking, but of supporting a major sector of the economy. At the same time the collapse of corporate governance was particularly severe with these farms. This probably explains why, despite falling inflation and improving terms of trade, the sector appears to be incapable of repaying loans. A similar situation is apparent with commodity wholesalers where demand for working capital and seasonal loans appears to be insatiable, but difficult to repay.

For the co-operative sector as a whole the level of non-performing loans is around 20 per cent: at the root of the financial problems in many of the co-operatives which are struggling is a small number of very large loans made during the years 1990-1992. These banks are also especially burdened by loan guarantees – mainly to the Bank Handlowy and the PKO SA for foreign transactions – which they will have to honour. New-found freedom after 1990 encouraged a number to engage in activities such as loan guarantees, whose price they had little experience to determine, and lending to non-members, about whom they had little knowledge. In addition related lending has also emerged as a factor promoting unsound lending practices. An estimate of such potential losses is not available.

The private banks – excluding the privatised ones which are in good financial condition – which have been established since 1989 were expected to maintain healthy balance sheets since they were not burdened by lending to large state-owned firms and by old credits. Even so, by 1992 bad debts accounted for around 30 per cent of the loan portfolio and a number of banks were insolvent. Others were experiencing liquidity problems as they were progressively excluded from the interbank market. A number of factors contributed to this situation even though it must be stressed that several private banks have been very successful. First, given the rapid growth of banking activity in general, lack of experienced staff became a severe problem. Second, although private banks were not burdened with old debt they still had to operate in a very uncertain environment characterised by unknown reputations of borrowers. Even if they had confined their activities to the private sector, a high rate of failure would have been inevitable. Under such conditions banks should have been well capitalised; this was not the case in some banks where the founders even had to borrow the start-up capital. In addition, the private banks were burdened by high start-up costs which did not allow them to build up capital from internally generated funds. All these factors might have encouraged a number of them to take on high-yield but high-risk assets.

In sum, the high level of non-performing loans arose during the transition in 1990/1991 as both firms and banks reacted slowly to the changing economic and systemic environment and were permitted to do so by the delayed tightening of banking supervision. In responding to the situation up to the present, the authorities have had to deal with three complex sets of policy issues: tighten prudential standards at a reasonable pace; deal with the immediate crises and signs of fragility which are a symptom of the bad debt problem; and, where appropriate, either recapitalise some of the major banks or take the debt of their balance sheets. At the same time, policy has been constrained by the need to be credibly "one off" – so that the problem would not quickly recur.

Tightening prudential regulations

An important contributing factor to the difficulties in the banking sector was the inadequate prudential framework which was mainly based on recommendations rather than directives. With the entry into force of amendments to the Banking Law in March 1992 the NBP has been able to take a number of measures which will contribute to the long-term soundness of the system. A major policy question has been the length of the transition period banks would be given to reach the required levels of capital adequacy, provisioning and exposure.

At first the NBP set very tight time limits, but these have been gradually relaxed in the light of experience.

To deal with the immediate problem of banks remaining in a captive relation with their clients and possibly extending new loans to them, bad debt work-out departments were established at all major banks in early 1992. The departments are the direct responsibility of a bank director and new lending is prohibited. Penalty interest also ceases to be charged on loans which must be transferred to this department. The NBP established criteria for assessing the lack of creditworthiness (inability to repay principal and interest on due dates, business situation of the client) and backed this with closer on-site supervision. By December 1992 over 4 400 enterprises, more than half of them private, were without creditworthiness. Given the difficult conditions of a transition economy, the departments can be rated a success. In some cases as much as 15 per cent of a banks' income has derived from the operations of the work-out department and there has been a steady though modest stream of enterprises returning to normal credit status. Moreover, it appears that enterprises do try and avoid losing creditworthiness if they can, indicating that the costs of losing it outweigh the benefits from interest no longer accruing.

The NBP also took steps to ensure soundness of the system by specifying capital adequacy requirements and increasing the required provisions for non-performing loans and minimum capital. Capital adequacy was set at 8 per cent of risk-weighted assets, although banks commencing operations after May 1993 will have to maintain 15 per cent during the first year of operations. By the end of 1993, 18 banks – excluding co-operatives – were beneath this level. In forming specific reserves against non-performing loans an initial deadline was set for the end of 1993. After it became apparent that most banks would not meet this deadline it was extended to March 1994. Although the shortfall was sharply reduced, many banks – including 60-70 per cent of co-operatives – will fail to meet the extended deadline. A problem faced by all banks is that their profits do not allow sufficient additional provisioning; if they show a loss even as a result of provisioning, the NBP may suspend their managements. In addition, the new taxation laws on provisioning only allow deductibility for new loans, not to loans prior to 1992 which is where the problem is concentrated. In 1992 the minimum founding capital for banks with foreign participation was set at $6 million so as to be broadly in line with EC requirements. For domestic banks the minimum capital requirement was raised from Zl 20 billion to Zl 70 billion. At the end of 1992 around 40 banks were capitalised below that level but this had been reduced to 23 by the end of 1993. A timetable has been set for each bank to meet these regulations.

Dealing with bank crises and fragility

By the end of 1993 the NBP had dealt with crises in ten private banks while a number of other banks were either under close scrutiny or were following recovery programmes: one was put into liquidation in 1992 and two in 1993, two were liquidated and taken over by other banks, and three were under administration. The policy objective has been to avoid bankruptcy for the larger banks but to liquidate the smaller ones or force them to merge with stronger banks. In several cases the NBP approached state-owned banks with requests that they take over a failing private bank, with some success. The NBP has at first sought to have the shareholders increase their capital contributions, but if this failed it has brokered a rescue scheme itself. In ten cases the NBP has invested its own funds (around Zl 3 trillion until mid-1994). In two of the larger cases it has taken over control of the bank by acquiring shares and using existing capital to cover losses. In other cases, secured loans and extended Lombard facilities have been granted to other banks to take over the problem ones. In each case the senior management of the bank in crisis has been replaced.

Apart from the desire to avoid any decline in confidence in the banking system, and especially the inter-bank market, the NBP's policy has been influenced by the lack of deposit insurance funds. For banks established since February 1989 there is no explicit deposit guarantee; for the others there is an unlimited state guarantee for all types of deposits by individuals, but not for enterprises and local government. Full compensation was in effect extended to depositors of the bank which failed in 1992 so that deposit insurance has been *de facto* extended to all banks – but at a cost to the NBP. Since mid-1993 there has been an agreement between the NBP and the Ministry of Finance to guarantee only a part of individual deposits. The result has been that in deciding how to handle a bank crisis the NBP has weighed the direct cost to itself of honouring the guarantee against the funds to be used in taking-over a bank – and up to now has decided in favour of the latter. Whether this sends the right signal to other banks is another question.

Although private banks in difficulty have posed some risk to confidence in the inter-bank market, the systemic problems associated with the co-operative banks have been of a different kind. In 1992 the NBP conducted an analysis of the level of guarantees offered by the co-operatives to other banks. On the basis of this analysis it issued a recommendation in July 1992 advising that such guarantees constituted a danger to the banking system and that they should not be accepted. In addition the regional associations of co-operative banks were also recommended to confine the banking activities of their members and especially to cease granting guarantees. The NBP does not at the moment have the power to issue regulations in these areas nor in the area of related lending, which is a particular problem in the co-operative sector.

Some co-operatives have experienced "runs" on deposits causing concern in the NBP that a domino effect could threaten even sound banks. In responding to the situation, by the end of 1993, 11 co-operative banks had been placed in bankruptcy and petitions had been submitted for a further six, while another 500 had gone into recovery programmes under the supervision of the NBP. Of this latter group around 300 may be candidates for bankruptcy. The NBP has committed its own money to managing the crisis: in March 1994 it decided to channel to the sector the Zl 0.5 trillion which had been set aside for supporting all problem banks in 1994. How these funds will be used is at present unclear. In managing the crisis the NBP has been hampered by the lack of legal powers and difficulties arising from the Co-operative Act. It is difficult to organise a merger or a take-over of an under-capitalised co-operative by another bank: in some cases the co-operative must first be liquidated and its capital distributed. Until mid-1994 deposit insurance has had to be paid in two cases, but, at the time of writing it was not known whether all deposits had been honoured.

Recapitalising the state-owned banks

The need to increase provisions for non-performing loans put a number of the state-owned banks in a difficult position. These banks were also effectively held hostage by their large debtors, and this relationship was clearly going to frustrate the policy goal to achieve increased efficiency of financial intermediation. Having decided that there would be neither general debt forgiveness nor the purchase of bad loans by a new body, the authorities proceeded with a recapitalisation of nine banks. Seven commercial banks were recapitalised in September

1993 through the issue of Zl 11 trillion in government bonds. The injection represented the estimated amount needed to achieve a capital risk weighted asset ratio of 12 per cent, including provisions for non-performing loans at the end of 1991. The savings bank (PKO BP) and the agricultural bank (BGZ) were partially recapitalised for their bad loans (excluding housing and agriculture) in December 1993 with the issue of a further Zl 10 trillion. Further recapitalisation of the BGZ was made dependant on its becoming incorporated and thereby controlled by the Ministry of Finance. It is proposed to issue a further Zl 19 trillion in recapitalisation bonds in 1994 – Zl 12 trillion to the BGZ and Zl 7 trillion to other "endangered" banks.

The recapitalisation bonds have a 15 year maturity and cannot be sold during the first three years without the approval of the Ministry of Finance. The bonds will pay a flexible interest rate based on the rediscount rate. Interest has accrued from the date of issue, but there will be no payments of interest and capital until January 1995. However, only 5 per cent per annum will be paid in cash, the remainder being capitalised. Income will not be taxable. After privatisation these bonds will be serviced by the converted stabilisation fund – the Polish Banks Privatisation Fund – which amounts to $700 million. While addressing the solvency and incentive issues of bad debts, and to a considerable extent the resulting loss of income, the recapitalisation will not greatly contribute to improving either the cash flow or liquidity of some of them.

To encourage banks to pass-on the benefits of the recapitalisation to their industrial clients the Bank and Enterprise Debt Restructuring Law came into force in February 1993. Under this law the bank initiates a conciliation procedure on the motion of the debtor which must be accepted by a majority – by value – of creditors. Enterprises must present restructuring programmes. If accepted by the bank a menu of options are available including a reduction of capital or interest and debt/equity swaps. If the restructuring plan is not accepted, the bank must either sell the debt on the secondary market (including the rights to collateral which it holds) or petition for bankruptcy.

To address the most pressing problems efficiently, the programme with its new legal powers for the banks has been targeted towards the largest debtors: the conciliation procedure can only be implemented in those cases where an enterprise's bank debt constitutes not less than 10 per cent of its total indebtedness and is not less than Zl 1 billion – or when the bank loan accounts for at least 20 per cent of the total debt.

Although the additional legal powers will be held by the banks for three years (the law specifies 13 banks including a non-bank, the Industrial Development Agency), the authorities felt that it was important to put the banks under increased pressure early in the programme. For those banks receiving recapitalisation bonds, reconciliation procedures had to be completed by a 31 March 1994 deadline (extended until April 1994); the savings banks (PKO BP) and the agricultural bank (BGZ) had until September 1994 to complete procedures. Consultants have been available from the PHARE and other bodies to help banks assess restructuring programmes.

One problem which has been encountered in the implementation of the programme is that large numbers of creditors have been involved – in some cases up to a thousand. As there is no minimum debt required to make formal objections to the courts, banks have proceeded cautiously.

Taxation and prudential rules appear to have had an important influence on the choice of debt restructuring options. However, the incentives do not appear to have been structured to achieve any particular outcome, only to minimise the fiscal impact. For the debt restructuring option, capital write-off is tax-deductible but affects the financial result of the bank; the reduction of interest arrears does not affect the financial result of the bank. For debt/equity swaps there are a number of considerations. First, no more than 25 per cent of a bank's equity may be held in enterprise shares although by special permission of the NBP this may be increased up to 50 per cent. Given the low equity levels of most Polish banks there is not much room for manœuvre. Second, if the company is not tradeable then the stocks will have a zero value for prudential purposes so that in practice full provisioning is still required; if they are tradeable no provisioning is necessary. When accrued interest is converted in a debt/equity swap this will be regarded as income for tax purposes; where capital is converted it is not. With respect to sales of debt on the secondary market, no tax deductions are available for the book loss.

The prudential treatment of conciliation agreements remains cautious. A restructured debt is not automatically regarded as good debt so that reserves set aside for the loan cannot be released immediately. Three months of normal servicing is required before the debt can be moved up a category and provisions reduced. However, unlike the case with other debts which are regarded as bad and doubtful, banks are permitted to extend new money to firms with a conciliation agreement.

Preliminary information indicates that the debt restructuring programme will cover 793 enterprises with loans totalling around Zl 16 trillion. Out of these, around 200 enterprises accounting for 45 per cent of the value of debt are expected to receive bank-led settlements – mainly debt write-offs since debt/equity swaps are less favourable from the taxation and bank provisioning perspective. Nevertheless, at the time of writing around 10 per cent of companies (20-25 per cent by value) may receive debt/equity swaps as part of their agreements. Most of the proposed swaps are being challenged in the courts. Around 170 liquidations accounting for about 12 per cent by value are expected. The debt of 80 companies, accounting for 7 per cent by value, is expected to be put up for sale.

It is still too early to judge the quality of the restructuring programmes agreed between enterprises and banks. Consultants only became available late in 1993 and in the rush to meet the deadline banks may have taken some short cuts. Very little new money is apparently being granted by the banks and most have time horizons for getting the firms in question off their books in around three years.

Table 20. **Progress in enterprise debt restructuring**
April 1994

	Principal	Interest	Total	Number of credits	Share of credit
	Trillion zlotys				(%)
Total debts in programme	13.06	2.68	15.74	792	100
Unfinished agreements	0.18	0.08	0.26	32	2
Concluded agreements	5.93	1.40	7.33	166	47
Resumed servicing	3.21	0.24	3.45	109	22
Repaid	1.61	0.16	1.77	203	11
Credits offered for sale	0.35	0.20	0.55	47	3
Sold credits	0.27	0.06	0.33	47	2
Unfinished liquidations or bankruptcies	0.08	0.02	0.10	14	1
Finished liquidations or bankruptcies	1.38	0.51	1.89	157	12
Debt/equity swaps	–	–	–	–	–
Not determined	0.05	0.01	0.06	17	0

Source: Ministry of Finance.

Policy issues in creating a sound universal banking system

In fostering the continued development of the banking system, the authorities will need to address three sets of issues bearing on the efficiency and soundness of financial intermediation: prudential standards, ensuring the soundness of the payment system, and the organisation of the banking industry. A number of policy initiatives are being undertaken in all three areas.

Prudential issues

Public expectations are high that the universal banking system – and especially one characterised by large banks – would enable banks to take large, long-term equity positions in Polish firms, or at least to extend a high volume of long-term credits. Whether this assessment corresponds to the situation is questionable, but of more interest here are the prudential issues. Allowing banks, which are also responsible for the payments system, to take large equity positions raises the possibility of conflict of interest as well as the question of loan concentration. At present a bank may take equity stakes in enterprises but both the magnitude of such holdings and lending to any one enterprise are subject to NBP approval if they exceed 25 per cent and 15 per cent respectively of bank capital – or if loans to a single company are greater than 10 per cent of its total loans. At this stage of development this appears reasonable and until the level of uncertainty declines substantially, warrants continuation.

An important aspect of bank balance sheets is foreign-denominated assets and liabilities, including deposits in foreign currencies. Around 58 banks are licensed to deal in foreign currency. Until 1992 banks had an exposed position since under the foreign exchange act they had to sell most foreign exchange to the NBP. The threat posed to the banks by open positions led to the gradual lifting of foreign exchange restrictions in 1992 and in 1993 to a new regulation which limited the total exposure of a bank in relation to its own funds.[105] As a result there was a substantial reduction in the open positions held by banks: although, at the end of 1993, 19 banks still exceeded the norms, this had been reduced to four banks by June 1994. These regulations will become increasingly important once the debt agreement with the London Club is finalised and the possibilities for Polish banks to raise funds on the world's capital markets increases. Large open positions by the banks will have not only implications for prudential regulations but also for the conduct of monetary policy.

A draft Deposit Insurance Bill which would extend deposit insurance formally to all banks but limit the liability is still under consideration: it proposes 100 per cent insurance for private persons on accounts up to 1 000 ECU, 90 per cent up to 3 000 and for amounts over 3 000 it would depend on special insurance. Approximately 50 per cent of deposits by value would be so covered. Presentation of the bill to the Parliament was delayed by controversy about whether the new deposit insurance organisation should be independent of the NBP and whether it would have any supervisory capacity. At the time of writing the draft included a proposal to establish a bank guarantee fund which would be able to take over directly bad loans and to buy the bonds of endangered banks, but it would not be able to acquire equity in the banks. The fund would be financed from bank contributions (0.4 per cent of amount used to calculate obligatory reserves) with an initial capitalisation of Zl 2.7 trillion. In this draft supervision functions would remain with the NBP, and the deposit insurance organisation would be a separate organisation.

Establishing an efficient payments system

The operation of the banking system has been significantly improved in recent years by organisational changes to the payments system which have facilitated development of the inter-bank market and a secondary market for government securities. The payments system at the start of the transformationin 1990 was ill-suited to the demands of a market economy.[106] In 1989 the dominance of credit transfers was replaced by the use of cheques which were intended to simplify settlements between customers and to reduce the chronic delays in transfer of funds. Initially, each branch of a commercial bank kept a clearing account at the regional branch of the NBP since settlement was on a branch-by-branch basis. For clearing purposes each commercial bank branch was allocated a threshold refinancing limit up to which it paid a basic rate. Reserve requirements were assessed on a branch basis and held in frozen accounts which could not be used for clearing purposes.

This system was inefficient and cumbersome, created significant credit risk exposure and made for a large and variable float which complicated the operation of monetary policy. The multiplicity of settlement accounts prevented an efficient management of bank reserves, forcing banks to hold large excess liquidity on which no interest was paid, thereby raising intermediation costs and slowing down the development of the money market. Positions arising from the debit float were left open for up to two weeks which exposed banks to significant credit risk, in addition to affecting banks' liquidity. The need for an urgent reform to the system was underlined in 1991 when the credit lent by the NBP for the float (about Zl 7 trillion) was equal to approximately 30 per cent of refinance credit. About half of the float was due to a fraudulent cheque clearing scheme.

Reform to the payments system has been far-reaching and is still continuing. In preparation for the operation of a National Clearing House in April 1993, during the period August 1991-September 1992 the NBP consolidated branch clearing accounts into a single account per bank, and accounts of the clearing house members were shifted to Warsaw. Moreover, the NBP forced banks to consolidate data on the current accounts of every branch on a daily basis, which taxed the underdeveloped communications network. Regulatory changes were introduced aimed at better synchronising the crediting and debiting of accounts. Most important of all, the NBP ended the automatic provision of settlement credit.

The National Clearing House began operations in April 1993, offering overnight clearing and settlement of some paper transactions. By the end 1993, around 2700 banking units were being served and clearing times have now decreased from two weeks to 1-6 days. Further improvements are expected as the telecommunications system is improved; since late 1993 large transactions including security transactions are handled electronically. The debit float has declined markedly although banks still need to maintain high current account balances to facilitate settlement. Improvements to the system are continuing; a series of inter-locking guarantees are now being established so as to reduce settlements risk further.

Reorganising the banking system

Looking to the longer term, the authorities are convinced that a reorganisation of the banking system is necessary to promote stable and efficient financial intermediation. Specific policy proposals are in some cases still tentative although a recurrent theme in all of them is the desire to consolidate the banking system through mergers.

The prospective opening of the domestic banking market to competition from EC-based banks in 1997 has led to a policy climate favouring the reduction of nine commercial banks to four. Whether the important specialised banks would also be involved in this restructuring is unclear, though given their extensive branch structures it would make sense to include them. At the same time, privatisation of a third commercial bank has been announced for late 1994. The modalities for any mergers are at the moment unclear. As sole owner, the authorities are free to reorganise seven of the banks, but two are already privatised. Public comment has pointed to the fact that the Treasury still maintains a 30 per cent shareholding in these, implying that the state could use this position to promote bank mergers.

In order to foster restructuring and to strengthen the banking system the NBP has been encouraging foreign banks to take over weak Polish banks rather than to apply for permission to establish a new bank. Up to now foreign banks appear luke-warm to the suggestion – though two foreign banks have bought significant stakes in Polish banks – preferring to remain absent from the Polish market. With the signing of the London Club agreement more foreign banks may be tempted to enter the Polish market, which will raise the issue how far the NBP will wish to pursue the concept.

The most far-reaching set of reforms concern the co-operative banks. The Act, which passed the Parliament in June 1994, represented a rather unwieldy compromise between two quite different draft laws. The most important elements are:

i) A three-tier system, with the individual co-operative banks at the local level; nine regional banks which would fully encompass all co-operative banks; and a national bank in which all regional banks are mandated to be members. The existing agricultural bank (BGZ), after incorporation and with 54 per cent share-holding by the Treasury, will be the national bank. The three existing regional banks, covering around 400 co-operative banks, had to decide whether to join this structure – there were strong financial incentives for doing so. At the time of writing it appears that they have decided to remain independent;

ii) The appointment of the directors for the individual co-operative banks would have to be approved by the president of the regional bank concerned. The presidents of the BGZ and the NBP will express an opinion about the appointment of the presidents of the regional banks, but it is not binding;

iii) The regional banks are obligated to prepare consolidated financial reports, which will include the reports of the affiliated co-operatives and it will become the tax entity. The risks and liabilities contracted by the banks of the whole group are to be borne by all member banks jointly. However, this will only occur after the restructuring which will take place first in 1996;

iv) Co-operative banks are to confine their lending activities to short-term loans, the remaining surplus of short-term deposits and all long-term deposits have to be passed on to the regional banks. They in turn may pass on all short-term deposit surpluses and 75 per cent of long-term deposits to the BGZ, in which case the latter must pay the inter-bank rate and not use the funds for its own purposes, but lend them to other regional banks;

v) The regional banks may receive recapitalisation bonds from the BGZ and will benefit from tax exemptions and lower reserves requirements on individual member banks in order to create a Solidarity Fund;

vi) Supervisory powers would be delegated from the NBP to both the regional banks and the BGZ, but it will retain supervisory powers over these banks.

The greatest unresolved issue remains the agricultural bank itself, the BGZ. One proposal saw the bank as fundamentally ceasing to exist, assets being disbursed to the new regional banks with a central bank remaining only to deal with large bad debts and loans. By contrast, the alternative draft saw the BGZ retaining its present role with regional banks having to remit surplus deposits to it. The final outcome does not do away with the dangers inherent in the latter proposal: the BGZ will remain in its present form for a number of years and might therefore be able to exert undue financial leverage over the new regional banks. At the same time, the urgent restructuring of this bank remains to be settled.

Assessment

In sum, the authorities have moved to deal with immediate threats to the solvency and liquidity of the banking system while at the same time seeking to change banking behaviour through a combination of tighter prudential regulations and bank recapitalisation. In pursuing the former objective the authorities have succeeded in avoiding any general run on the banking system even though they have been hampered in their efforts by the lack of suitable legal powers and, in the absence of a deposit insurance fund, by the desire to minimise costs to both the budget and the NBP. Much remains to be done with those parts of the banking system which are in a fragile state or a crisis but experience in other countries – and also in Poland – suggests that mergers of weaker with "stronger" banks may not be the best path to pursue. Banks expanding through such acquisitions run the risk of becoming weaker, not stronger, in the process.

There are indications that bank behaviour has changed and that – with two important exceptions – the characterisation of the banks as passive lenders committed to old state-owned clients is a thing of the past. This does not necessarily imply that corporate performance will improve – that banks will be able single-handedly to improve corporate governance – but it does mean that the payments system and basic levels of financial intermediation are more secure than before. The outstanding question is whether the incentives are sufficiently strong for this state of affairs to be maintained: have the banks been recapitalised sufficiently to be able to deal with new bad debts and with enterprises which, despite conciliation agreements, will ultimately not succeed. There are some indications that the level of bad debts is in fact greater than the recapitalisation of the major banks. However, the amount involved is not likely to be large enough to change bank behaviour, especially as the exposure of banks to enterprise loans has generally fallen. A second recapitalisation, with all that it would imply for moral hazard, may not therefore prove necessary. For the immediate future the recapitalisation is not likely to substantially lower spreads – greater provisions are still necessary and bank profitability in relation to capital is low – but over the medium-term continued competition for sound borrowers should lead to a reduction.

There are three major issues to which a policy response is currently being debated. The most immediate concerns the recapitalisation of the PKO BP and the BGZ: preliminary estimates point to the need for an additional Zl 10-15 trillion for the former and Zl 25 trillion for the latter, over and above the sums they have already received in 1993 (Zl 10 trillion). Nevertheless, it appears premature on two grounds to proceed with a further injection of funds. First, the flow problem of enterprises in both housing and agriculture must be improved: financial discipline on the part of both housing co-operatives and the agricultural sector appears to be particularly poor, and to lag behind that in the remainder of the economy. Enterprises in both sectors seem to still hold the view from the past that there is an inherent need for their activities which transcends financial considerations. Until financial discipline is established, it seems pointless to proceed with a solution to the stock or balance sheet problem of the banks. Second, the behaviour of the two banks must be put on a commercial footing, replacing the symbiotic relations with borrowers which prevail at the moment. The long overdue incorporation of the BGZ, with the Ministry of Finance as the majority shareholder, is a step in the right direction. In the meantime the authorities are placed in the difficult position of having to ensure that these two large banks are able to remain solvent while at the same time avoiding any moral hazard problems with these banks – and indeed banks more generally.

The second set of issues concerns the structure of the banking sector. In terms of formulation, the most advanced to date is the law to restructure the co-operative banking sector. The law represents an uneasy compromise, but does overcome the worst features of an earlier draft which would have subordinated the co-operative banks to the BGZ. How the nine new regional banks will function is unclear as is the extent to which co-operative banks will be restricted in their behaviour. As risks will be jointly covered, it will be important to avoid moral hazard on the part of the individual co-operatives. The attention given to solving the problem of co-operative banks has not been reflected in the drive to solve the difficulties at the BGZ, a much larger and potentially more damaging problem.

With respect to the other banks, there are a some grounds for believing that the current structure may not be conducive to efficient financial intermediation and stability: the major banks are too regionally concentrated and the branch networks limited. Operating cost/asset ratios are high in comparison with other countries, and there might be some economies of scale to be reaped, although the history of administrative measures to achieve such economies in other countries have often been disappointing. Some reduction in the number of banks might be necessary although a simple comparison of the banking structure with that in western Europe should not be taken as proof of this. That being said, it is important to bear in mind that a consolidation would not automatically bring sound banks with increased lending power for investment. Consortia are a method currently being utilised to spread risk and to maintain exposure limits. What is lacking is perhaps not large banks but sound projects.

Finally, the establishment of an explicit deposit insurance fund should serve to clarify the limited nature of the guarantee and to minimise the danger of moral hazard. At present, implicit and explicit deposit insurance must appear to economic agents to be universal. Current proposals call for a fund separate from the NBP with powers to acquire bad debts and to extend loans to endangered banks. To avoid dangers of misuse, the constitution of the new institution needs to be carefully formulated. This applies in particular to the relations with banking supervision and to the NBP's role as lender of last resort.

IV. Medium-term policy issues

Introduction

The Economic Transformation Programme launched in 1990 has been extremely successful in stabilising the economy and in establishing the conditions for market-based growth to occur. This success has been accompanied by a steady shift in policy goals towards promoting economic growth – especially by facilitating investment and exports – and reducing unemployment and alleviating social costs, while at the same time consolidating gains on inflation. Such goals are clearly desirable. However, their attainment will require policy measures whose benefits will take some time to become evident and which may involve short-term costs. In Poland – as in other countries – the formation of economic policy is subject to strong pressures to implement measures with a short-run pay-off. In order to stay the course with policy objectives, as well as to ensure that policy instruments are internally consistent, other countries have often found it useful to adopt a medium-term policy framework.

The Strategy for Poland, announced in June 1994, sets out the elements of such a framework and should serve to focus public debate on key medium-term issues, and thereby hopefully help to create the necessary consensus for policy to be effective. This chapter seeks to contribute to the debate by discussing some of the main medium-term issues confronting Polish policy-makers, emphasising the interrelationships between competing goals and the potential trade-offs involved. The first section focuses on macroeconomic balance, outlining the constraints within which economic policy, including fiscal and monetary policy, will have to be set. The second section deals more directly with the ability to achieve final policy objectives: it discusses the institutional and policy requirements to ensure that growth will have the greatest possible impact on reducing the present high levels of unemployment over time, while simultaneously leading to a steady improvement in the environment. Other medium-term issues including privatisation, the development of financial markets, and measures to improve governance of state-owned enterprises (SOEs) have been discussed in the preceding chapters.

Macroeconomic balance

Medium-term economic policy must address three inter-related issues which will constrain the room for manœuvre: high inflation, the need to service a significant volume of foreign debt while at the same time limiting the growth of domestic debt, and the low level of monetisation and financial intermediation. At the same time, the desire to place the economy on a high and sustainable growth path raises additional issues and options relating to savings and investment.

Costs and benefits of reducing inflation more quickly

The government's medium-term policy framework reaffirms the commitment to a gradual reduction of inflation, with the goal of reaching single-digit levels by 1997. There is, it seems, a presumption that the costs of reducing inflation more rapidly are high and policy-makers have shown great caution not to threaten the recovery. The short-term "benefits" of slow progress on inflation have to be weighed against the potential costs. Two factors need to be considered in this regard. First, in the experience of comparable countries, Polish inflation is now in the range (25-35 per cent) which risks becoming persistent[107] and also carries with it the danger of rapid re-acceleration in the face of adverse external shocks. Policy-makers in such situations often appear to feel that inflation is sufficiently low so as not to warrant the political and economic costs of continued reduction, especially when institutions such as a crawling peg exchange rate and widespread indexation appear to make the problem less pressing. Second, but closely related – faster progress might be perceived by private agents as more credible. The importance of these considerations depends on the likely costs of inflation in the Polish context.

The costs of high – though gradually decelerating – inflation largely relate to the disincentives to hold domestic currency and to save and invest, as well as to its distributional consequences. High inflation, and uncertainty about its future path, have reduced the willingness of the public to hold domestic currency.

Following the near hyper-inflation in 1990, the level of monetisation (*i.e.* money/GDP ratio) fell and the income velocity increased to around 3.2 in 1993. This is much higher than in either the Czech Republic or in Hungary, and it is declining only gradually. Another possible reason that savings are lower is that financial assets are predominantly short-term, carrying negative real rates of interest.[108]

The low level of money demand has significant economic costs. First, it is one factor contributing to a low level of financial intermediation; a low level of intermediation of savings and investment serves to depress potential growth.[109] Second, the budget is deprived of resources which must be replaced either by other more costly sources of income or by lower expenditures. The low level of money demand reduces seigniorage which arises from the increased demand for money as real incomes grow. This has led to a greater dependence of the budget on damaging inflation taxes – the amount of money which must be acquired by economic agents to keep their real money balances constant in the face of inflation.[110] Despite a relatively low budget deficit, the Polish budget appears particularly dependent on inflation taxes: assuming that real money demand will grow by 4.5 per cent in 1994, the inflation tax may account for some 40 per cent of budget financing.

In combination with uncertainties arising from the transition and lagging improvements in governance, high inflation has created disincentives to invest. High levels of inflation have been accompanied by significant instability in relative prices, with the variance reinforced by the move from controlled to market prices. This has led to high real rates of interest on borrowing for a number of industries and considerable uncertainty about the *ex post* real rate of interest they might face. High nominal interest rates associated with high inflation also effectively shorten the duration of loans.[111] This creates particular problems in housing and construction, by creating front-loaded repayments streams which are impossible for most households to meet. As noted in Annex I, high levels of inflation interact with an accounting system which does not adequately differentiate between real and nominal capital gains to increase effective tax rates on capital. In tandem with the inflation tax on corporate money balances, important disincentives for investment are created.

Set against these benefits which would accrue from a reduction in inflation are the potential costs in terms of foregone output and income, which although possibly short-term in nature figure prominently in decision-making. Tighter credit policies, higher interest rates and slower exchange rate devaluation can reduce real demand and GDP, resulting in lost potential output and higher unemployment. However, as discussed in Chapter I, current growth appears to be driven not so much by exogenous demand forces as by strong supply-side impulses, based on efficiency gains from the reallocation of fixed assets and highly productive investments, and by the exploitation of new entrepreneurial opportunities. At the same time, economic recovery in western Europe and continued market opening by the European Community is increasing export demand, and this is likely to continue for the next few years, suggesting a window of opportunity for risking some short-term contraction of domestic demand. Arguing further for a more ambitious goal for disinflation, many domestic observers are concerned that Poland will not be able to take advantage of market opening because of inadequate export capacity: export growth and growth in general may only be sustainable with an acceleration of investment. With nominal interest rates already high, savings relatively responsive to real interest rates, and with most savings not intermediated, a more ambitious disinflation goal is likely to result in a substantial increase in savings, supporting investment and relieving pressures on financing the public sector borrowing requirement. On balance, it appears clear that the potential benefits of more rapid disinflation outweigh the costs.

A high level of public debt

As noted in Chapter I, even after the Paris and London Club debt reduction agreements the level of public debt remains high and this must constitute an important consideration in formulating medium-term policies. Foreign debt service will grow at more than 7 per cent per annum in dollar terms over the next five years and will form an increasing burden on the budget. Domestic debt – about a quarter of which is denominated in dollars – is also a serious problem, amounting to 23 per cent of GDP at the end of 1993. This is set to rise, in part because the balance sheets of state-owned banks and enterprises have still not been fully restructured through the issue of budget debt, so that the public sector borrowing requirement (PSBR), is likely to remain greater than the general government deficit, continuing the pattern of recent years.

The high level of public debt and the rapidly increasing debt service have several implications for policy. First, an additional restriction is placed on exchange rate policy since any real devaluation to stimulate exports, or to improve a current account deficit, will have important repercussions on the level of foreign debt, debt service, and the budget. A real devaluation will increase the ratio of foreign debt to GDP and will restrict the room for external financing if the debt-output ratio is to be maintained at a particular level.[112] Second, the relation between the real interest rate and the rate of growth becomes extremely important, constraining interest rate policy in both the short and medium terms. Real interest rates greater than the growth rate of GDP, which may prove necessary for extended periods, would lead to an explosive growth of public debt. Third, high levels of foreign debt in particular may, *ceteris paribus*, decrease access to foreign saving, making it necessary to increase the role of domestic saving for any level of investment.

For these reasons the proposal in the government's medium-term strategy to steadily reduce the public debt/GDP ratio between 1994 and 1997 seems appropriate. Moreover, the proposal to substantially reduce the level of foreign debt through debt/equity swaps should be pursued, although numerous administrative barriers are likely to arise.[113] The important issue for a medium-term strategy is the consistency between inflation and debt targets, fiscal and monetary policy, and growth objectives. These questions are taken up in the following sections.

Setting a consistent fiscal policy

The government's medium-term strategy sets out goals for inflation, GDP growth, budget revenues and expenditures and the ratio of public debt to GDP. To investigate the consistency of these plans and their likely sustainability, the Secretariat has utilised a small steady-state model (see box) augmented by a number of equations defining budget expenditures and receipts as a function of both inflation and the growth of GDP. The real exchange rate and the real interest rate are assumed constant at 1994 levels while GDP growth rates are exogenous and taken from the government's medium-term scenario (Table 21). The key government budget identity has been solved sequentially for each year till 1997 with level variables such as debt updated after each model solution. While the model might give the impression of simulating the dynamics of inflation, budget balances, etc. this is not the case. The budget identity is rather used to solve for one particular variable which is thereby consistent or sustainable with the others such as inflation, debt and the budget deficit.

The relation between inflation, debt and the budget

To analyse the complex interrelationship between domestic and external debt, the non-interest budget deficit and inflation, the Secretariat utilised a representation of the public sector budget identity developed by Anand and Wijnbergen.

The simplest budget identity

$$D + iB + i*B*E \equiv \overline{B*E} + \overline{DC} \tag{1}$$

states that the non-interest deficit (primary deficit) plus internal and external debt service (where i and $i*$ are the domestic and foreign interest rate respectively, and E the exchange rate) must be financed from either an increase in domestic or foreign debt (where "—" represents a change in the level of a variable), or by central bank lending to the government, DC. Consolidating the balance sheets of the government and the central bank clarifies the linkage with the money supply:

$$D + iB + i*(B* - NFA*)E \equiv \overline{B} + (\overline{B*} - \overline{NFA*})E + \overline{M} \tag{2}$$

where NFA is net foreign assets held by the central bank and M is the monetary base adjusted for credit to commercial banks and other private agents.

In the presence of inflation, the budget identity, which should represent only current transactions, may include capital payments, as for instance when the repayment of principal takes place through inflation eroding the real value of a loan. Incorporating the effect of both inflation and capital losses due to changes in the real exchange rate yields

$$d + rb + (r* + \hat{e})(b* - nfa*)e \equiv \overline{b} + \Delta(b* - nfa*)e + \left(\frac{\overline{M}}{P}\right) \tag{3}$$

where lower-case letters represent the real value of a variable, r and $r*$ the real domestic and foreign interest rate respectively and e the real exchange rate.

For analytical purposes (3) must be augmented by assumptions about the demand for money. The Secretariat has assumed that there is a fixed relationship between base money and broad money supply: the money multiplier is constant. The demand for money is in turn a simple function of real income (unit elasticity) and real interest rates. These assumptions allow the last term of (3) to be decomposed into the increase in the real balances consequent upon the growth of income – seignorage – and the amount of nominal balances which must be accumulated just to keep the real value of the money stock constant – the inflation tax.

Table 21. **Medium-term strategy: targets and consistency**

	Source	Programme targets			
		1994	1995	1996	1997
GDP, constant prices (per cent)	SFP	4.5	5.0	5.2	5.5
CPI, Dec. on Dec. (per cent)	SFP	23.6	16.1	12.0	8.7
Budget revenues, constant prices (per cent)	SFP	5.3	4.3[1]	4.8	5.5
Budget expenditures, constant prices (per cent)	SFP	8.0	8.4[1]	1.8	2.1
Change in debt/GDP	SFP	−7.9	−0.8	−2.8	−1.7
	Source	Model assumptions			
		1994	1995	1996	1997
Income velocity	OECD	3.2	3.1	3.0	2.9
Money multiplier	OECD	3.3	3.3	3.3	3.3
Domestic real interest rate (per cent)	OECD	2.6	2.6	2.6	2.6
		Simulation results			
		1994	1995	1996	1997
Sustainable budget expenditures					
– Strategy for Poland scenario (per cent)		8.0	6.3	5.8	4.1
– 4 per cent GDP growth (per cent)		8.0	4.4	3.0	2.0

1. These growth rates are not compatible with the target deficit but were included in the Strategy document in order to show the adjustments which would be required. The growth of expnditures in planned to be in the range of 5 per cent in 1995.
Source: Strategy for Poland (SFP), Warsaw, 1994 and OECD Secretariat calculations.

For most of the following analysis the model has been solved for the growth rate of government expenditures, including interest,[114] which is consistent with the underlying economic assumptions. The reason for focusing on fiscal adjustment in terms of reducing expenditures is that substantial progress has already been made to increase revenues; since 1991 they have risen steadily as a share of GDP. The fairly thorough nature of these reforms means that the scope for future gains are limited and the marginal cost of taxation revenues might now be increasing: the share of total revenues in GDP is near 46 per cent, close to the European average, and tax rates are quite high and contributing to evasion. The government's medium-term assumption that revenues will grow less rapidly than GDP during 1995-1997 thus appears plausible.

Analysis of the medium-term framework indicates that the projected deficit and disinflation path to 1997 are broadly consistent with each other, but that the projected growth rate of expenditures indicated in the strategy for 1995 (8.5 per cent) will have to be lowered to meet the deficit target. At the time of writing it appears that the proposed draft 1995 budget has made the necessary adjustments, though again this is measured by the deficit and not the PSBR.

The consistency between budget deficits and the disinflation path is highly sensitive to the assumptions made about GDP growth. The government's scenario foresees growth rising steadily to 5.5 per cent in 1997 (Table 21). Given the difficulties in projecting growth – and therefore the need to remain flexible in the implementation of policy – the Secretariat evaluated a scenario of constant 4 per cent growth with budget revenues adjusted accordingly. In this scenario, the inflation goals and debt/GDP targets are only consistent with a growth path of real government expenditures some 2 percentage points less than planned each year. Alternatively, if expenditures were maintained they could not be financed unless inflation remained at around 25 per cent per annum. The simple lesson appears to be that declining inflation – and with it lower inflation taxes – requires that total expenditure growth converges to rates lower than GDP growth.

A key assumption – and one which is likely to be violated in practice – is that the real interest rate on government debt is lower than the growth rate of GDP: real interest rates are assumed to be 2.6 per cent (the level in 1993 on average) relative to the GDP deflator, compared with an assumed GDP growth rate of around 5 per cent. Changing this assumption increases substantially the degree of adjustment required of the primary deficit, either forcing significant changes in the growth rate of expenditures or alternatively raising the targets for inflation and debt accumulation.

Changing the level and composition of expenditures

In achieving consistency, much attention has been devoted to the need to shift the composition of non-interest expenditures to investment which, it is hoped, would stimulate growth: fiscal policy in 1992/1993 was heavily biased towards supporting consumption, with at best passive effects on growth. The empirical evidence linking the overall level of public-sector investment to economic growth, or to positive externalities promoting private-sector investment, is weak.[115] Indeed the evidence linking investment, *per se*, to growth is also weak, indicating that what matters most are policies which ensure efficiency and high rates of return. Nonetheless, there are strong reasons to believe that individual public-sector investment projects might exhibit high rates of return[116] and contribute to growth. However, the government still has neither a consolidated investment budget, nor the facilities to perform project evaluations using discounting or cost-benefit analysis.

In the medium-term the redirection of expenditures towards investment, and the need to restrict the growth of non-interest expenditures, cannot be achieved unless pension and social welfare expenditures are more tightly controlled. Reform of the pension and social welfare systems in Poland is vital for the medium-term prospects for the economy. Such reform can contribute to increasing private and public savings, improving the quality of life for Polish citizens, and generating greater support for the reform process. The greatest problem is that the current system of retirement pensions is not self-financing and is unsustainable given current benefit levels and demographic trends, while the disability system is widely abused and effectively operates a form of supplementary social insurance. Pensions and social welfare expenditures are highly redistributive but not well-targeted – the overwhelming majority of recipients are not poor – so that despite high expenditures little is done to alleviate actual poverty or to cushion the effects of the transition. The current system of retirement pensions is not transparent to the employee, who does not see his or her contribution or any relation between contributions and benefits. Nothing in the current pension system encourages additional personal savings. Similarly, little reform has taken place in the administration or delivery of other social services like health or education, so that funds are allocated on the basis of ministerial needs, with no evaluation of programme goals, targets or effectiveness.

Most of these problems are recognised in the Strategy for Poland, and appropriate solutions prescribed. Most important are the proposals to: 1) make contributions transparent and place the burden jointly on both employers and employees; 2) shift the retirement pension scheme towards insurance and away from redistribution, encouraging private supplemental schemes; and 3) curtail early retirement and the abuse of social insurance by dubious invalidity claims.

Savings, investment and the balance of payments

One of the most important unresolved questions for Poland concerns the probable relationship between growth and investment and the likely sources of finance: domestic or foreign. Completion of agreements with both the Paris and London Clubs, which at least formally clears the way for access to international capital markets, increases the immediate relevance of the policy issue, as does the large current account deficit which Poland incurred in 1993.

Some guide to the general policy issues involved can be obtained by examining the experience of other middle-income countries, even though they did not experience structural transformation on anywhere near the scale which Poland is undertaking. By and large, in the early stages of growth investment needs have been large but were financed predominantly by domestic sources. Foreign financing only becomes significant later in the growth process in the face of proven high profitability, at which time the current account has moved strongly into deficit and the real exchange rate has appreciated.

The medium-term issue in Poland would appear to be the need to strengthen domestic savings. Revised GDP estimates for 1992 indicated gross domestic savings of around 15 per cent; gross and net household savings were 15.4 per cent and 11.6 per cent of estimated household income, respectively. Higher household saving could be encouraged through increased real domestic interest rates, pension reform and the further development of financial markets. However, the prospects for increasing household saving rates appears limited given that the marginal propensity to consume appears to be high. The weakness of savings appear to be primarily due to low corporate profitability which can only be indirectly influenced by policy measures.

Achieving policy objectives through growth

The experience in many countries, including those in the OECD area, is that GDP growth is a necessary though probably not sufficient condition for achieving a number of policy goals. These include lowering an already high level of unemployment, absorbing pockets of unemployment, relieving groups in poverty and improving environmental conditions. Rather, a number of additional institutional and policy issues have to be addressed.

Raising the impact of growth on employment creation

In the coming years there will be several urgent needs over and above the need to reduce the high level of unemployment. It will be necessary to re-absorb large numbers of former farmer-employees from small-scale agriculture to promote employment and labour mobility in areas of extremely high unemployment, and to cope with increasing numbers of employees who are not permitted to, or who do not wish to, retire early. At the same time, the expansion of new jobs will have to be much greater than the net increase; many industries and enterprises still need to close or to reduce further their workforce, increasing the flows into unemployment. While specific policy measures targeted to particular groups are certainly useful – for example, retraining, regional subsidies for new firms, measures to facilitate labour mobility – the historical experience has been that a rapidly rising level of employment is the key factor. Mobility and retraining usually follow. At very high levels of GDP growth such as in East Asia, rapid employment growth seems guaranteed but at moderate levels of growth the relationship is much more variable and appears to depend on a number of policy and institutional choices. In forming a medium-term policy framework the authorities need to consider some of these factors.

Crucial to the medium-term performance will be the labour intensity of production and the need to economise on the use of capital. Particularly important in this respect is the relative price of capital and labour. Two considerations need to influence policy deliberations in this area. First, a number of proposals to stimulate output and exports rely on incentives to invest through special depreciation allowances, loan guarantees, access to low-cost funds and trade protection. Unless carefully structured, these could reduce the labour intensity of production since the price of labour would be raised relative to capital, favouring both capital-intensive industries and the choice of technology. Some well-meaning proposals for social legislation – including employment guarantees – might also have the same effect. Second, the growth of real wages must remain beneath the growth of productivity for some time, thereby increasing profitability and providing funds for investment. The medium-term strategy goes some way in this direction by proposing that real wages only increase by half the growth rate of GDP. The policy question remaining is how to achieve this objective.

Achieving moderate growth of aggregate real wages will require real wage flexibility in the face of unemployment. The evidence is still mixed about the relative costs and benefits of decentralised *versus* centralised wage formation systems in achieving this. This is often not a policy choice at all but simply the result of spontaneous social action, and Poland is no exception. For a variety of reasons including anti-inflation policy and governance of SOEs, wages are decided in a highly decentralised manner at enterprise level. In such a system wages need to respond to local conditions. This requires above all financial discipline on the part of enterprises. The power of insiders must not be overwhelming so that local employment conditions play a role in determining wages. Particularly important will be whether enterprises with above-average productivity pass it on exclusively via wage increases, or whether relative prices fall and output and employment expand instead, as is usual in market economies.[117] What is needed are actions to create a unified labour market to go hand-in-hand with decentralised wage formation.

Improving environmental quality

Achieving a high, employment-generating, growth over the medium-term raises the issue of whether there might be a trade-off between growth and the state's objective to improve the environment, adopted in 1991 as the National Environmental Policy.[118] As growth continues a key environmental challenge will be to stabilise or reduce further the main emissions. From this perspective, the likely growth in motor vehicle traffic suggests that the transport sector, particularly urban transport but also motorway construction, should receive priority attention. Consumption has been less environmentally damaging than in OECD countries, but pressures will tend to increase in line with growth.

The authorities have recognised that policy conflicts are bound to arise unless environmental considerations are integrated into public policy. However, by and large, the major ministries do not appear to have internalised a commitment to the environment; existing arrangements have not been effective in holding them accountable for the environmental consequences of their policies.[119] The environment has been seen as an expensive ''add-on'' which is the responsibility of another Ministry.

The medium-term policy issue concerns less the establishment of new programmes than to make implementation more effective. This will probably require setting fewer priorities and establishing clearer targets. Over the medium term the Polish authorities are committed to harmonising environmental standards with those of the EC. However, the target concerns the enactment of legislation, not necessarily its implementation. The costs and benefits of alternative compliance schedules, particularly as they apply to existing plants, need to be carefully weighed.

V. Conclusions

Assessment

Despite difficult economic and social conditions during the first three years of transition, all Polish governments have remained steadfast in their commitment to stabilisation and to the rapid structural transformation of the economy. The rewards to this perseverance are now becoming evident and are impressive: Poland was the first country in the region to return to growth, experiencing a cumulative increase of GDP by some 6.5 per cent in 1992 and 1993, and prospects appear good that growth will be in the vicinity of 4 per cent in 1994. At the same time, inflation has been brought down from 76 per cent in 1991 to 35 per cent in 1993, and in 1994 it is likely to be in the range of 27-30 per cent. Substantial current account convertibility of the zloty has been maintained and progress has been made in liberalising the capital account. Thanks in part to forgiveness and rescheduling on foreign debt, net official reserves have continued to increase and a large current account deficit in 1993 was kept within financing limits. Above all, the faith in entrepreneurship and in the ability of market forces to develop spontaneously if provided the opportunity to do so has been amply justified: a number of state-owned enterprises (SOEs) have started adjusting to the new situation, but it is the private sector which has shown the way and now accounts for about half of output and employment.

GDP growth, which was achieved barely two years after the implementation of the Economic Transformation Programme, has been accompanied by increased labour productivity and by important changes in the structure of the economy. The share of output accounted for by heavy industry has declined while trade, services and construction have all expanded strongly, even according to official statistics which are probably conservative. In line with the dynamic growth of the private sector, economic organisation has started to shift from over-dependence on large-scale enterprises to a greater – though still modest – role for small and medium-sized enterprises. Production has also become more cost-conscious reflecting a new approach to management: energy intensity has declined, raw materials and transport services are now used more sparingly and adjustment of the labour force has been proceeding. Investment, though growing strongly in 1994, remains low. An important element in the recovery appears to have been efficiency gains from the reallocation of the capital stock through asset sales, liquidations, and privatisation. These gains have been augmented by a small volume of high-yield investments, concentrated in plant and equipment in small and medium-sized firms. This investment, and restructuring more gener-ally, has occurred despite a decline in real bank credit to the economy, through self-financing.

Underpinning these structural changes and contributing to their sus-tainability has been a marked improvement in financial discipline. Inter-enterprise credit has not increased abnormally and firms are now very active in seeking payment from each other. Expectations of a general forgiveness of enterprise debt to banks were finally extinguished during the review period. Instead, bad debt work-out departments were established by banks and a prohibition was placed on new lending to non-performing clients. As a result, the level of non-performing loans held by banks has stabilised, except for loans extended to co-operative housing, to commodity wholesalers and to agriculture. To minimise risk, many enterprises have either repaid their bank loans or avoided bank credit altogether. Improved financial discipline has also influenced the development of wages: over the last two years many small and medium SOEs were often below their wage norms. Running counter to these developments, tax arrears increased markedly over the review period, concentrated in a number of very large enterprises (mining, shipbuilding, steel), which also account for a disproportionate level of debt to banks and to other enterprises. These enterprises have also consistently exceeded their wage norms and have accumulated large excess-wage tax arrears.

Financial discipline has extended to the restructuring process. On a number of occasions the authorities have sought to make firms and managements respon-sible for themselves and to break the previous feeling of dependency on the state. Financial restructuring has emphasised decentralised agreements between banks and enterprises, conditional on the negotiation of a plan for corporate reorganisa-tion. Industrial restructuring programmes developed by the government for the coal, steel and power generation sectors have been mainly indicative; large budgetary expenses and major distortions of market signals have generally been avoided. However, the overriding concern to maintain fiscal discipline has, in some cases, resulted in distortions to competition when, for example, holding companies have been established which enable cross subsidisation to occur. The use of trade protection has been limited although it has probably increased and there is the distinct risk of further moves in this direction as interest groups become better organised.

While many firms are now bound by hard budget constraints, there is still some way to go in establishing the first pillar of a market economy: reorienting enterprise behaviour toward being profitable in a competitive market environment and developing corporate governance to support this. The well-established private sector and new entrepreneurs are undoubtedly concerned with profitability, but most SOEs and some newly privatised ones appear to continue to pursue goals of increasing wages and maintaining employment – albeit subject to increased financial discipline. While the evidence is somewhat unclear, it appears on balance that commercialisation of firms has often not resulted in hoped-for improvements in governance. Progress has been comparatively slow in privatisation. In addition to its impact on governance, these delays have meant that foreign direct investment has remained modest and many enterprises uncertain about the future.

Social costs of the transition have undoubtedly been high for a substantial portion of the population. The level of unemployment has reached over 16 per cent and is highly concentrated by age, location and gender; average real wages have fallen in the last two years, and many pension recipients cannot live on their remittances alone. Particularly hard hit have been small part-time farmers who have been squeezed on two fronts: by losing industrial jobs and by the more competitive agricultural environment. These developments have contributed to a widespread feeling in the population that they are not benefiting from the recovery. In turn, this perception has increased public resistance to raising the returns on capital and to high entrepreneurial incomes. At the same time, the excess-wage tax has become highly unpopular, being regarded, incorrectly, as a punitive tax on SOEs. In order to maintain popular support for continuing enterprise reforms in these circumstances, the government reached agreement with the unions in early 1993 on the Pact on State-Owned Enterprises. The Pact required that an enterprise's future transformation be decided within a given period, but with the particular route chosen by the employees. In return they would receive a free distribution of the shares, representation on the supervisory board, and a relaxation of wage controls. The most important parts of the Pact had not been implemented by June 1994 when the new government introduced its Strategy for Poland, which is discussed below. Like the earlier Pact, the Strategy is concerned to maintain support for changes in the governance of state-owned firms, although a greater role for the state in this is foreseen. However, the policy measures proposed in the Strategy are more wide-ranging, the objective being to lower the social cost of transition.

Macroeconomic policy has successfully supported the continued deceleration of inflation although inflation remains unacceptably high. Fiscal discipline has largely been maintained: the expansion of the deficit witnessed in 1991 and 1992 was reversed in 1993, in large measure due to the completion of wide-ranging tax reforms. Nonetheless, although the budget deficit and public sector borrowing requirement (PSBR) are reasonable by international standards, they remain high in comparison with what the economy is able to finance. Expenditures have been, and continue to be, under enormous pressure to deal with the social costs of the transition: social security expenditures are set to rise further, responding to demands for increased benefits. The debt burden is growing – in part due to the need to resume servicing a reduced, but still very substantial, foreign debt.

Monetary policy has steered a careful path between several objectives. Monetary growth has been set to maintain inflation on a gradual downward path while supporting the recovery. At the same time, the National Bank of Poland (NBP) has been kept under pressure to lower nominal interest rates to support both budget financing and enterprise borrowing. Exchange rate policy has had to balance the need for a nominal anchor with the desire to avoid a significant real appreciation in the face of continuing inflation momentum Despite a marked deceleration of inflation from the near hyper-inflation levels in early 1990, remonetisation has proceeded slowly: the ratio of money to GDP is only around 30 per cent and a substantial proportion of the money supply is held in the form of foreign currency. Negative real interest rates on a wide range of deposit maturities discourage holding of domestic currency, and savings more generally, while periodic devaluations have increased the potential returns from holding foreign currency.

In the period immediately following the introduction of reforms the balance of trade was in surplus, but this has now been reversed for both structural and business cycle reasons. Despite widespread public belief, protectionist measures in the OECD area and trade liberalisation by Poland are of only relatively minor significance in explaining this development: trade policies have relatively limited effects on trade balances, though of course important effects on the structure and efficiency of trade. In this respect, limitations on market-access in the OECD area, while substantially less than before, continue to be damaging to Poland's transition. Polish products are generally quite competitive at present levels of the real effective exchange rate, and given still low market shares for most products, reasonable export growth rates could be expected for the medium-term. The downturn in exports from mid-1992 to the end of 1993 was mainly due to the recession in western Europe, and they have recovered strongly in 1994 in line with European recovery. Import growth has partly reflected the steady integration of Poland into the world economy – as represented by increased intra-industry trade, especially trade in industrial supplies. However, the rapid growth of imports in 1993 also reflected increased domestic absorption; the household saving rate declined and the marginal propensity to consume appeared to be quite high.

Although the recovery has been impressive – and economic policy has contributed importantly to this – several key medium-term issues have to be considered in developing policy for the next stage of the transition:

- Even after the debt reduction and rescheduling agreements with both the London and Paris Clubs, Poland will remain a heavily indebted country with significant servicing commitments. At the same time, imports can be expected to exhibit an underlying tendency to increase faster than GDP, quite independently of the level of domestic absorption, as the economy is integrated into the world economy. Under these circumstances it is important that exports grow rapidly and domestic absorption remain restrained. The key question for policy will be to judge the current account deficit which would be sustainable and the degree to which foreign borrowing opportunities should be utilised. The decision will need to be influenced by the rate of return which can be earned on foreign savings (borrowing) and this will in turn depend on progress in establishing corporate behaviour oriented toward profitability;

- As simple efficiency gains become exhausted, demand for investment funds will increase. This factor, together with pressures for increased consumption, suggest that a high real rate of interest can be expected over the medium-term. Increased household saving would reduce these pressures but financial intermediation is likely to remain limited for some time to come. Both factors point to the need to maintain high corporate profitability thereby increasing savings and ensuring a high level of self-finance;

- The low level of monetisation makes financing the budget deficit and public borrowing difficult and impedes the efficient allocation of resources, thereby lowering the long-term growth potential. Declining inflation is necessary for remonetisation and would, furthermore, reduce price uncertainty, thereby lowering the risk premium demanded by savers and increasing investment.

The government adopted in June 1994 a medium-term economic framework – Strategy for Poland – which shares some of these assessments. The Strategy recognises the constraints arising from the high level of indebtedness, as well as the need to increase domestic saving and to maintain a high growth rate of exports. A great deal of emphasis is placed on reducing interest rates both to lower the possibility of a debt trap as well as to stimulate investment. Although the assessment underlying the Strategy differs in some respects from the one presented here, there is general agreement on the overriding requirements: continued progress is needed on stabilisation, and macroeconomic policies must be supported by continued structural reforms to improve corporate governance and to raise the rate of return on investment. With these goals in mind, the following recommendations consider fiscal, monetary and structural policy measures which maintain and enhance the most dynamic elements of growth to date, while at the same time seeking to minimise the negative consequences arising from ongoing structural adjustment which will entail continuing decline for some enterprises. At the time of writing – September 1994 – the government is still involved in preparing detailed decisons to implement the Strategy. The recommendations which follow have sought to take into consideration current proposals, but these will certainly change in the coming months.

Recommendations

Fiscal Policy

The Strategy for Poland identifies the objective for fiscal policy as supporting monetary policy and disinflation through a steady reduction of both the state budget deficit and the share of it financed by the central bank. To this end, the intention to reduce the deficit by about half a percentage point of GDP each year until 1997 is sound. Several further actions are desirable:

- It is important to establish credibility at an early stage. To this end it is necessary to avoid any slippage in setting and implementing the 1995 budget. Credibility would also be enhanced if the government were to accept binding legal restrictions on central bank financing of the deficit. The present law restricting financing to 2 per cent of current expenditure is entirely ineffective because it is automatically suspended by the budget bill;

- Although the state budget deficit attracts the greatest notice, it is equally important to reduce the public sector borrowing requirement. In 1995 the PSBR could be in the range of Zl 150 trillion, in comparison to a planned state budget deficit of Zl 87 trillion. A high PSBR serves to increase interest rates and to crowd-out credit to the economy;

- The task of the budget to support monetary policy in reducing inflation should not extend to maintaining administered prices at uneconomic levels. Costly distortions would only be prolonged and the apparent advance in controlling inflation might lead to pressures for a premature easing of policy.

To improve growth prospects it is important to restructure expenditures and revenues. The present composition does not appear to support growth, and thereby a steady decline in unemployment. General government revenues and expenditures (including transfers) comprise around a half of GDP, reducing the role of the market in resource allocation, while consumption (mainly supported through transfers) is supported at the expense of investment. A number of measures are necessary to redress the situation:

- Comparatively little progress has been made in improving efficiency in the central administration and in the provision of services such as health and education. A prerequisite is reform of the public administration which, although announced on a number of occasions, is still pending. Action is long overdue;

- Infrastructure investment remains low and needs to be increased. Before doing so it is important to establish a suitable regulatory framework (notably in telecommunications, gas distribution and highways) and to select projects on the basis of rate-of-return analysis. Continuation or resumption of support to old central investment projects needs to be treated in a similar manner.

A focal point for concern about the costs of transition is the social security system, and pensions in particular. The medium-term strategy identifies pension reform as a major priority and makes a large number of proposals which merit support, including curtailing early retirements, tightening the criteria for disability pensions, establishing a full multi-tier system comprising both basic compulsory pensions and supplementary voluntary schemes, and indexing pensions to prices rather than wages. It is realistic to expect that such a wide-ranging package will take some time to implement but in the meantime there would appear to be several priorities:

- Public sentiment – in part fuelled by earlier announcements – appears to expect that the minimum level of pensions will be raised further. The present pay-as-you-go system is already unsustainable beyond the end of the decade because of demographic trends, and an increase in benefits will simply bring this date forward. If the government's commitment to lower the social cost of the transition is to be met, it will need to be carefully targeted and perhaps allocated through social assistance rather than through increased pension entitlements which create long-term claims by broad segments of the population;
- Given the likelihood that it will take some time to achieve a consensus on the reform package, the way should at least be cleared for a voluntary pillar to be established by passing relevant legislation permitting the establishment of private pension funds;
- The high rate of social security contributions (45 per cent) has encouraged widespread evasion and in the long term needs to be reduced substantially if employment creation is to be encouraged. In the shorter term, the contributions should be restructured so that employees contrib-

ute explicitly – even if wages have to be increased initially so as not to reduce the net wage for employees. At a later stage benefit rights need to be directly related to proof of payment of contributions, which is presently not the case.

With the successful introduction of a VAT in 1993, Poland has almost completed a thorough restructuring of its tax system. The current system is, however, characterised by high marginal rates of both personal and corporate taxes, which encourages distortionary behaviour on the part of tax payers, and a lack of transparency of tax incidence for policy-makers. While the medium-term strategy recognises the need to reduce these rates it also relies to a considerable extent on what could be a significant increase in tax expenditures covering areas such as insurance, all forms of investment relief, encouragement of exports, regional incentives, and human capital formation. Experience elsewhere shows that such policy instruments often lack transparency, are ineffective, and put revenues at risk. Priority needs instead to be given to reducing the tax burden by reducing tax rates rather than by increasing allowances. Several other policy changes should also be considered as priorities:

- Double taxation of dividends on inter-enterprise distributions needs to be discontinued so as to foster the development of investment and venture capital funds;
- Current and prospective high rates of inflation create very high marginal effective tax rates on capital, thereby discouraging investment. A number of measures could ameliorate such side-effects of inflation including last-in-first-out valuation of inventories (LIFO) and more adequate revaluation of depreciation allowances;
- The need for high profitability and for reinvestment (self-financing) suggests that long-term capital gains on investments could be taxed at a lower rate than income. This would be preferable to investment tax credits since it would remain neutral as between capital- and labour-intensive projects.

Monetary policy

The low level of money supply relative to income suggests that the authorities might reconsider existing targets for a gradual reduction of inflation – reaching single digits first in 1997 – with a view to achieving a faster and more credible path for disinflation. While the caution of the authorities to avoid any action which might slow growth is understandable, a gradual disinflation may be counterproductive in the medium-term and inappropriate in view of the steady increase in financial discipline and signs that the recovery is based on sound economic behaviour. A gradual disinflation from high rates of inflation often lacks credibility and this may be the case in Poland, leading both to low money demand and relatively large holdings of foreign currency. Tightening the targets for disinflation would require several policy measures which would have to be undertaken together:

–   the pre-announced crawling devaluation of the exchange rate needs to be reduced further and the practice of unannounced devaluations ended to bring down the risk premium demanded by holders of domestic currency;

–   the immediate impact may be a real appreciation of the currency in terms of price deflators. Policy measures should not brake or otherwise hinder the ongoing increase in labour productivity which would serve to mini-mise any real appreciation of unit labour costs measured in a common currency;

–   exchange rate policy needs to be supported by a firmer commitment to maintaining positive real interest rates on zloty deposits. This would have the additional benefit, in the medium-term, of increasing monetisa-tion of the economy, and possibly savings. (While in many OECD countries the empirical relationship between savings and interest rates is weak, this relationship appears to be stronger in Poland.);

–   a more ambitious path for disinflation would have to be supported by a reduction of the budget deficit, and the public sector borrowing require-ment. This would allow increased lending to the economy: ''crowding-in''.

As the Polish economy continues to develop it will be beneficial to further liberalise exchange convertibility so that rewards – and necessary disciplines – may be gained from closer integration into the world economy. The pace of liberalisation should depend upon institutional and economic improvements including further progress on stabilisation, ensuring a sound banking system, improving financial discipline of large SOEs, and in developing effective instruments of monetary policy. The recommendations made in this report all move in this direction. A number of specific measures need to be considered:

- The remaining steps should be taken to achieve full current account convertibility and Article VIII status with the IMF;
- Poland is still characterised by multiple exchange rate practice, even though the exchange rates have not diverged markedly: the foreign exchange offices (kantors) are not permitted to purchase foreign currencies from the banking system. Plans should be formulated to lift this restriction while at the same time developing a full-fledged foreign exchange market, especially for inter-bank transactions;
- Progress has already been made in liberalising the capital account: foreign investors may now purchase securities of all maturities, and are free to remit the full proceeds of resale – as well as interest and dividends – without a special foreign exchange license. Capital outflows, however, remain restricted, although there is *de facto* a rather liberal regime for individuals – via the foreign exchange offices and household foreign exchange accounts. Further liberalisation *de jure* might best be progressive, beginning with trade-related finance, direct investment abroad and investment diversification by pension funds and other recognised institutional investors.

Improving corporate governance of state-owned firms

Although growth is deriving primarily from the private sector it is still necessary to undertake measures to improve the performance of SOEs. This must be viewed not as a substitute for privatisation, but as a second-best solution which will permit improved economic performance – especially through the more rational development of wages and more effective restructuring measures. The government attaches priority to policy changes in this area, and under the circumstances this is entirely appropriate. At the time of writing, few concrete decisions had been taken. However, in general terms the intention is to incorporate a great number, if not all, state-owned enterprises, thereby ending the role of Employees' Councils. The enterprises would then be subject to effective ownership by a new institution, the State Treasury, exercised through a system of management contracts. While the plan appears sound in principle, there are a number of risks which need to be considered at the crucial implementation stage:

–   Fundamental to success of the plan is the development of a new admin-
    istration (the State Treasury) which will act as an effective owner. Such
    an institution would have to be non-political, focusing solely on eco-
    nomic objectives, for example, the rate of return on invested resources.
    The experience in a number of countries has been that such an institu-
    tion has great difficulty in monitoring enterprises and in specifying
    appropriate management contracts – indeed, this has been the experience
    to date in Poland since there is little convincing evidence that incorpora-
    tion has improved enterprise performance. Moreover, in view of the
    emphasis the Strategy places on limiting social costs and the preserva-
    tion of employment, it could be expected that non-economic objectives
    would exercise an important role, involving the Treasury in old-style
    bargaining with enterprises about performance criteria. When develop-
    ing plans for dealing with bad debts to banks the government doubted its
    ability to create an effective non-political institution, and these doubts
    are still appropriate;
–   The potential risks would be reduced by holding to a minimum the
    financing powers of the Treasury and, to a lesser extent, by decentralis-
    ing its operations. Giving the Treasury significant financial resources
    runs the risk of recreating line ministries and could compromise efforts
    to improve financial markets, particularly the banking system. It would
    also increase the incentive for firms to engage in non-market behaviour.
    Decentralisation is useful, but given the regional concentration of some
    industries might nevertheless result in the creation of powerful lobby
    groups without an interest in promoting competition;
–   The current proposal treats all enterprises in the same manner yet there
    is a great deal of evidence that behaviour differs as between small and
    medium enterprises on the one hand, and large ones on the other. Even
    though the former are in many cases *prima facie* worker-controlled and
    not oriented primarily to profitability, they have nevertheless demon-
    strated a capacity to adjust to a market environment and to meet a hard
    budget constraint. Given the lack of administrative resources which
    characterises any new institution, it might be best to exclude such
    companies from the Treasury. Otherwise, the plan risks damaging the
    internal, incipient market-oriented structure of these enterprises without
    putting anything obviously better in its place. The status of these

153

enterprises needs to be finally resolved through the privatisation programme.

Large SOEs – including perennial loss-makers – present additional issues suggesting a more differentiated approach to corporate governance. In this area Poland has taken some promising steps. With the bank-led debt restructuring programme, banks have been forced to assume a governance role with respect to around 700 companies, although it is too early to assess the extent to which the programme will change corporate performance. Particularly innovative is the creation of National Investment Funds as part of the mass privatisation programme. These funds are designed to be active managers of enterprises and, in contrast to the proposed State Treasury, are subject to a strong incentive structure to increase wealth and to privatise their enterprises. Any further slippage in establishing these funds or any dilution of their commercial character needs to be avoided. Further measures need to be implemented to improve corporate governance since the surrogates – wage controls and a capital charge (dividenda) – have become increasingly ineffective.

- Some large enterprises retain political influence because of various forms of economic power, often as the sole regional employers, and have a backlog of unpaid taxes, bank debts, interenterprise arrears, or combinations thereof. Wage controls are no longer functioning effectively here, and are really not the issue: what is crucial is the political will to enforce financial discipline and its attendant consequences. Incorporation of such enterprises has not up until now solved these issues;
- Many of these firms are now participating in some form of restructuring programme, either bank-led or state-organised (*e.g.* coal), and in coming months some may also receive financial support from the Intervention Fund. The Fund needs to remain closely focused on social problems and issues of down-sizing, treating new investment very cautiously. It is essential that the various programmes include some measures to improve governance. Where privatisation or liquidation is not possible, management contracts, including controls such as cash limits, should be established. Incorporation would facilitate this but could not replace any lack of political will – and indeed might make it worse;
- For other large firms with less political influence the situation is different. Complex internal structures and interest groups have rendered

management difficult and this might be improved through incorporation. But the risks are also great that new dependencies on the state might be re-created. Increased coverage by the National Investment Funds would be more appropriate.

No matter what the size of the firm it is necessary to recognise formally the interests of employees in the future transformation of their enterprise and to structure these in a more efficient manner. To this end the issue of free shares is sound, and preferable to the current practice of selling shares to employees only at the time of privatisation for a preferential price. Since the issue price is unknown there is no incentive for workers to make sacrifices in order to improve the value of the enterprise: with free shares they automatically participate. However, once employee interests are recognised in this manner and are compensated, it is important that expectations of higher wages solely on account of changes in ownership be discouraged.

The government's role in promoting competition has at times been ambivalent, monopolistic market structures and trade protection sometimes being viewed as necessary for international competitiveness and for sectoral restructuring programmes. In principle, there is nothing wrong with the state, in its ownership role, accelerating the transition by transforming industrial organisation. This needs to be done, however, with the right priorities. In several restructuring programmes, too much emphasis has been placed on avoiding the social costs of closing down weak firms (through cross-subsidisation via a holding company), and too little on promoting competition. This practice may have advantages in terms of preserving the fiscal balance, but the long-run costs could be large in terms of distorted investment and losses of dynamic efficiency. Moreover, some enterprises have abused their monopolistic position to earn rents, which are often passed to employees in the form of higher wages.

- To promote competition, the Anti-Monopoly Office needs to be more closely involved in privatisation, industrial restructuring and trade policy, including decisions on anti-dumping and safeguard measures;
- In the case of true natural monopolies, or in cases where contestable markets cannot be created, an appropriate regulatory framework needs to be created. While the Anti-Monopoly Office has done a good job highlighting problems in these industries, it does not have sufficient powers

to resolve them. Either the powers of the Office need to be extended, or a new regulatory agency (or agencies) needs to be created, as exist in many OECD countries;

– In other instances, ministries and lower levels of government have been instrumental in either forming cartels or supporting cartel-like behaviour. These are often based on general powers so that the Office has been powerless to act. This situation needs to be remedied.

Wages and employment

Wages policy – in the form of an excess-wage tax levied on SOEs – has been used since the start of the transition both as an anti-inflation instrument and for indirect governance of enterprises. Such controls in their present form are likely to lapse at the end of 1994 but in any case they have by now outlived their usefulness. As noted above, financial discipline of many SOEs is now established and the fact that they are less concerned with profitability suggests the need for better governance, not wage controls. For these firms it will be necessary to maintain financial discipline through rigorous collection of taxes and by ensuring a competitive environment. Removal of wage controls on some very large or monopolistic enterprises, on the other hand, carries with it the real danger of large wage increases, with damaging spillover effects on other sectors of the economy. These firms, however, already largely flout current policy and the proposal to include wage limits in future management contracts may not by itself improve the situation. What is necessary in their case is flanking financial and competition policy measures, and above all the political will to act.

A major priority for Poland will be to reduce the high level of unemployment and to absorb a significant number of people from the low-productivity agricultural sector. Real wage growth must be restrained in the short run to avoid loss of competitiveness, while profits must be channelled into real investments to increase productivity and growth. One method of achieving these objectives is through national negotiations between labour and representatives of capital – both private and SOEs. While this idea is appealing there must remain uncertainty about whether the conditions exist for such a social contract. If they do not exist, a wide range of economic instruments must shoulder the burden, including privatisation and other changes in corporate governance. Of particular importance is the development of a unified competitive labour market. Several steps need to be taken:

- the legal framework to support collective bargaining at either enterprise, branch or regional level, is now in place. OECD experience suggests that either decentralised or centralised wage systems can work satisfactorily depending on countries' institutions and traditions, but that mixed systems tend to behave poorly. Close monitoring will be necessary to ensure that efficient institutional arrangements evolve;
- while the government is rightly concerned to increase employee welfare, the experience in other countries is that the unintended consequence can be to reduce employment and to give an upward push to wage levels. Legislative proposals in the medium-term strategy need to be reviewed in this light;
- labour and social legislation needs to encourage labour mobility both inter-regionally and inter-firm. The proposal in the Strategy to introduce employment undertakings as part of the privatisation process needs to be closely examined since it is likely to increase labour market segmentation further;
- regional policy needs to recognise that some areas are not viable, and to encourage mobility through improved housing opportunities. Resources to encourage regional development need to be tightly focused not necessarily in the worst areas, but in those with most potential;
- although expectations from active labour market measures should remain modest, more needs to be done in this area. Current policy instruments favour direct subsidisation of employment and public works at the expense of training and labour mobility. This needs to be rebalanced.

Privatisation

The government's declared aim is to accelerate privatisation. To this end a number of detailed proposals are under consideration and a number of decisions are expected in the near future. Several aspects need to be closely considered if the government's objective is to be achieved:

- privatisation has been delayed by a multitude of decision-making centres, which have created an institutional bottleneck. The proposed State

Treasury, as sole owner, is intended to clarify the situation. However, privatisation may not accelerate unless the Treasury is given an explicit mandate, or the Ministry of Privatisation is given increased powers to push privatisation plans ahead. Clarity in this area is required as a matter of some priority;

- current proposals to obtain from investors social, investment, and employment guarantees would seem to run counter to accelerating privatisation and to run the risk of further segmenting the labour market;
- the prospective implementation after a delay of two years of the Mass Privatisation programme is welcome, and further slippage would be damaging. However, more needs to be done to encourage the development of capital markets which will facilitate the expansion of institutional investors;
- the large-scale equity participation by commercial banks needs to be avoided, at least at this stage of development. Their capital base is too low and the risk posed to the fledgling universal banking system by conflicts of interest appear excessive;
- there is now widespread resistance to normal asset sales by SOEs. This needs to be countered by the authorities, and indeed such sales need to be facilitated by lifting remaining tax and administrative barriers.

Many small and medium firms have been privatised through management/ employee buyouts, usually through lease/purchase agreements. Some results are positive, although in the initial phase wages have often been raised substantially and the diversified worker/shareholder structure has not always been conducive to changes in enterprise behaviour. This is a transitional problem which could be improved by increasing the possibilities for trading shares in unlisted companies, thereby facilitating a more rapid concentration of ownership and a more timely introduction of new investors. There are a number of proposals to improve this privatisation technique, some of which are commendable and others less so. Among the former is the plan to grant some title to the enterprise dependent on the level of repayments accomplished. This would provide the firms with much-needed collateral and needs to be implemented. By contrast, the commitment to decrease further the capital required to be contributed for a buy-out is questionable and could increase the risk of early insolvency.

Banking and capital markets

The authorities have taken a number of appropriate measures to recapitalise the commercial banks, thereby reducing their dependence on old debtors – in particular large SOEs. At the same time, prudential regulations have been implemented and banking management changed which should ensure that non-performing loans do not recur on anywhere near the scale that they had reached by 1992. Moreover, the NBP has pursued a pragmatic policy in dealing with banks in difficulty and has successfully avoided any systemic threats. Nevertheless, a great deal remains to be done to create and maintain an efficient and sound universal banking system. Four areas in particular deserve consideration:

– Although the main commercial banks have been placed on an improved financial footing and new lending behaviour has probably improved, this does not apply to the three large "specialised" banks which account for around half the assets of the banking system. Recent reform measures with respect to the bank dealing with the agricultural sector (BGZ) appear to be inadequate and to pose an undue risk to the co-operative banks by giving it important economic power over the new regional banks, which will oversee co-operatives. Moreover, in both the housing and the agricultural sectors the pre-conditions do not yet appear to exist which would support a credible "one-off" recapitalisation of the banks concerned. Indeed, there is every indication that new funds would be rapidly wasted. Wide-ranging measures are necessary in these banks and also with respect to their main clients, co-operative housing, agricultural purchasing organisations and agriculture.

– While prudential regulations have been considerably improved, vigilance with respect to their implementation will be required, and prudent banking behaviour needs to be steadfastly encouraged. In particular it will be important for banks and supervisors to remain relatively cautious in the face of any pressures for more investment loans to be granted or for greater "long term" equity positions to be taken. The foreign exchange exposure of banks is now more tightly controlled than earlier but experience in other countries suggest that the situation needs to be closely monitored. Any tendencies for banks to acquire "cheap" funds abroad for on-lending to investment needs to be watched to ensure that all risks are duly accounted for.

159

- Interest rate spreads remain high – although not nearly as high as some would believe – and this issue has now entered the political agenda. Rather than using direct controls or suasion to reduce these, it is preferable to treat the source. Recapitalisation bonds will lead to a reduction of the spread, but the need to accumulate additional reserves will delay this for a while. In the meantime, consideration should be given to paying banks interest on compulsory reserves, or if monetary policy considerations permit, to reduce them. With respect to the high level of costs, it is important that competition be encouraged to reduce these and this might on occasion warrant mergers of state-owned banks. However, caution needs to be exercised to avoid the creation of large banks which are ostensibly required for competition with foreign banks, but which would in reality remain protected.
- Deposit insurance needs to be put on a sound basis. At present deposit insurance *de facto* covers all banks and gives full coverage, features which easily lead to moral hazard on the part of banks. Present proposals call for only limited insurance of private accounts but this will be difficult to enforce, especially in the presence of large state-owned banks. Adequate disincentives for banks to engage in overly risky activities still need to be developed and a clear division of responsibilities between the NBP and a new insurance institute established. In particular, the power of the latter to aid ailing banks needs to be carefully defined.

Considerable progress has been made in establishing capital markets and 1994 should see a marked increase in companies raising fresh capital on the stock exchange. Nevertheless, the ability of the capital markets to support privatisation, restructuring and corporate finance remains limited. Several policy initiatives might contribute to improving the situation.

- The development of institutional investors may be facilitated in several ways. Taxation regulations have hindered the development of venture and capital funds while the lack of an appropriate legal framework has held back the creation of both closed-end investment funds and pension funds. With respect to the latter, it is important that rigorous liquidity requirements and prudential rules be established and that they not be viewed as a source of cheap funds for privatisation. Outdated regulations

- and high inflation – appear to have retarded the development of a market in corporate bonds and need to be reviewed.
- The legal and to some extent institutional framework for an over-the-counter market (OTC) is in place. The mass privatisation programme presents a valuable opportunity to establish this market. Beyond that, the authorities should seek to encourage the development of this market for small firms, not only as a means of privatisation, but as a channel for post-privatisation restructuring.

The success of the Economic Transformation Programme – due in part to the perseverance of successive governments since 1990 – has brought significant rewards and laid the basis for the future growth and structural transformation of the economy. At the same time, new policy issues have become apparent which must be tackled during the second phase of the transition, if growth is to be firmly established and increased still further. Many of these issues have been diagnosed, and appropriate solutions identified, in the government's medium-term policy document, Strategy for Poland. However, much will depend on implementation and in important areas policy intentions are still unclear. In many ways the policy-making environment is now more difficult than at the start of the transition. Some of the most important issues concern distributional questions and the need to maintain high profits and saving rates for some time to come, at a time when the population understandably demands increased consumption. Yet these questions must be resolved against the background of an increasingly pluralistic economy and society. Social contracts such as that represented by the Pact on State-Owned Enterprises are thus valuable and should be utilised, but indirect economic policy instruments will have to increasingly shoulder the burden. Over the past four years the Polish economy and society have demon-strated an impressive flexibility and capacity to adapt and this is likely to con-tinue. Poland has shown the way to other countries with a resolute commitment to transformation and has been the first to enter the stage of growth. The way thus seems open for Poland to start down the path of convergence with the OECD area.

Notes and references

1. GDP figures for 1991 and 1992 were revised in early 1994. Consistent industrial production and 1993 estimates are not yet available.

2. Table 1 indicates that banking and finance made a negative contribution to value-added. This is a statistical artefact arising from the inability of the statistical authorities (GUS) to calculate intermediate consumption of banking services by other sectors – and industry in particular. The value-added of these other sectors is therefore over-stated.

3. Calculated from FØ1 data which only includes large firms. Analysis of 20 industrial branches indicates that in 1992 double-digit growth was recorded in fuel, metal products, transport equipment, building materials, wood and wearing apparel. By contrast, nine branches experienced a decline in output: mining, coal, ferrous and non-ferrous metallurgy, engineering, precision instruments, leather products and textiles. In 1993, all but three branches had substantial growth.

4. According to estimates by the Ministry of Foreign Trade, roughly 21 per cent of total imports were composed of investment goods. Multiplying this figure by total imports on a national accounts basis, and dividing by total gross fixed investment, gives an estimate that in 1992 and 1993, 28 and 32 per cent, respectively, of domestic investment was based on imports.

5. The comparable figures in the former Czechoslovakia and in Hungary were between 15 and 17. This is not simply a result of scale effects as inflation decelerates: the coefficient of variation has also declined from 0.5 in 1991 to 0.20 in 1993.

6. Production, financial and price data are collected on a monthly basis for industrial enterprises with more than 50 employees and 20 employees in other sectors including services. The data collection is called FØ1. Data on small firms are collected only on an annual basis and are released with a delay of around nine months. This series, which presents a more complete view of the economy, is called FØ2.

7. The correlation of the change in gross financial result/income with the growth of real output was 0.41 in 1992 and significantly different from zero. There was no correlation between the change in output and in relative prices. See Annex IV for details.

8. See Marian Ostrowski, ''Investment demand'', in *Transforming the Polish Economy*, IRISS, Warsaw, 1993, Chapter 4.

9. For some evidence for this, see J. Dabrowski *et al.*, ''Privatisation of Polish State-Owned Enterprises: Progress, Barriers and Initial Effects'', *Economic Transformation*, No. 33,

Gdansk, 1993. Such sales are likely to have increased the inter-sectoral reallocation of assets in contrast to privatisation procedures which presumably keep assets in the same sector.

10. There are several possible explanations for this. The most popular is that profit is simply concealed. Deniszuk and Kudrycka estimate that incomes from privatised firms in fact grew some 70 per cent in 1992 (''Individual incomes and consumer demand'', Chapter 3, IRISS *op. cit.*). Further, in the first semester of 1994 reported profits suddenly surged, coinciding with the introduction of an investment tax credit which required a minimum profit threshold (see Annex I). Another reason is that profit margins actually convey little or no information about the rate of profit which is more relevant for the actions of private owners. However, there is some reason to doubt that the Polish economy has as yet matured to a situation of low margins and market rates of return.

11. In 1992, 527 Chapter 11 actions were settled and 215 were carried over. The average duration of a proceeding decreased from 8.5 months in 1991 to 3.8 in 1992. It increased to 7.2 months in 1993 reflecting the fact that large enterprises started using the procedure. For bankruptcy 850 of the 1 250 motions in 1991 were filed in the second half. In 1992, 2 150 motions were decided. The average duration of a bankruptcy proceeding was seven months. The share of state and private enterprises utilising each procedure is not available.

12. Unemployment data in Poland come from two sources: monthly unemployment registers and quarterly labour force surveys. These sources have been fairly close in their estimates of total unemployment, though their profiles have differed slightly.

13. The unemployment rate does not adequately reflect the employment problem in rural areas. Only farmers with less than two hectares of land (quality-adjusted) may register as unemployed: above this limit they can only be registered as looking for work.

14. However, even in low unemployment voivodships like Katowice, there are numerous pockets of high unemployment centred around the shutdown or restructuring of a dominant local factory.

15. Three quarters of those exiting to employment went to normal jobs with a further 14 per cent going to subsidised positions called intervention jobs. (See Chapter II for a description.) The remainder went to public works programmes.

16. In 1992 mass layoffs constituted 23 per cent of inflows or 356 000 persons. In 1993 this declined to 13 per cent or 261 000 persons.

17. Unemployment among youths may be overstated as many register for unemployment in between studies or over the summer. Thus two-thirds of the 1993 summer surge in school-leaver unemployment was maintained through December, though presumably some of these actually found jobs, and the rest returned to school.

18. Customs statistics have been affected by numerous data collection problems such that in 1992 a trade deficit of $2.7 billion was registered as opposed to a cash surplus of $512 million. In the course of 1993 the differences between the two sources have become better understood but the differences remain large: in 1993 on a customs basis the trade deficit was US $4.6 billion, almost $2.4 billion greater than on a cash basis.

19. Expectations of devaluation undoubtedly had an important impact on the timing of receipts because of lagged repatriation of earnings by exporters prior to August 1993. Delaying

receipts pending a devaluation appears to be quite well-established in Poland but is difficult to explain given the tightness of bank credit. An explanation might be found in the dominance of highly liquid trading companies in both exporting and importing.

20. Very rapid import growth was registered in chemicals, agriculture and light industry: the last of these possibly reflecting increased reprocessing in the clothing industry.

21. The kantors are not permitted to purchase foreign currency from the banking system so that Poland still maintains multiple currency practices. If vendors deposited the receipts from trade or tourist activities in their foreign currency accounts, they would be recorded as private transfers.

22. The Agreement was fully described in the last Economic Survey. Under the first stage there was a reduction of 30 per cent in net present value, including an 80 per cent decrease in interest payments for three years.

23. Up until now any bank willing to grant credit had to accumulate high reserves (up to 60 per cent) – and thereby increase interest charges – since Poland was classified as a high-risk country.

24. Contract employees are not on the payroll and firms are not required to make unemployment and social security contributions for them.

25. No doubt most of this was explained by widely diverging savings rates.

26. For the same period, ownership of colour televisions went from 37.6 to 74.2, freezers from 44 to 59.9, video cassette players from 6.9 to 36.9. Strangely enough, ownership of automatic washing machines was flat.

27. Although budgetary units finished 1993 with significant cash balances, the situation in the last quarter had initially appeared quite different. At first the government experienced great difficulty in selling bills but was unwilling to increase interest rates since it was believed that this would threaten the recovery. The surge in revenue thus obviated the need to make some difficult fiscal policy choices.

28. The Labour Fund is financed by a 3 per cent contribution based on wages. In addition there is a newly established fund, and accompanying contribution, to guarantee wages to workers in the event of bankruptcy of the enterprise.

29. The average number of recipients of wage earners' pensions is expected to rise from 6.7 million in 1993 to 6.875 million in 1994 while for the farmers it will increase from 2.06 million to 2.09 million.

30. Though the budget deficit to GDP ratio dropped in 1993, the PSBR increased because of banks' recapitalisation.

31. This includes the increase in the zloty value of dollar-denominated Treasury bills as a consequence of the pre-announced devaluation of the exchange rate and the further issue of recapitalisation bonds to the banks of Zl 19.5 billion.

32. Among the areas which are still restricted are non-trade related services such as insurance and banking.

33. Table 9 must be treated with care since credit to the government has expanded considerably as a result of several balance sheet transactions: in 1992 the budget took over a debt of

Zl 20 trillion owed by Bank Handlowy to the NBP and in 1993 recapitalisation bonds for Zl 21 trillion were issued to nine banks by the Ministry of Finance.

34. See Gomulka, *op. cit.*

35. The shortfall was for each quarter Zl 2.2, Zl 5.3, Zl 6.7 and Zl 7.9 trillion respectively.

36. The issues were examined in detail in the last *Economic Survey* and also in *Industry in Poland*, OECD, 1992.

37. For evidence which must remain somewhat impressionistic about these trends see J. Dabrowski *et al.* "State owned companies in the process of transition: 1992-1993 survey results", *Transformation of Economy*, No. 38, Warsaw (in Polish).

38. See the *Economic Survey of Poland*, OECD, 1992. Under conditions in which the employees controlled the firm prior to privatisation, the future sales of shares to them at a preferential but unknown price provided no incentive to increase the value of the enterprise: on the contrary, some of the incentives could lead to a decapitalisation of the enterprise. By contrast, the value of free shares will increase with any successful restructuring.

39. Only for the larger firms is incorporation a first step to privatisation. Smaller firms can be privatised directly without this intermediate step.

40. The Commission has already discussed and agreed to changes in withholding of personal income taxes. At the time of writing, it was considering the question of fuel and energy pricing.

41. From March to June 1993 the rate was reduced to 0.7 per cent, but for the rest of the year it was increased to 1.4 per cent.

42. The penalty tax rates were 20 per cent less for enterprises which were incorporated.

43. According to the Act on State-Owned Enterprises from September 1981.

44. The IDA was founded in 1991 as a joint-stock company, serving as the restructuring agency for the Ministry of Industry, see OECD *Economic Survey of Poland*, 1992, p. 118.

45. Total loans by the IDA (and its forerunner institution) have totalled Zl 1.7 trillion. As of June 1993, Zl 1 trillion were classified as bad loans. (This figure is primarily the original principal; interest is not being capitalised on these loans.) Three enterprises account for 47 per cent of bad debts, 81 out of 180 debtors are in default.

46. This process is not automatic, but requires development of a viable restructuring plan, though in some cases political pressures have played a role. The IDA suffers from similar problems as commercial banks: it has to pay income taxes of 40 per cent on write-offs of capitalised interest, since this counts as income received. The IDA is, for the purposes of the Enterprise Debt Restructuring Law, classified as a bank and has the same legal powers.

47. See "Industrial Policy", Chapter 6 in *Economic Policy of Poland*, Polish Policy Research Group (PPRG), Warsaw University, July 1993, pp. 131-132.

48. *Op cit.* pp. 131-32.

49. Grants will mostly be available in cases of liquidation.

50. Funds are generally not available for firms which have access to other sources, especially conciliation agreements with the banks, the principle being that banks are not to benefit from the Intervention Fund. Interpretation of this clause will be on a case-by-case basis,

largely dependent on the degree of bank debt forgiveness and if the IDA holds the majority of the debt. Other criteria for access to the fund are: a review and possible replacement of the current management team, review of the firm's restructuring plan to assure viability, and application for commercialisation or plans for privatisation. Applications are initially screened by the IDA, the founding body and an inter-ministerial committee headed by the Ministry of Finance. Their recommendations must then be approved by the Council of Ministers. The loans will be administered by the Ministry of Finance, with monitoring by the IDA.

51. It appears that there will be no difficulty disbursing the funds allocated. As of June 1994 the IDA had received 55 applications requesting nearly the entire amount available for the three-year period, the zloty equivalent of $330 million.

52. Coal accounts for 60 per cent of electric energy production, 80 per cent of heat, and is the basis for nearly all metallurgy.

53. Outstanding liabilities were Zl 51.6 trillion at the end of 1993 and losses in 1993 were Zl 15 trillion.

54. Some mines with higher quality coal and low transport costs preferred instead to concentrate on exports.

55. By comparison, the average level of registered unemployed was 2.7 million people.

56. Intervention support has the additional benefit that employers do not have to pay the 3 per cent contribution to the Labour Fund on this portion of wage payments.

57. High unemployment regions cover about 15 per cent of all townships (gminas), accounting for about 21 per cent of the unemployed.

58. Firms can apply for greater amounts, which have to be approved by the Labour Council. They must present guarantees for the repayment of these loans. Firms which have undertaken mass layoffs in the previous year are prohibited from applying, as are firms in liquidation or bankruptcy.

59. Kawalec, S., S. Sikora and P. Rymaszewski, *Dealing with bad debts: the case of Poland,* Conference on Building Sound Finance in Emerging Market Economies, Washington, 10-11 June 1993.

60. The share of employment has remained at around 27 per cent of total since 1988. Total employment in agriculture has dropped by 600 000 or 13 per cent, about the same as the labour force, with many older agricultural workers benefitting from early retirement.

61. Farmers with less than 7 hectares receive an average 70 per cent of total income from non-farm sources. See *Agricultural Survey of Poland,* OECD, 1994 (forthcoming), Table 14.

62. The goals and practice of Poland's agricultural policies are described in greater detail in Chapter III of the *Agricultural Survey of Poland,* OECD, Paris, 1994.

63. The result of the subsidies was that farmers paid only 17 per cent of the cost of calcium fertilisers in 1993. Fuel subsidies were allocated to farmers on the basis of hectarage, rather than fuel usage, and were intended to offset the cost of fuel price increases. These subsidies only occurred in 1993 and were terminated in 1994.

64. The Polish authorities feel that such future contracts, used at the insistence of the World Bank, are ineffective without the institutional framework supporting a futures market.

65. See J. Dabrowski *et al.*, "Privatisation of state-owned enterprises: Progress, barriers, initial effects", *Economic Transformation*, No. 33, 1993, Gdansk.

66. During the first two years only 30 per cent of due interest may be paid but in the third year arrears must be cleared.

67. *Privatisation in Poland*, October 1993. These figures should be treated only as indicative since the sample of enterprises was quite limited.

68. Dabrowski *et al.*, p. 52.

69. The PAIZ reports an additional $4.3 billion in commitments. According to the GUS, these figures do not include an estimated $2.3 billion in small investments.

70. Survey sponsored by the Friedrich Ebert Foundation and PAIZ.

71. The Privatisation Council noted that the delay sometimes prevents foreigners from taking part in privatisation bids. They recommended (in April 1994) liberalisation, but also noted that changes in the foreign exchange law would also be required to make it easier to draw medium-and long-term credits from abroad and for foreign entities to open time deposits at Polish banks.

72. A duty-free import quota for cars was also offered, but was withdrawn after protests from the EC.

73. Dabrowski J., "State Enterprises in the Process of Economic Transformation, 1992-1993", *Economic Transformation*, No. 38, Warsaw, 1993. These results are somewhat at odds with Pinto *et al.*who believe that large SOEs have also made important advances in restructuring.

74. The bonds would be similar to the compensation warrants issued in Hungary, with the important exception that some assets are being set aside. Whether these would be sufficient is unclear.

75. The bounding level is higher in the case of agricultural lines since to the tariff is added tariffication of non-tariff measures and minimum access.

76. Indicative lists which were part of the trade system introduced in 1991 have not been prepared in 1992 and 1993.

77. There is a draw-back system for tariffs on inputs, and industrial assembly is zero-rated. However, this does not alter the fundamental point that protective tariffs will eventually tax some activities, including potential and actual exporters. If for example an input is manufactured locally and is protected, then any industry using the product as an input will be taxed. Draw-backs will in turn discriminate against import-competing industries in favour of export-oriented ones.

78. N. Nagarajan, "EU-CEEC trade in textiles and clothing", forthcoming in *European Economy*.

79. See *Agricultural Survey of Poland*, OECD, Paris, forthcoming, for details.

80. For more details on the enforcement of competition policy see *Annual Reports on Competition Policy*, 1993-1994, OECD, Paris, forthcoming.

81. The rapid development of financial markets more generally is discussed in Annex II.

82. There are 58 banks which have a foreign exchange licence, and 23 are also involved in the stock exchange through broker affiliates.

83. The process of divesting the NBP of all its commercial operations was only completed in 1993 with the spinning-off of the Polish Investment Bank, which remains wholly owned by the former. The bank took over Zl 18.5 trillion in liabilities from the NBP (mostly foreign exchange accounts) together with a similar amount of dollar denominated bonds issued by the Ministry of Finance. The NBP contributed Zl 500 billion in capital and a similar amount in kind: the bank acquired 26 local branches and 2 200 staff. It did not take over any bad or doubtful loans.

84. Despite the obvious dangers of regionally based banks – and often by extension industry-based – there seemed at the time to be no alternative, since telecommunications problems prevented a more disbursed structure.

85. The directors are appointed by the supervisory boards which are in principle able to establish performance-related incentive structures for bank management.

86. The commercial code to which the incorporated banks are subject also requires directors to act only in the commercial interests of the bank.

87. The Treasury retains a substantial holding of 30 per cent. Recent public comments in Poland suggest that the Treasury might use this strong minority holding to influence bank mergers.

88. These areas include bank strategic plans, credit policies, marketing, balance sheet management, managerial information systems, accountancy, personnel policy and computerisation.

89. These include the Polish Development Bank. There are a few other highly specialised banks but they remain insignificant in comparison to the roles they were intended to fulfil. This is mainly due to a difficult external environment in their target areas. The Bank for Social Economic Initiatives was intended to support small enterprises. To assist in this difficult area the NBP has since 1990 offered partial guarantees on some bank credit to private enterprises: up to 60 per cent of the difference between the face value of the loan and the value of collateral. Losses have been high, leading the NBP to sharply reduce the facility, which is now in effect moribund. There is also a bank to support environmental projects and one (Budbank, partly owned by the Ministry of Construction) to facilitate mortgage lending for housing. All three banks remain insignificant, due in part to the very low demand for loans, and the high risks associated with lending.

90. For more details on the behaviour of Polish banks over the period 1990-1991 and the policy of the NBP, see *Economic Survey of Poland,* OECD, Paris, 1992.

91. This indeed appears to have happened just prior to the collapse of the Bank Handlowo Kredytowy in Katowice.

92. Speech delivered by the President of the NBP to the Plenary Session of the Sejm, February, 1994. With respect to the private banks she also noted that they had losses of Zl 5.5 trillion against a capital base of only Zl 1.3 trillion.

93. Such ratios must be interpreted carefully. For a guide to the many pitfalls see D. Vittas, Measuring Commercial Bank Efficiency; Use and Misuse of Bank Operating Ratios, *Policy Research Working Papers,* World Bank, WPS 806, 1991.

94. Such rates of return are reported in Pawel Wyczanski, *Polish Banking System*, 1990-1992, Friedrich Ebert Foundation, Warsaw, 1993.

95. See Wyczanski, *op. cit.*

96. A big credit is defined by NBP banking supervision as a loan above Zl 10 billion or a loan exceeding 15 per cent of a bank's funds where these are less than Zl 70 billion.

97. Figures here taken from *The Financial Voice*, No. 3 (21), March 1994.

98. S. Gomulka, "The financial situation of Polish enterprises 1992/1993 and its impact on monetary and fiscal policies", Paper presented to the Conference on Output Decline in Eastern Europe, IIASA, Austria, 1993. Forthcoming.

99. Nine banks earned rates of return higher than the rate of inflation in the period 1990/1991.

100. It should be noted that the NBP did make a number of sound recommendations in 1990 but without effect. Moral suasion from other quarters was also placed on banks to extend loans especially to the new private sector.

101. The amendment to the Banking Law in 1992 removed the chapter dedicated to state and co-operative banks but extended the period for the BGZ to become an incorporated bank. As of May 1994 this has still not occurred so that the BGZ is without legal status.

102. As quoted in Gomulka *op. cit.* p. 14.

103. For a discussion of the system for financing new housing construction via double indexed mortgages see the *Economic Survey of Poland,* OECD, 1992, Annex V.

104. Under the old system which was terminated in March 1992 co-operatives received a 43-year housing loan at 2 per cent with a three-year grace period during which interest was capitalised. A remarkable feature of the programme was the length of time buildings were under construction: in 1991 76 per cent of the loans were under disbursement.

105. The net foreign currency position cannot exceed 30 per cent, and for individual currencies 15 per cent, of a bank's own funds.

106. For further detailed information on the system, see S. Topinski, *Payment system reform in Poland*, Warsaw, 1993. For a discussion on wider payments-related issues, see J. Tomas, "The payments systems reforms and monetary policy in emerging market economies of central and eastern Europe", *IMF Working Paper*, WP/94/13.

107. For a review of the experience in countries with such levels of inflation, see Rudiger Dornbusch and Stanley Fischer, "Moderate Inflation", *Policy Research Working Papers*, World Bank, 1991, WPS 807.

108. This is arguably not a result of inflation *per se* but of the interest rate policy which has been pursued and which has led to some financial repression. Financial assets with longer maturities earn positive real rates of interest.

109. On this point there is by now compelling international evidence. See for example Nouriel Roubini and Xavier Sala-i-Martin, "Financial repression and economic growth", *Journal of Development Economics*, 39 (1992) and the references therein. Financial intermediation is also undertaken in Poland through inter-enterprise credit, but even taking this into account intermediation remains comparatively low.

110. The public choice theory views inflation from another perspective: low money demand increases the inflation rate which governments seek to achieve in order to meet budgetary demands. This is risky since money demand – the tax base – will decline at the same time.

111. There are two reasons for this. First, for any given term of a loan, a higher nominal interest rate will increase interest payments at the start of the servicing , and lower the repayment of capital. Second, with inflation declining, borrowers will not wish to lock themselves into long-term fixed-interest loans but will seek to roll over short-term ones.

112. This link also points to a potential conflict between fiscal consolidation and increasing external competitiveness through devaluation in the presence of substantial foreign debt. See Ritu Anand and Sweder Wijnbergen, "Inflation and the financing of government expenditure: an introductory analysis with an application to Turkey", *The World Bank Economic Review*, 3, 1989.

113. In Latin America, debt/equity swaps have played an important role in reducing the level of external debt. However, the effect was primarily to attract back to the country capital flight. This may have been more politically acceptable than the prospect of foreign investors purchasing domestic firms with debt bought in the secondary markets. Indeed, extra conditions are already being added to the proposal, thereby reducing its attractiveness.

114. The model does not use the PSBR, which would be technically correct. The PSBR has been consistently well above the general budget deficit because of continued internal and foreign debt restructuring, but these have been a series of one-time events, making them difficult to model.

115. See David Lindauer and Ann D. Velenchik, "Government spending in developing countries", *World Bank Research Observer*, Vol. 7, No. 1 (January 1992), pp. 59-78. Their review of the literature shows that positive correlations often found between government investment spending and economic growth are often either statistically weak, or involve questionable assumptions separating the effects of demand from the externality effects.

116. Public-sector investment is about 2 per cent of GDP, well below the level of other middle-income countries. Moreover, a great deal is still allocated to old, uncompleted projects whose potential value remains uncertain.

117. W. Salter, *Productivity and Technical Change*, Cambridge, 1964.

118. The *Economic Survey of Poland, op. cit.*, 1992, contains a description of the plan.

119. See *Environmental performance review of Poland*, OECD, Paris, forthcoming.

Annex I

Development of the tax system

With the introduction of the VAT in July 1993 and excise bands on domestic products in 1994, the general reform of the tax system is largely complete; the personal income tax came into force in January 1992 and important amendments to the corporate income tax in February 1992 (both were described in the last Economic Survey). However, numerous modifications and improvements in collection procedures continue to be introduced for all taxes.

Personal income tax is progressive, and at the time of its introduction, was levied in three brackets: 20, 30 and 40 per cent. The threshold for entry into each bracket was not adjusted in 1993 for inflation, resulting in some tax creep. A correction for price increases during 1993 was made in the 1994 budget at the same time as the rates were increased to 21, 33 and 45 per cent respectively. There are some anomalies and exemptions in the system with respect to taxation of income by source: interest on bank deposits and government securities, and profits on stock exchange transactions are not taxed, while interest on securities, loans and dividends are taxed at a 20 per cent flat rate. Capital gains on real estate held for less than five years are taxed as normal income as are government bonds if sold before redemption; unemployment benefits and pensions are also treated as normal income. There are a large number of deductions which are rather important as incentives: subscriptions to Treasury bills and shares may be deducted up to Zl 12.4 million per annum (raised to Zl 15 million in 1994)[1] and a number of capital expenditures to do with housing are deductible. Overall, the system could be distorted with high marginal tax rates being matched by a number of important exemptions and deductions.

Tax collection appears to have worked reasonably well and tax offices were able to process ten million tax declarations in 1993. Tax collection is on a monthly pay-as-you-earn basis with the tax rate based on the accrual of income at one place of employment in the course of the year. In 1992 income was taxed at 20 per cent and a final calculation was rendered in 1993 – this is one reason for the surge in tax revenue in 1993. However, during the second full year of operation many more individuals will be paying higher rates from the beginning.

An important amendment has been made to the system in 1994 with respect to the self-employed, a significant sector in Poland. If for certain occupations income is less than Zl 1.2 billion per annum, tax is calculated as a flat rate only on income. The statutory maximum is 9 per cent but three rates have been determined depending on the profession: 7.5, 5.0 and 2.5 per cent.[2] Literary, artistic, advertising and scientific professions continue to be taxed at the 20 per cent flat rate on net income. The objective of the change was not to encourage particular professions, but to reduce administrative costs for taxpayers by reducing the need to maintain a full set of accounts regarding costs. The personal income tax exemptions listed above are also available to the professions. While the need to encourage simplicity in an economy in transition is an important objective, new distortions to the tax structure might have been introduced.

At the time of writing no analysis of the tax schedule faced by a typical worker was available so that judgements about distortions must necessarily remain tentative. However, rough estimates can be made of the effective marginal tax rate on labour income. The contribution to the Social Insurance Fund (FUS) is 45 per cent of the gross payroll and the contribution to the Labour Fund is 3 per cent. Assuming an average income tax rate of 30 per cent and an effective VAT of 15 per cent yields an effective marginal tax rate on labour income of 62 per cent. This is not high in comparison with countries in the region[3] and is the same as countries in western Europe although the latter do have much higher levels of income. However, it is certainly high enough to create work disincentives and tax evasion and avoidance.

The high rate of contribution to the Social Insurance Fund (FUS) is a powerful motive for tax evasion. The rate of contribution (45 per cent) is greater than the rate for profits tax (40 per cent) so that there is an incentive for firms to understate wages. There is also an incentive for workers to collude: pension rights are only very weakly related to contributions and workers' gross pay does not even include the contribution. For both reasons most observers believe that there is massive avoidance of social security contributions, which additionally lowers registered wages and leads to reduced income taxes.

There have been few changes in corporate income tax over the survey period: the basic corporate tax rate has remained at 40 per cent and asset revaluation for the effects of inflation, after being skipped in 1992 as part of budget savings, was reintroduced in 1993[4]. While there has been no general programme of investment relief over the period, anecdotal evidence suggests that the practice of treating investment as a current cost is widespread. Since mid-1993 in designated areas affected by large scale unemployment, investment relief can be granted for 50 per cent of the costs provided that people who are registered as unemployed are given jobs.

A new investment relief was introduced in January 1994. An economic unit can deduct from taxable income investment spending which has been undertaken since 1 January 1994, if two conditions are fulfilled:

- the ratio of gross profit to income is not lower than 4 per cent in food processing or housing construction, and 8 per cent in other activities; and
- there are no arrears on taxes and contributions to FUS and the Labour Fund.

The whole amount or a part of the investment spending up to 25 per cent of gross profit can be deducted from taxable income. If export revenues exceed 50 per cent of total income, or if income from exports is higher than ECU 10 million, taxpayers can deduct from taxable income the costs of investment up to 50 per cent of the gross profit (a right to this kind of deduction has been obtained also by units which do not fulfil the condition about the ratio of profit to income). If a taxpayer benefits by other investment reliefs from corporate income tax, they cannot gain by this regulation. The Council of Ministers made an amendment to the scheme on 20 May 1994. According to this, half of the investment spending borne in the previous year can be deducted from gross profit in the current year, but it cannot be more than 25 per cent of the gross profit. The second possibility is that 50 per cent of investment spending on a licence or research activity can be deducted from gross profit. The two primary conditions have to be fulfilled.

Over the period of the review the taxation system may have interacted with inflation to discourage investment. One channel has been through the partial adjustment of depreciation allowances to inflation but two other channels may have been more important. First, nominal rather than real capital gains have been taxed thereby serving to increase the pre-tax real rate of return required of investment in order to achieve any given post-tax rate of return. Second, money balances have been taxed by inflation, the seignorage gains accruing to the budget both directly and indirectly. While they must be regarded as only suggestive, some estimates suggest that the required pre-tax rate of return over the period was around 60 per cent with the two inflation factors accounting for 45 percentage points of this[5]. At these rates of return, the number of viable investment opportunities would have been substantially reduced.

The taxation treatment of banks has also affected behaviour in an undesirable direction but has contributed to maintaining budget revenues. In particular, provisioning for non-performing loans has not been tax-deductible, contributing to under-provisioning by banks and decapitalisation. (See chapter III for details). Since January 1994 tax regulations have been partly relaxed with respect to bad loan provisioning.

The turnover tax, which had been continually broadened, was replaced by a value-added tax in July 1993[6] comprising three bands: a basic 22 per cent, 7 per cent[7] and zero rate on exports and a few other goods. In order to facilitate its introduction the threshold for paying VAT was set quite high at Zl 4.75 billion[8], but in view of accumulating administrative experience this has been lowered to Zl 1.2 billion for 1994.

The Polish authorities took a very cautious and thorough approach to introducing the VAT, which has paid off handsomely. Based on a close examination of Czech, Japanese and Canadian experience a widespread publicity and education programme was undertaken and temporary powers to deal with any price surges were introduced: until September 1993 any price increases not resulting from official price increases or exchange rate movements could be punished. Despite these measures there was a boom in retail sales and imports in the months preceding the introduction of the tax. In the event, consumer prices did not rise (producer prices rose by the amount foreseen) and no strengthening of inflation was noticeable after the removal of the temporary price surveillance.

Following its introduction, VAT receipts grew from month to month and quickly exceeded the revenues collected from the old turnover tax by around Zl 2 trillion per month; expectations were that it would be revenue neutral. Enterprises appear to have understood the rules quickly (although there were cases of mistakes which were corrected by tax offices) and after a few months increasing numbers of those who had chosen not to pay the tax because they were below the threshold started to register. By late 1993 there were about 300 000 registered taxpayers. Unlike other taxes, enforcement has been vigorous and as a consequence there are no problems with tax arrears. For state-owned firms, managing directors may be dismissed for failure to pay and this has been carried out on two occasions with clear demonstration effects[9].

Notes

1. The deduction is adjusted each year so that it remains four times the monthly average wage in the economy during the third quarter of the previous year.
2. Pharmacists, accountants, lawyers and currency traders are excluded from the system. The rate of 7.5 per cent applies to services, 5 per cent to construction, lending and some forms of transport and 2.5 per cent on restaurants and catering, excluding those where alcohol is sold.
3. EBRD Economic Review, *Annual Economic Outlook*, September 1993, p. 49.
4. Assets which were brought into operation after December 1989 were revalued by 43 per cent in 1993 and by 25 per cent in 1994.
5. See EBRD, *op. cit.*
6. Turnover tax was completely abolished on this day.
7. It applies to coal, fuel and energy, food products, some commodities connected with agriculture and forestry, with health care and products for children, some construction materials and services.
8. Those undertakings with turnover between Zl 820 million and the threshold had the option of registering.
9. In addition, novel approaches have been used: the authorities have impounded enterprise cars and this has usually brought rapid payment of overdue taxes.

Annex II

The non-bank financial sector

Capital markets

Early in the transition, the Polish authorities took a number of steps to promote the development of capital markets, culminating in the opening of the Warsaw stock exchange in April 1991. The general approach pursued by the authorities has been first to assure that regulatory safeguards meeting international standards were in place in such areas as disclosure and prospectus requirements, flotation procedures, licensing of brokers and centralisation of supervisory authority in the Securities Commission. This may have slowed the development of markets somewhat, but it was felt that it would assure against the risks inherent in the unregulated development of securities markets. In line with this strategy, the powers of the Securities Commission were further enhanced in December 1993 with a pre-emptive widening of the scope for penalising stock exchange offences; untruthful financial reporting and insider trading are now punishable with imprisonment of six months to five years in addition to a fine.

Stock exchange

The Warsaw stock exchange (WSE) has grown rapidly since 1991 and by June 1994 comprised 46 brokerage houses employing around 600 licensed security brokers. Brokerage houses are often owned by banks in which case they must operate as financially and organisationally independent units. The exchange is organised as a three-tier market depending on the registered capital of the enterprise and the number of shareholders.[1] Public trading of securities outside the exchange is only permitted under exceptional circumstances, which distinguishes Poland from other countries in transition.

The rules of operation of the exchange are adapted to the needs of a small market with limited liquidity: they are based on the Lyon exchange. Dealing is conducted in a manner similar to the French "par casier" or German "Einheitspreis" systems, quotations being guided by the objective to maximise the trading volume. Each quotation may vary by no more than 10 per cent from the quotation of the previous day. If in the course of setting the day's quotations the ratio of supply and demand is greater than 5:1, trading in the given security is suspended. Following increased experience, the 10 per cent rule was suspended for some companies for one or two sessions in order to facilitate a more rapid convergence of the market price to equilibrium. Trading in securities is performed electronically rather than by actual physical transfer of documents of title. Recording transactions is the responsibility of the State Securities Deposit.

From September 1994 foreign investors may engage in transactions on the exchange on the same terms as domestic investors; up to then, permission was nominally required for around six listed companies since these corresponded to sectors in which there are still licensing requirements for foreign direct investment. Before placing an order foreign investors must open a Securities Account with one of the brokerage houses and deposit a 30 per cent coverage, with the remaining 70 per cent due three days after the transaction. Personal and corporate income from capital gains are tax-free until the end of 1994 and foreigners are free to repatriate these gains without a foreign exchange license.

Since its founding, the exchange has grown at an uneven pace reflecting the changing tempo of the privatisation programme and the surge of prices in 1993: the number of listings has doubled since autumn 1992. At the start of 1994, 24 companies were listed on the first tier, 19 of which had been privatised through public offering. Only one company was listed on the second tier. Not only has trading volume increased but also the number of participants: the number of brokerage accounts increased from 150 000 in March 1993 to 250 000 in October and to 560 000 in February 1994 following the privatisation of Bank Slaski.

Beginning in March 1993 share prices rose dramatically before collapsing from March 1994. The index of share prices rose from 1 299 in March 1993, reaching a peak of 20 000 points in March 1994. Price/earnings ratios surged from around 2.5 into the high 30s, making shares very expensive by OECD standards. By June 1994 the index had fallen to 8 000 points. The rise in share prices, while certainly to some extent speculative, was probably driven by the acute lack of financial instruments available to domestic investors. The cut in deposit interest rates in March 1993 led to increased domestic demand which, on a small market, caused rapid price increases. The excess demand was reinforced by increased interest on the part of foreign investors who may now account for around 20 per cent of the market's capitalisation. An additional indicator for generalised excess demand in 1993 was the variability of the P/E ratio across enterprises: the relative P/E ratio was correlated with earnings and this did not change greatly in the course of the bull market.

The collapse of the stock market may be attributed to several factors. Among those most often cited in Poland is the lack of large institutional investors and an excessive reliance on small shareholders. The former point, taken alone, is not altogether convincing since large foreign institutions contributed powerfully to the price increase in 1993. As any large institution would, they withdrew as prices became increasingly expensive. More important, at least in terms of establishing the dynamics, was possibly the reactions of the numerous small participants.

The increase of stock market prices and trading volume, and the subsequent collapse, has raised a number of regulatory and policy issues. The most actively debated in Poland is whether the authorities could and should have sought to dampen the rise in prices by increasing the supply of securities in 1993. Even if new issues could not have been accelerated it would have been easy to increase supply by selling the Treasury's 30 per cent holding in most of the privatised companies. The position taken by the authorities was one of concern to avoid losses by individual investors once the price turned downward, which it was expected would happen. While it is certainly prudent in transition economies to protect and enhance the reputation of new financial markets, losses were in any case expected to occur as the "bubble burst". It is therefore difficult to view this as a valid reason for not using a bull market to increase share sales and so to dampen a demand-driven rise.

A second set of issues arose with the flotation of Bank Slaski in January 1994; the first fixing in February exceeded the issue price by more than 13 times. Whilst it is inappropriate to comment on all aspects of this case several need mentioning. First, the brokerage system was overwhelmed by the large number of new investors and by the need to register all new holdings before they were tradeable. As a result only 0.35 per cent of the issue was traded on the opening day while potential sellers remained in queues to register their holdings. Workers in companies to be privatised may in the future receive around 10 per cent of the equity free. Unless the trading infrastructure is improved, a barrier to privatisation may be developing. Second, the method of issue has been criticised. Rather than auctioning the shares on the exchange the authorities chose to set an issue price and to accept huge excess demand (there was an oversubscription of around 7:1). The authorities decided to do this rather than risk losses to investors who would have bought at what was regarded an unrealistic price. Plans for a further bank privatisation in November 1994 envisage that shares will be auctioned.

Up until the end of 1993 the stock exchange had been scarcely used to raise new capital, but this changed during the first half of 1994. The Securities Commission granted permission for 30 issues including 14 capital increases by public companies, seven listings of private companies, and five by employee-controlled companies. More than 20 new applications were awaiting approval. At the time of writing it is unclear how the collapse of stock market prices since March 1994 will influence these plans. In an attempt to ease strict prospectus requirements which have discouraged many prospective applicants from seeking a listing, the law was amended in December 1993 to provide for a regulated over-the-counter (OTC) market. Companies will be able to offer their shares to the public via brokerage houses upon issuing an information memorandum which is less demanding than a prospectus. In addition, a third tier to the stock exchange was established in August 1994. Trading on the third floor will be almost totally unrestricted.

Money market

The Polish money market has developed quite rapidly, in part in response to the need to finance the budget deficit. It now comprises an inter-bank market and markets for both Treasury bills and bonds. Only the latter is regulated by the Securities Commission. The market in corporate bonds is still in its infancy,[2] discouraged by the tax system, outdated regulations and high inflation.

An important change in the organisation of the banking system has been the steady development of the inter-bank market. The decline in the refinancing facility of the NBP and the imposition of high reserve requirements in 1990/1991 made banks much more sensitive to managing their balance sheets and this led eventually to the development of the market. Progress has been furthered by the increasing reliance of the NBP on market instruments for the conduct of monetary policy, and in 1994 by the move to reserve averaging for the purpose of monetary control. By 1992 the volume of deposits on the market was already quite significant accounting for 6-19 per cent of all deposits: at the end of each month in a range of Zl 7-12 trillion. Since 1992 the market has broadened to include 38 banks although it is dominated by the ten largest. During 1992, small banks, including co-operatives, sought inter-bank deposits vigorously, mainly from the very large banks. As discussed in chapter III, difficulties in the banking system have meant that the smaller banks have had little access to the market in 1993.

To encourage a secondary market in Treasury bills, the NBP established a brokerage facility. It provides screen-based information on bids and offers, and facilitates the transfer of funds for the trades that have been concluded. The transfer is undertaken by the National Clearing House without the physical movement of securities by issuing an equivalent security to the buyer against payment.

Since June 1992 a market in Treasury bonds has developed in one-and three-year bonds. The secondary market is dematerialised with different markets for small and large investors. The primary market is by invitation only – and up to the present has only been extended to banks. The one-year bonds are indexed on the CPI inflation over a 12-month period ending two months before redemption, plus 5 per cent. The three-year bonds have been on issue since April 1993. Interest is based on the average rate on three month T-bills over the proceeding four auctions, multiplied by 1.1.

Foreign investors were at first permitted to purchase only bonds with a maturity longer than one year. However, since 1993 the restriction has been removed. Profits on all maturities can now be repatriated without the need for a special foreign exchange permit.

Capital and venture funds

Capital and venture funds have been slow to develop but this is gradually changing: by early 1994 around six venture funds were said by observers to be either in operation or in the process of formation, each with a capitalisation of around $50-$100 million. One reason for the delay has been the absence of regulation covering closed-end investment funds. A clause setting up the legal framework for both pension funds and closed-end investment funds was removed from the amendment to the Securities Public Trading Act which was enacted by the Sejm in December 1993. An even greater barrier, which is still not yet resolved, is the double taxation on the transfer of dividends between companies, which substantially lowers prospective returns.

Investment funds are nevertheless developing and the Pioneer Mutual Fund has been very successful. One of the most significant developments, apart from the National Investment Funds (chapter II), is the SRP programme (Stabilisation, Restructuring, Privatisation). In 1994 the EBRD, in combination with the government, proposes to establish three to four investment companies each with a major domestic commercial bank as a partner. The banks will transfer their equity holdings in some enterprises in poor financial condition (often acquired as part of a debt restructuring scheme), as will the Treasury, so that the enterprises will become fully owned by the funds. It is envisaged that around 40 enterprises will enter the scheme. The EBRD will inject new capital into the funds as will the banks.[3] The SRP funds will be responsible for restructuring and privatising the enterprises. It is intended that the funds will introduce new management and capital into the firms and there will be a success fee at the time the companies are privatised. Only when the firms are sold will the capital gains be distributed. A waiver from double taxation will be necessary to make the scheme viable.

Insurance

Poland was the first Partner in Transition to promulgate a law on insurance. The regulation is often described as the most liberal one in the region. A new law is, however, awaiting parliamentary consideration. The requirements for new firms wishing to carry out insurance activity will be tightened, in addition to increased regulation of existing firms. The proposals include the requirement of a detailed activity plan for new companies, the creation of a new supervisory body which will be independent of the Ministry of Finance, an increase of capital requirements, the legalisation of the status of actuaries, and several measures concerning the Insurance Protection Fund and the Guarantee Fund. An order of the Ministry of Finance concerning brokers' permitted activities has also been issued recently (23 December 1993).

Insurance tariffs are not regulated. OECD experts stressed at a recent meeting the importance for central and eastern European countries to supervise tariffs and products. This control should, however, be adapted to the specific situation of each country and be reconsidered in line with the development and modernisation of each market. Supervision is currently conducted by the Ministry of Finance in accordance with the standards adopted by the EC. Insurance companies are forbidden from offering life and non-life insurance cover at the same time. Capital adequacy must correspond to the solvency margin (the ratio of equity and reserve capital to premiums, adjusted for reinsurance) depending on the type of insurance sold. If a company's capital falls below this margin it may be closed; this occurred in the case of one private insurer in February 1993. Every company is required to create a capital or standby reserve, and a claims reserve, and the investment policy is quite closely regulated: investments may only be undertaken in Poland and the total value of the investment in securities cannot exceed 30 per cent of the insurance companies funds. In the case of unlisted securities, the investment cannot exceed 15 per cent of funds; for real estate (except farms), the limit is 25 per cent.

The industry itself is still in a development stage: premium income in 1993 amounted to some Zl 31 trillion and of this 30 per cent is estimated to be life insurance. By the middle of 1993 some 25 companies (31 by the middle of 1994) were active on the insurance market including seven (10 by the middle of 1994) with foreign participation. However, the dominant company remains the state-owned PZU with a market share of 67.7 per cent of non-life premium earnings; it is about 99 per cent in life assurance (PZU Life). An important feature of the market is the strong equity involvement by banks which have been very active in investing in insurance companies. As a result of the still under-developed capital market, insurance companies have invested around 75 per cent of their funds in bank deposits. By the middle of 1993, shares in companies listed on the exchange amounted to only 1.6 per cent of funds. The Ministry of Finance must be notified if an insurance company wishes to acquire an interest of over 10 per cent in any registered company.

The dominance of the state-owned firm PZU has raised a number of policy issues. At the time of its founding in December 1991 the Anti-Monopoly office gave its approval subject to the proviso that it be split into life and non-life firms as soon as possible; something which is in any case necessary under Polish law. Moreover, at the time of its incorporation the company also did not meet capital adequacy requirements and still remains some Zl 3 trillion short of this sum. The management of this state-owned company responded by establishing a 99 per cent-owned subsidiary for life insurance and has vetoed proposals by the Ministry of Finance – its formal owner – to divide the firm arguing that its scale should be measured in relation to west European standards since in 1999 these companies will be able to offer their policies directly on the Polish market. Recently the Ministry of Finance has approved a programme for the recapitalisation of the PZU. The main goal of the programme is to meet capital adequacy requirements before July 1996. Privatisation of the PZU will follow.

Notes

1. Zl 30 billion listed capital for the first tier and at least Zl 10 billion for the second tier.
2. The market, which is usually for securities of less than one year, is organised by the Polish Development Bank. Recently one international company has issued three-year bonds.
3. For this purpose they will acquire a loan, guaranteed by the Treasury, from the EBRD.

Annex III

Calculating the interest rate spread

On the basis of published data it is extraordinarily difficult to estimate the interest rate spread. The OECD Secretariat's assumptions are outlined here in detail.

Effective lending rate

Dividing total income on credits by average credits of the banking system, excluding NBP, yields:

1992	1993
31.8%	30%

The figures do not include interest due but not paid, estimated to be Zl 12 trillion and Zl 25 trillion respectively. This implies contract rates of 37 and 38 per cent. By contrast, the published loan rates in 1992 ranged from 40 to 58 per cent.

Effective borrowing rates

Simply dividing interest costs by end-of-year deposits yields an interest rate of 17 per cent. Using the correct denominator, average deposits, raises the rate to 20 per cent in both 1992 and 1993. However, this is seriously flawed as an estimate of the cost of funds since foreign currency deposits are not adequately accounted for, as are "other deposits". Interest on foreign currency accounts is paid in foreign currency but for accounting purposes is converted into zlotys along with the value of deposits. In this case the derived interest rate will only be that in foreign currency: 3-5 per cent in 1992. Capital losses for the bank – the crawling devaluation was 26 per cent in 1992 and there was a 12 per cent step devaluation – will not be registered as an interest charge but as a revaluation loss. The interest rate on foreign currency deposits after making this correction was around 30 per cent in both 1992 and 1993, and more than 42 per cent in 1992 if the step devaluation is included.

Refinance was available from the NBP at 38 and 35 per cent respectively and amounted to Zl 47 trillion and Zl 62 trillion respectively, while the average cost of funds on the inter-bank market was 38.7 and 31.5 per cent respectively.

Excluding demand deposits – which although not carrying interest are not costless – yields a total deposit base of Zl 326 trillion and Zl 454 trillion. The percentage allocation across groups and assumed interest rates are summarised in Table A.1.

Table A.1. **Deriving interest rate spread**

	1992	Interest	1993	Interest
Interest-bearing deposits	0.48	20%	0.44	20%
Foreign currency deposits	0.36	30%	0.42	30%
NBP	0.14	38%	0.14	35%
Weighted average		25%		26%
With step devaluation		30%		29%
Effective interest rate spread				
Lending	32		30	
Borrowing	25		26	
	7		4	
With step devaluation	2%		1%	
Nominal interest rate spread				
Lending	37		38	
Borrowing	25		26	
	12		12	
With step devaluation	7		9	

Annex IV

Sectoral adjustment

This annex presents data on the performance of industrial branches in 1992 and 1993. The data only reflects a small fraction of Polish firms. Comprehensive reporting for all firms, called the FØ2 survey, is only collected annually and results for 1993 will not be available before the end of 1994. To provide for comparability between 1993 and previous years, the data presented in this annex were drawn from the more narrow monthly FØ1 survey, which is available on a much more timely basis. All calculations were derived from annual averages.

The FØ1 data only covers firms with 50 or more employees in industry and construction, and with 20 or more employees in other sectors of the economy. In total, roughly 20 000 firms meet these criteria, about one-third of which are in industry. This limit on firm size means that the FØ1 data excludes a large proportion of the private sector, which is dominated by firms of under five employees, while disproportionately representing large state-owned firms. In the FØ1 database, public enterprises accounted for 79 per cent of total income in industry in 1993, 40 per cent in construction, 85 per cent in transport and 46 per cent in trade. By contrast, preliminary estimates indicate that for the economy as a whole, the comparable figures are 63, 14, 56 and 11 per cent, respectively. Because of this bias, the data from the FØ1 survey present a fairly accurate picture of developments in large enterprises, but exclude the more dynamic small private sector, and therefore are not representative of trends in the economy as a whole.

Table A.2. Indicators of industrial performance[1]
(By industrial branch and economic sector)

	Industry (total)	Mining	Manufacturing	Fuel and power (total)	Coal	Fuel	Power	Metallurgical (total)	Iron and steel	Non-ferrous metallurgy	Electroengineering (total)	Metal products	Engineering	Precision instr. and apparatus	Transport equipment	Elec.eng/electronics	Chemical	Mineral total
								Percentage										
Real output[2]																		
1992/91	4.1	-2.7	4.8	0.4	-8.8	11.0	-4.0	-2.9	-1.1	-6.2	4.3	9.6	-7.7	-7.5	17.5	2.0	4.5	8.2
1993/92	7.9	-2.6	8.7	0.4	-1.2	5.7	-4.5	-0.2	0.8	-2.3	13.6	11.9	4.7	16.7	20.6	17.3	9.8	8.6
Labour productivity																		
1992/91	12.1	2.1	14.0	3.7	-4.5	8.1	-4.2	5.5	8.6	-0.2	19.9	15.4	6.4	11.0	35.4	26.8	12.6	13.0
1993/92	10.5	4.5	9.9	1.5	3.4	-9.9	-5.9	11.9	10.0	15.5	19.7	11.6	15.0	32.8	23.0	26.3	11.3	12.5
Real average producer monthly wages																		
1992/91	7.2	1.5	7.3	n.a.	2.4	-8.1	4.8	n.a.	13.7	5.3	n.a.	13.4	13.6	7.7	21.0	17.6	15.3	n.a.
1993/92	3.5	-7.7	3.2	n.a.	-11.8	-2.1	7.1	n.a.	0.3	13.0	n.a.	3.7	2.5	9.2	2.5	6.7	7.3	n.a.
Real investment[3]																		
1992/91	-16.4			-0.5				-22.9			-30.7						-25.5	
1993/92[4]	-3.4			15.8				-29.6			-34.1						6.7	
Gross financial results/total income																		
1991	4.4	6.8	4.1	6.2	3.2	4.5	8.9	4.8	-2.4	18.8	-0.7	4.4	5.2	3.5	-10.7	-1.0	10.8	7.8
1992	1.4	-8.4	2.6	3.6	-14.5	5.4	10.7	2.6	-3.7	13.9	-4.8	2.8	-2.5	-0.2	-11.8	-4.2	6.7	2.9
1993	2.6	-3.3	3.3	6.5	-7.1	9.9	10.8	4.1	0.7	10.6	-3.8	1.6	-2.2	2.6	-9.3	-0.5	5.3	3.9
Employment																		
1992/91	-7.1	-4.7	-8.1	-3.2	-4.5	2.7	0.2	-8.0	-8.9	-6.0	-13.0	-5.0	-13.2	-16.7	-13.3	-19.5	-7.1	-4.2
1993/92	-2.4	-6.8	-1.1	-1.1	-4.5	17.4	1.5	-10.8	-8.4	-15.4	-5.0	0.3	-8.9	-12.1	-1.9	-7.1	-1.3	-3.4
Relative PPI[5]																		
1992/91	125.8	102.0	99.8	108.9	102.3	112.3	112.7	91.9	86.8	102.0	92.8	93.2	92.0	99.8	92.5	92.2	94.8	97.0
1993/92	132.3	110.7	99.4	107.6	116.5	103.9	104.5	101.3	103.6	87.6	99.5	97.4	98.0	97.0	103.0	97.7	97.1	96.3

Real stocks																	
1992/91	−12.8	n.a.	n.a.	n.a.	4.0	6.3	−18.6	n.a.	−5.4	−14.1	n.a.	−13.0	−21.7	−21.9	−8.8	−15.8	−0.0	n.a.
1993[6]/92	−1.8	−38.6	1.1	n.a.	−44.1	1.8	17.6	n.a.	5.9	2.9	n.a.	−3.4	−11.2	−14.6	−0.4	−9.7	−1.4	n.a.

Exports																	
1992/91	−5.7				0.0				4.0							9.3	−25.2
1993/92[7]	9.4				−15.1				13.6							−6.0	23.0

1. Growth rates for all categories except rate of return on income.
2. Deflated by branch PPI, except where noted.
3. Deflated by overall (not branch) PPI.
4. Sept./Sept.
5. Total industry: PP = 100; branches PPI: Total PPI = 100 through November in 1993.
6. Nominal stocks full-year, PPI through Nov. 1993.
7. June/June.
Source: Central Statistical Office, FØ1 (annual averages, not adjusted).

Table A.2. **Indicators of industrial performance** [1] (cont.)

(By industrial branch and economic sector)

Percentage

	Building materials	Glass Products	Pottery, China and earthenware	Wood and paper (total)	Wood	Paper	Light industry (total)	Textile	Wearing apparel	Leather	Food	Other industries	Construction	Transport	Communication	Trade total	Community services
Real output [2]																	
1992/91	10.0	2.6	6.2	14.7	16.7	9.8	1.0	-2.2	12.9	-6.1	9.2	2.5					
1993/92	9.1	5.6	10.0	9.7	11.7	4.9	9.5	11.3	13.4	-1.0	11.8	18.7					
Labour productivity																	
1992/91	11.6	9.4	28.9	15.3	14.8	20.3	15.2	22.3	13.6	11.1	4.0	15.8					
1993/92	12.4	11.8	11.1	7.6	8.7	9.5	11.1	18.8	5.0	10.6	9.1	24.7					
Real average producer monthly wages																	
1992/91	10.1	7.8	20.4	n.a.	12.7	15.8	n.a.	13.1	8.3	10.9	1.4	n.a.					
1993/92	3.3	10.7	8.1	n.a.	3.2	6.3	n.a.	5.9	1.1	2.2	0.5	n.a.					
Real investment [3]																	
1992/91				-18.7			-10.2				-13.7		13.8	-35.1	109.7	7.4	-9.7
1993/92 [4]				68.2			21.7				-14.0		-44.1	-18.4	68.9	5.7	-4.2
Gross financial results/total income																	
1991	9.0	6.0	2.6	0.4	-0.3	2.1	-8.4	-14.0	3.3	-8.1	7.4	n.a.	11.6	-1.3	34.3	2.4	12.0
1992	3.1	2.0	3.4	0.2	-0.9	2.6	-7.8	-12.5	3.2	-10.3	2.9	n.a.	4.6	0.5	30.2	1.6	9.9
1993	4.5	-0.3	8.9	1.7	1.1	3.2	-4.3	-6.9	5.8	-13.6	2.5	n.a.	2.5	0.3	26.7	2.0	8.8
Employment																	
1992/91	-1.4	-6.2	-17.6	-0.6	1.6	-8.7	-12.3	-20.1	-0.6	-15.5	4.9	-11.5	-4.2	-16.5	2.7	-4.7	-27.2
1993/92	-2.9	-5.6	-1.0	1.9	2.8	-4.2	-1.5	-6.3	8.0	-10.5	2.5	-4.8	-8.6	-5.9	0.4	-3.7	-6.9
Relative PPI [5]																	
1992/91	98.0	95.5	93.3	95.1	94.7	96.0	93.7	92.3	97.7	92.4	105.8	n.a.	n.a.	n.a.	n.a.	n.a.	n.a.
1993/92	97.7	92.1	95.3	98.2	98.1	97.6	97.2	94.9	100.9	97.1	95.9	n.a.	n.a.	n.a.	n.a.	n.a.	n.a.

Real stocks											
1992/91	−16.4	−13.3	−1.1	n.a.	−16.7	−10.8	n.a.	−15.1	−17.4	−17.4	−6.1
1993[6]/92	−5.2	−3.5	8.3	n.a.	4.1	6.4	n.a.	−4.6	−1.4	−16.1	11.4
Exports											
1992/91			8.3			2.4					−14.4
1993/92[7]			29.1			95.0					−17.7

1. Growth rates for all categories except rate of return on income.
2. Deflated by branch PPI, except where noted.
3. Deflated by overall (not branch) PPI.
4. Sept./Sept.
5. Total industry: PP = 100; branches: Total PPI = 100 through November in 1993.
6. Nominal stocks full-year, PPI through Nov. 1993.
7. June/June.

Source: Central Statistical Office, FØI (annual averages, not adjusted).

Table A.3. **Correlation of indicators of structural change**

	Real output	Labour produc- tivity	Monthly wages	Rate of return on income	Employ- ment	Relative PPI	Real stocks
1 – by industrial sub-branches							
1992/91							
Real output	1						
Labour productivity	0.53	1					
Monthly wages	0.17	0.74	1				
Rate of return on income	0.44	0.47	0.22	1			
Employment	0.40	−0.57	−0.64	−0.07	1		
Relative PPI	−0.01	−0.43	−0.67	−0.03	0.47	1	
Real stocks	0.19	−0.03	−0.25	−0.19	0.23	0.13	1
1993/92							
Real output	1						
Labour productivity	0.58	1					
Monthly wages	0.13	0.42	1				
Rate of return on income	0.23	−0.02	−0.50	1			
Employment	0.19	−0.68	−0.38	0.25	1		
Relative PPI	−0.10	−0.27	−0.53	0.34	0.22	1	
Real stocks	0.05	−0.23	0.51	−0.28	0.32	−0.25	1

	Real output	Labour produc- tivity	Real investment	Rate of return on income	Employ- ment	Exports
2 – By all major industrial branches						
1992/91						
Real output	1					
Labour productivity	0.31	1				
Real investment	−0.16	−0.58	1			
Rate of return on income	−0.14	0.21	0.35	1		
Employment	0.58	−0.59	0.36	−0.31	1	
Exports	−0.11	0.38	−0.24	0.55	−0.43	1
1993/92						
Real output	1					
Labour productivity	0.57	1				
Real investment	0.04	−0.55	1			
Rate of return on income	−0.03	0.21	0.21	1		
Employment	0.48	−0.45	0.63	−0.26	1	
Exports	0.21	0.04	0.47	0.88	0.18	1

Source: Central Statistical Office, FØ1, OECD Secretariat calculations.

Table A.3. **Correlation of indicators of structural change** *(cont.)*

	Real output	Labour produc- tivity	Real investment	Rate of return on income	Employ- ment	Exports
2 – By all major industrial branches						
1992/91						
Real output	1					
Labour productivity	0.31	1				
Real investment	−0.16	−0.58	1			
Rate of return on income	−0.14	0.21	0.35	1		
Employment	0.58	−0.59	0.36	−0.31	1	
Exports	−0.11	0.38	−0.24	0.55	−0.43	1
1993/92						
Real output	1					
Labour productivity	0.57	1				
Real investment	0.04	−0.55	1			
Rate of return on income	−0.03	0.21	0.21	1		
Employment	0.48	−0.45	0.63	−0.26	1	
Exports	0.21	0.04	0.47	0.88	0.18	1

Source: Central Statistical Office, FØ1, OECD Secretariat calculations.

Annex V

A simplified model of Polish banks

Starting from a highly stylised representation of the balance sheet of Polish banks, the model estimates the spread between deposit and lending rates as a function of inflation, the proportion of bad loans and reserve requirements.

Banks are assumed to have four categories of assets: bad loans (*BL*), performing loans (GL), required reserves (RES) and government securities (GV) (Table A.4). Bad loans account for a proportion (*bl*) of total assets. The reserve requirement is specified as a fixed proportion (*res*) of deposits. On the liability side, banks have three sources of funding: deposits (DEP), the bank's own capital (CAP) and other borrowings (BOR). For simplicity, it is assumed that bank deposits and borrowings bear the same interest rate. In the model, deposits are specified as a fixed proportion (*dep*) of total assets. The capital-to-asset ratio is also a fixed parameter.

Only performing loans yield interest income to the banks [at the lending rate (*il*)]. In addition, bank reserves at the National Bank of Poland bear an interest rate (*nbp*), currently zero per cent, and government securities (in relation to assets, *gv*) earn interest at the rate *ig*. Bank costs comprise the interest paid to depositors and creditors [at the deposit rate (*ib*) where *1-ca* equals the sum of deposits and borrowing in relation to assets], and operating costs. The balance of costs and revenues as a percentage of assets is expressed as follows:

Revenues	Costs
Interest on performing loans: **(1 – bl – res.dep).il**	Interest paid to depositors and creditors: **(1-ca).ib**
Interest on reserves: **res.dep.nbp**	Operating cost: **cost**
Interest on securities: **ig.gv**	

The rate of return on assets (*RORA*) is expressed as the difference between bank revenue and costs as a percentage of assets:

$$RORA = (1 - bl - res.dep).il + ig.gv + res.dep.nbp - (1 - ca.).ib - cost \qquad (1)$$

190

It is next assumed that the bank sets its lending rate (il) equal to its borrowing rate (ib) incremented by a margin (s). This margin is calculated so as to achieve a given real rate of return on equity ($RRORE$) considered as a target and defined as:

$$RRORE = \frac{(1 + RORA/ca)}{(1 + If)} - 1 \tag{2}$$

with If being the inflation rate.

By solving equations (1) and (2), the bank spread between deposit and lending rate is calculated:

$$s = \frac{ca.[(1+If).RRORE + If] - res.dep.nbh - (ca - bl - res.dep).ib + cost - ig.gv}{(1 - bl - res.dep)} \tag{3}$$

Expression (3) makes it possible to simulate the effects of increased bad loans and reserve requirements. It can be seen that increasing the proportion of bad loans together with the amount of required reserves raises the spread between lending and deposit rates by more than the sum of the effects from these increases applied separately. Table 19 shows the contribution of each of these elements, including that of their interaction, given the assumptions:

Inflation	43%
Effective borrowing rate	25% and 30%
Interest on reserves	0.0
Required reserves as percentage of deposit	7.7%
Capital/total assets	4.7%
Deposits/liabilities	50%
Operating costs as a percentage of assets	4.0%
Non-performing loans/assets	11%
Government securities/assets	15.6%
Interest on government securities	48% (5% real)

Table A.4. **Simplified balance sheet for Polish banks**

Assets	Liabilities
Bad loans: BL = bl.A	Deposits: DEP = dep.A
Performing loans: GL = (l-bl-res.dep).A	Own capital: CAP = ca.A
Required reserves: RES = res.DEP	Borrowings: BOR
Securities: GV = gv.A	
Total total assets (A) = total liabilities (L)	

EMPLOYMENT OPPORTUNITIES

Economics Department, OECD

The Economics Department of the OECD offers challenging and rewarding opportunities to economists interested in applied policy analysis in an international environment. The Department's concerns extend across the entire field of economic policy analysis, both macro-economic and micro-economic. Its main task is to provide, for discussion by committees of senior officials from Member countries, documents and papers dealing with current policy concerns. Within this programme of work, three major responsibilities are:

- to prepare regular surveys of the economies of individual Member countries;
- to issue full twice-yearly reviews of the economic situation and prospects of the OECD countries in the context of world economic trends;
- to analyse specific policy issues in a medium-term context for theOECD as a whole, and to a lesser extent for the non-OECD countries.

The documents prepared for these purposes, together with much of the Department's other economic work, appear in published form in the *OECD Economic Outlook, OECD Economic Surveys, OECD Economic Studies* and the Department's *Working Papers* series.

The Department maintains a world econometric model, INTERLINK, which plays an important role in the preparation of the policy analyses and twice-yearly projections. The availability of extensive cross-country data bases and good computer resources facilitates comparative empirical analysis, much of which is incorporated into the model.

The Department is made up of about 75 professional economists from a variety of backgrounds and Member countries. Most projects are carried out by small teams and last from four to eighteen months. Within the Department, ideas and points of view are widely discussed; there is a lively professional interchange, and all professional staff have the opportunity to contribute actively to the programme of work.

Skills the Economics Department is looking for:

a) Solid competence in using the tools of both micro-economic and macro-economic theory to answer policy questions. Experience indicates that this normally requires the equivalent of a PH.D. in economics or substantial relevant professional experience to compensate for a lower degree.

b) Solid knowledge of economic statistics and quantitative methods; this includes how to identify data, estimate structural relationships, apply basic techniques of time series analysis, and test hypotheses. It is essential to be able to interpret results sensibly in an economic policy context.

c) A keen interest in and knowledge of policy issues, economic developments and their political/social contexts.

d) Interest and experience in analysing questions posed by policy-makers and presenting the results to them effectively and judiciously. Thus, work experience in government agencies or policy research institutions is an advantage.

e) The ability to write clearly, effectively, and to the point. The OECD is a bilingual organisation with French and English as the official languages. Candidates must have excellent knowledge of one of these languages, and some knowledge of the other. Knowledge of other languages might also be an advantage for certain posts.

f) For some posts, expertise in a particular area may be important, but a successful candidate is expected to be able to work on a broader range of topics relevant to the work of the Department. Thus, except in rare cases, the Department does not recruit narrow specialists.

g) The Department works on a tight time schedule and strict deadlines. Moreover, much of the work in the Department is carried out in small groups of economists. Thus, the ability to work with other economists from a variety of cultural and professional backgrounds, to supervise junior staff, and to produce work on time is important.

General Information

The salary for recruits depends on educational and professional background. Positions carry a basic salary from FF 262 512 or FF 323 916 for Administrators (economists) and from FF 375 708 for Principal Administrators (senior economists). This may be supplemented by expatriation and/or family allowances, depending on nationality, residence and family situation. Initial appointments are for a fixed term of two to three years.

Vacancies are open to candidates from OECD Member countries. The Organisation seeks to maintain an appropriate balance between female and male staff and among nationals from Member countries.

For further information on employment opportunities in the Economics Department, contact:

Administrative Unit
Economics Department
OECD
2, rue André-Pascal
75775 PARIS CEDEX 16
FRANCE

Applications citing "ECSUR", together with a detailed *curriculum vitae* in English or French, should be sent to the Head of Personnel at the above address.

MAIN SALES OUTLETS OF OECD PUBLICATIONS
PRINCIPAUX POINTS DE VENTE DES PUBLICATIONS DE L'OCDE

ARGENTINA – ARGENTINE
Carlos Hirsch S.R.L.
Galería Güemes, Florida 165, 4° Piso
1333 Buenos Aires Tel. (1) 331.1787 y 331.2391
Telefax: (1) 331.1787

AUSTRALIA – AUSTRALIE
D.A. Information Services
648 Whitehorse Road, P.O.B 163
Mitcham, Victoria 3132 Tel. (03) 873.4411
Telefax: (03) 873.5679

AUSTRIA – AUTRICHE
Gerold & Co.
Graben 31
Wien I Tel. (0222) 533.50.14

BELGIUM – BELGIQUE
Jean De Lannoy
Avenue du Roi 202
B-1060 Bruxelles Tel. (02) 538.51.69/538.08.41
Telefax: (02) 538.08.41

CANADA
Renouf Publishing Company Ltd.
1294 Algoma Road
Ottawa, ON K1B 3W8 Tel. (613) 741.4333
Telefax: (613) 741.5439
Stores:
61 Sparks Street
Ottawa, ON K1P 5R1 Tel. (613) 238.8985
211 Yonge Street
Toronto, ON M5B 1M4 Tel. (416) 363.3171
Telefax: (416)363.59.63

Les Éditions La Liberté Inc.
3020 Chemin Sainte-Foy
Sainte-Foy, PQ G1X 3V6 Tel. (418) 658.3763
Telefax: (418) 658.3763

Federal Publications Inc.
165 University Avenue, Suite 701
Toronto, ON M5H 3B8 Tel. (416) 860.1611
Telefax: (416) 860.1608

Les Publications Fédérales
1185 Université
Montréal, QC H3B 3A7 Tel. (514) 954.1633
Telefax : (514) 954.1635

CHINA – CHINE
China National Publications Import
Export Corporation (CNPIEC)
16 Gongti E. Road, Chaoyang District
P.O. Box 88 or 50
Beijing 100704 PR Tel. (01) 506.6688
Telefax: (01) 506.3101

DENMARK – DANEMARK
Munksgaard Book and Subscription Service
35, Nørre Søgade, P.O. Box 2148
DK-1016 København K Tel. (33) 12.85.70
Telefax: (33) 12.93.87

FINLAND – FINLANDE
Akateeminen Kirjakauppa
Keskuskatu 1, P.O. Box 128
00100 Helsinki
Subscription Services/Agence d'abonnements :
P.O. Box 23
00371 Helsinki Tel. (358 0) 12141
Telefax: (358 0) 121.4450

FRANCE
OECD/OCDE
Mail Orders/Commandes par correspondance:
2, rue André-Pascal
75775 Paris Cedex 16 Tel. (33-1) 45.24.82.00
Telefax: (33-1) 49.10.42.76
Telex: 640048 OCDE
Orders via Minitel, France only/
Commandes par Minitel, France exclusivement :
36 15 OCDE

OECD Bookshop/Librairie de l'OCDE :
33, rue Octave-Feuillet
75016 Paris Tel. (33-1) 45.24.81.67
(33-1) 45.24.81.81

Documentation Française
29, quai Voltaire
75007 Paris Tel. 40.15.70.00
Gibert Jeune (Droit-Économie)
6, place Saint-Michel
75006 Paris Tel. 43.25.91.19
Librairie du Commerce International
10, avenue d'Iéna
75016 Paris Tel. 40.73.34.60
Librairie Dunod
Université Paris-Dauphine
Place du Maréchal de Lattre de Tassigny
75016 Paris Tel. (1) 44.05.40.13
Librairie Lavoisier
11, rue Lavoisier
75008 Paris Tel. 42.65.39.95
Librairie L.G.D.J. - Montchrestien
20, rue Soufflot
75005 Paris Tel. 46.33.89.85
Librairie des Sciences Politiques
30, rue Saint-Guillaume
75007 Paris Tel. 45.48.36.02
P.U.F.
49, boulevard Saint-Michel
75005 Paris Tel. 43.25.83.40
Librairie de l'Université
12a, rue Nazareth
13100 Aix-en-Provence Tel. (16) 42.26.18.08
Documentation Française
165, rue Garibaldi
69003 Lyon Tel. (16) 78.63.32.23
Librairie Decitre
29, place Bellecour
69002 Lyon Tel. (16) 72.40.54.54

GERMANY – ALLEMAGNE
OECD Publications and Information Centre
August-Bebel-Allee 6
D-53175 Bonn Tel. (0228) 959.120
Telefax: (0228) 959.12.17

GREECE – GRÈCE
Librairie Kauffmann
Mavrokordatou 9
106 78 Athens Tel. (01) 32.55.321
Telefax: (01) 36.33.967

HONG-KONG
Swindon Book Co. Ltd.
13–15 Lock Road
Kowloon, Hong Kong Tel. 366.80.31
Telefax: 739.49.75

HUNGARY – HONGRIE
Euro Info Service
Margitsziget, Európa Ház
1138 Budapest Tel. (1) 111.62.16
Telefax : (1) 111.60.61

ICELAND – ISLANDE
Mál Mog Menning
Laugavegi 18, Pósthólf 392
121 Reykjavik Tel. 162.35.23

INDIA – INDE
Oxford Book and Stationery Co.
Scindia House
New Delhi 110001 Tel.(11) 331.5896/5308
Telefax: (11) 332.5993
17 Park Street
Calcutta 700016 Tel. 240832

INDONESIA – INDONÉSIE
Pdii-Lipi
P.O. Box 269/JKSMG/88
Jakarta 12790 Tel. 583467
Telex: 62 875

ISRAEL
Praedicta
5 Shatner Street
P.O. Box 34030
Jerusalem 91430 Tel. (2) 52.84.90/1/2
Telefax: (2) 52.84.93
R.O.Y.
P.O. Box 13056
Tel Aviv 61130 Tél. (3) 49.61.08
Telefax (3) 544.60.39

ITALY – ITALIE
Libreria Commissionaria Sansoni
Via Duca di Calabria 1/1
50125 Firenze Tel. (055) 64.54.15
Telefax: (055) 64.12.57
Via Bartolini 29
20155 Milano Tel. (02) 36.50.83
Editrice e Libreria Herder
Piazza Montecitorio 120
00186 Roma Tel. 679.46.28
Telefax: 678.47.51
Libreria Hoepli
Via Hoepli 5
20121 Milano Tel. (02) 86.54.46
Telefax: (02) 805.28.86
Libreria Scientifica
Dott. Lucio de Biasio 'Aeiou'
Via Coronelli, 6
20146 Milano Tel. (02) 48.95.45.52
Telefax: (02) 48.95.45.48

JAPAN – JAPON
OECD Publications and Information Centre
Landic Akasaka Building
2-3-4 Akasaka, Minato-ku
Tokyo 107 Tel. (81.3) 3586.2016
Telefax: (81.3) 3584.7929

KOREA – CORÉE
Kyobo Book Centre Co. Ltd.
P.O. Box 1658, Kwang Hwa Moon
Seoul Tel. 730.78.91
Telefax: 735.00.30

MALAYSIA – MALAISIE
Co-operative Bookshop Ltd.
University of Malaya
P.O. Box 1127, Jalan Pantai Baru
59700 Kuala Lumpur
Malaysia Tel. 756.5000/756.5425
Telefax: 757.3661

MEXICO – MEXIQUE
Revistas y Periodicos Internacionales S.A. de C.V.
Florencia 57 - 1004
Mexico, D.F. 06600 Tel. 207.81.00
Telefax : 208.39.79

NETHERLANDS – PAYS-BAS
SDU Uitgeverij Plantijnstraat
Externe Fondsen
Postbus 20014
2500 EA's-Gravenhage Tel. (070) 37.89.880
Voor bestellingen: Telefax: (070) 34.75.778

NEW ZEALAND
NOUVELLE-ZÉLANDE
Legislation Services
P.O. Box 12418
Thorndon, Wellington   Tel. (04) 496.5652
                              Telefax: (04) 496.5698

NORWAY – NORVÈGE
Narvesen Info Center – NIC
Bertrand Narvesens vei 2
P.O. Box 6125 Etterstad
0602 Oslo 6   Tel. (022) 57.33.00
                              Telefax: (022) 68.19.01

PAKISTAN
Mirza Book Agency
65 Shahrah Quaid-E-Azam
Lahore 54000   Tel. (42) 353.601
                              Telefax: (42) 231.730

PHILIPPINE – PHILIPPINES
International Book Center
5th Floor, Filipinas Life Bldg.
Ayala Avenue
Metro Manila   Tel. 81.96.76
                              Telex 23312 RHP PH

PORTUGAL
Livraria Portugal
Rua do Carmo 70-74
Apart. 2681
1200 Lisboa   Tel.: (01) 347.49.82/5
                              Telefax: (01) 347.02.64

SINGAPORE – SINGAPOUR
Gower Asia Pacific Pte Ltd.
Golden Wheel Building
41, Kallang Pudding Road, No. 04-03
Singapore 1334   Tel. 741.5166
                              Telefax: 742.9356

SPAIN – ESPAGNE
Mundi-Prensa Libros S.A.
Castelló 37, Apartado 1223
Madrid 28001   Tel. (91) 431.33.99
                              Telefax: (91) 575.39.98

Libreria Internacional AEDOS
Consejo de Ciento 391
08009 – Barcelona   Tel. (93) 488.30.09
                              Telefax: (93) 487.76.59
Llibreria de la Generalitat
Palau Moja
Rambla dels Estudis, 118
08002 – Barcelona
       (Subscripcions) Tel. (93) 318.80.12
       (Publicacions) Tel. (93) 302.67.23
                              Telefax: (93) 412.18.54

SRI LANKA
Centre for Policy Research
c/o Colombo Agencies Ltd.
No. 300-304, Galle Road
Colombo 3   Tel. (1) 574240, 573551-2
                              Telefax: (1) 575394, 510711

SWEDEN – SUÈDE
Fritzes Information Center
Box 16356
Regeringsgatan 12
106 47 Stockholm   Tel. (08) 690.90.90
                              Telefax: (08) 20.50.21
Subscription Agency/Agence d'abonnements :
Wennergren-Williams Info AB
P.O. Box 1305
171 25 Solna   Tel. (08) 705.97.50
                              Téléfax : (08) 27.00.71

SWITZERLAND – SUISSE
Maditec S.A. (Books and Periodicals - Livres
et périodiques)
Chemin des Palettes 4
Case postale 266
1020 Renens   Tel. (021) 635.08.65
                              Telefax: (021) 635.07.80

Librairie Payot S.A.
4, place Pépinet
CP 3212
1002 Lausanne   Tel. (021) 341.33.48
                              Telefax: (021) 341.33.45

Librairie Unilivres
6, rue de Candolle
1205 Genève   Tel. (022) 320.26.23
                              Telefax: (022) 329.73.18

Subscription Agency/Agence d'abonnements :
Dynapresse Marketing S.A.
38 avenue Vibert
1227 Carouge   Tel.: (022) 308.07.89
                              Telefax : (022) 308.07.99

See also – Voir aussi :
OECD Publications and Information Centre
August-Bebel-Allee 6
D-53175 Bonn (Germany)   Tel. (0228) 959.120
                              Telefax: (0228) 959.12.17

TAIWAN – FORMOSE
Good Faith Worldwide Int'l. Co. Ltd.
9th Floor, No. 118, Sec. 2
Chung Hsiao E. Road
Taipei   Tel. (02) 391.7396/391.7397
                              Telefax: (02) 394.9176

THAILAND – THAÏLANDE
Suksit Siam Co. Ltd.
113, 115 Fuang Nakhon Rd.
Opp. Wat Rajbopith
Bangkok 10200   Tel. (662) 225.9531/2
                              Telefax: (662) 222.5188

TURKEY – TURQUIE
Kültür Yayinlari Is-Türk Ltd. Sti.
Atatürk Bulvari No. 191/Kat 13
Kavaklidere/Ankara   Tel. 428.11.40 Ext. 2458
Dolmabahce Cad. No. 29
Besiktas/Istanbul   Tel. 260.71.88
                              Telex: 43482B

UNITED KINGDOM – ROYAUME-UNI
HMSO
Gen. enquiries   Tel. (071) 873 0011
Postal orders only:
P.O. Box 276, London SW8 5DT
Personal Callers HMSO Bookshop
49 High Holborn, London WC1V 6HB
                              Telefax: (071) 873 8200
Branches at: Belfast, Birmingham, Bristol, Edin-
burgh, Manchester

UNITED STATES – ÉTATS-UNIS
OECD Publications and Information Centre
2001 L Street N.W., Suite 700
Washington, D.C. 20036-4910 Tel. (202) 785.6323
                              Telefax: (202) 785.0350

VENEZUELA
Libreria del Este
Avda F. Miranda 52, Aptdo. 60337
Edificio Galipán
Caracas 106   Tel. 951.1705/951.2307/951.1297
                              Telegram: Libreste Caracas

Subscription to OECD periodicals may also be
placed through main subscription agencies.

Les abonnements aux publications périodiques de
l'OCDE peuvent être souscrits auprès des
principales agences d'abonnement.

Orders and inquiries from countries where Distribu-
tors have not yet been appointed should be sent to:
OECD Publications Service, 2 rue André-Pascal,
75775 Paris Cedex 16, France.

Les commandes provenant de pays où l'OCDE n'a
pas encore désigné de distributeur peuvent être
adressées à : OCDE, Service des Publications,
2, rue André-Pascal, 75775 Paris Cedex 16, France.

11-1994

PRINTED IN FRANCE

•

OECD PUBLICATIONS
2 rue André-Pascal
75775 PARIS CEDEX 16
No. 47587
(09 94 03 1) ISBN 92-64-14314-9
ISSN 0376-6438

•